GREAT CATS

GREAT CATS

MAJESTIC CREATURES OF THE WILD

CONSULTING EDITORS
Dr. John Seidensticker and Dr. Susan Lumpkin

ILLUSTRATIONS
Frank Knight

MEREHURST

LONDON

Published 1991 by Merehurst Limited
Ferry House, 51/57 Lacy Road, Putney, London, SW15 1PR

By arrangement with Weldon Owen
Produced by Weldon Owen Pty Limited
43 Victoria Street, McMahons Point NSW 2060, Australia
Telex 23038; Fax (02) 929 8352
Weldon Owen Inc.
90 Gold Street, San Francisco CA 94133, USA
Fax (415) 291 8841
Members of the Weldon International Group of Companies
Sydney • San Francisco • Paris • London

President: John Owen
General Manager: Stuart Laurence
Publisher: Wendely Harvey
Production Director: Mick Bagnato
Project Coordinator: Tracy Tucker
Editors: Margaret Jones, Tracy Tucker,
Jill Wayment
Proofreader: Glenda Downing
Editorial Assistants: Tristan Phillips,
Julia Burke

Picture research: Jenny Mills
Captions: Susan Lumpkin, John Seidensticker
Designer: Andi Cole, Andi Cole Design
Series design: Sue Burk
Maps and tables: Greg Campbell Design
Extra illustrations and diagrams:
Tony Pyrzakowski
Index: Dianne Regtop
Senior Editor Foreign Editions:
Derek Barton

Printed by Kyodo Printing Co. (S'pore) Pte Ltd
Printed in Singapore

A Weldon Owen Production

Mitsuaki Iwago

Front jacket: A puma (*Felis concolor*) displays the running speed it can achieve to capture prey.
Photo by George Lepp/Comstock

Endpapers: Adapted for jumping, the puma thrives in steep broken terrain.
Photo by George Lepp/Comstock

Back jacket: Requiring huge expanses of African plains habitat to survive, lions (*Panthera leo*) face
an uncertain future on that crowded continent. Photo by Anthony Bannister/Oxford Scientific Films

Page 1: Largest of the cats, the tiger (*Panthera tigris*) stays cool by lounging in water.

Page 2: From the vantage of a thorn tree, a leopard (*Panthera pardus*) surveys the African plains.

Page 3: Group living in lions helps protect cubs from predation by African carnivores.

Pages 4 –5: Young cheetahs (*Acinonyx jubatus*) and their mother on the Serengeti Plains in Africa,
during the rainy season.

Page 7: A serval (*Felis serval*) listens for prey in the tall grass of Africa's Serengeti Plains.

Pages 8 –9: Wildebeest are a mainstay in the diet of lions in Africa.

Pages 10 –11: North American lynx (*Lynx canadensis*) specialize in hunting snowshoe hares.

C O N T E N T S

FOREWORD

S ince the beginning of recorded history cats have fascinated and inspired us. Cats so captivated the Egyptians that they adopted them for their deities, welcomed them in their homes for companionship, and erected spectacular cat-like monuments. Throughout Asia the tiger is considered a symbol of a king's power and in Hinduism it is associated with the main female deity, Durga.

Unfortunately, man's coexistence with the great cats has not always been harmonious. They continue to be hunted as pests. The furs of the spotted cats have been hunted for fashion accessories. All cats are threatened through loss of habitat due to human activities. It would be a great tragedy if we were to lose any species of this diverse and elegant family from which we have drawn so much cultural richness and enjoyment. Furthermore, as predators they play key roles in natural ecosystems.

When World Wide Fund for Nature (WWF) was founded 30 years ago, much of our work focused on the large, more spectacular, forms of wildlife. In 1973 WWF started funding Project Tiger which with the assistance and financial support of the Indian Government and people led to an increase in tiger numbers from less than 2,000 in 1969 to more than 4,000 in 1989.

WWF also funds the worldwide TRAFFIC network, which monitors both the legal and illegal trade in wildlife products. Trade in the furs of spotted cats is a focus for TRAFFIC's activities. WWF also draws public attention to this issue through its publications and this has helped make these furs so unfashionable that their trade has fallen dramatically. Regrettably, the fur trade of some spotted cats, such as lynx and bobcat, continues at disturbing levels.

Nevertheless, the case of the spotted cats shows just how effective good communications can be in achieving conservation objectives. *Great Cats* will promote a wider appreciation of the beauty of cats and their importance to us and add to the enjoyment the great cats have provided to humans through the centuries.

Charles de Haes
DIRECTOR GENERAL, WORLD WIDE FUND FOR NATURE

"There are certain things in Nature in which beauty and utility, artistic and technical perfection, combine in some incomprehensible way: the web of a spider, the wing of a dragon-fly, the superbly streamlined body of the porpoise, and the movements of a cat."

Konrad Lorenz

Young children can identify a cat as a cat, whether it is a tiny rusty-spotted cat or a huge lion, so similar in form are these carnivores. But the diversity of species in the family Felidae and the relationships among them are a source of continuing wonder and study for specialists. Lions and tigers, the largest cats, can be seen in most zoos, but most of the smaller cats are not maintained by zoos. Some are represented only by a few specimens in the world's museums. Modern field studies have been undertaken with many of the large and medium-sized cats; the small cats remain virtually unknown. Aside from domestic cats, lions, tigers and perhaps a few of the medium-sized cats such as leopards and cheetahs, few of the other members of the family are familiar or easily identified except as "some kind of cat." *Great Cats* introduces these neglected members of the Felidae.

Great Cats covers the origins of cats, their form and function, and includes details for each species — what we know about them and what we don't know — together with a stunning collection of photographs and illustrations. Experts who have studied cats first-hand share their observations and wonder. The relationship between cats and people are explored — cats in art, history, and culture, and the conservation prospects of cats. Entire or subspecies of 23 cat species are threatened or endangered with extinction. Seeing their beauty, and discovering their diversity and life processes are essential steps toward saving all cats.

John Seidensticker and Susan Lumpkin
CONSULTING EDITORS

▲ A female North American lynx (*Lynx canadensis*) and her cub explore a western Montana stream. In habitats as diverse as the boreal forests of North America, the mountains of Europe, the steamy jungles of Asia, the pampas of South America, and the savannas of Africa, the world's 37 species of cats find homes.

EVOLUTION

AND BIOLOGY

THE CATS AND HOW THEY CAME TO BE

NANCY A. NEFF

Among the carnivores, the cats are among the most dramatically adapted for a predatory lifestyle — sleek runners or stealthy ambush hunters, with lethal teeth and razor claws. For all their diversity in coat pattern, size, and habit, the felids (or true cats) are also remarkably uniform in body and skull shape and proportions, and especially so in dentition and postcranial skeleton. Although they are obviously specialized as predators, their success is also due to how generalized they are in many other features: they are not structurally extremely adapted as either runners or climbers, for example, and they retain many primitive features from the earliest ancestors of the entire order Carnivora. This state of affairs presents some problems for biologists as they try to deduce the evolutionary relationships among the cats because there is frequently little strong anatomical evidence for specific relationships.

▼ The phylogenic relationships among the families in the order Carnivora are shown here against a geological timetable to indicate when the families split. The Carnivora contains two major subdivisions: the cat-like carnivorans, the Aeluroidea, and the bear-like carnivorans, the Arctoidea.

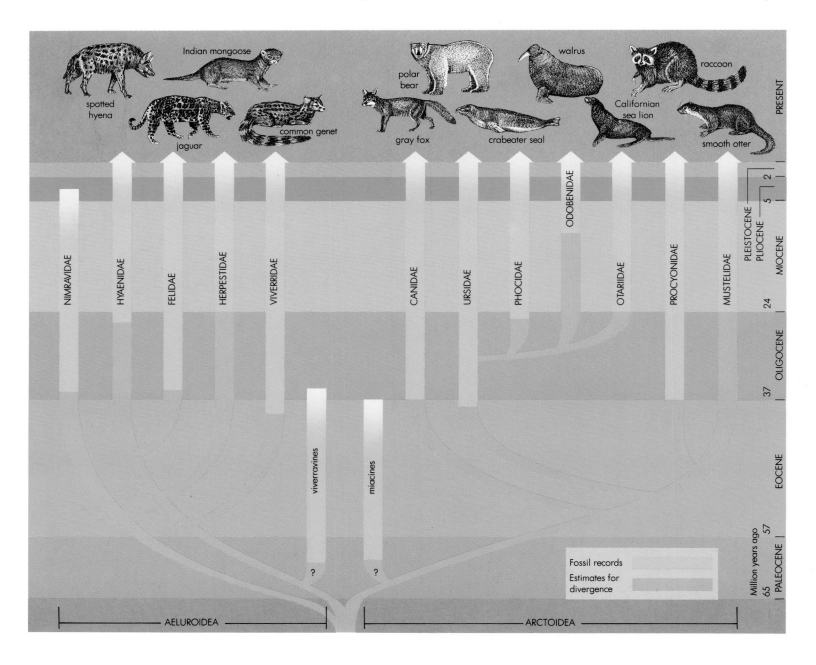

C.R. Knight/American Museum of Natural History

PLACE OF THE FELIDAE WITHIN THE ORDER CARNIVORA

The modern and extinct families of Carnivora fall into two major groups, a cat-like group (aeluroids) and a bear-like group (arctoids), each of which arose from a group of early, primitive carnivorans usually collectively termed miacids. These small mammals were similar in appearance and size to modern genets, with a long body and tail, short flexible limbs, and small brains. They were arboreal (probably with retractile claws), with wide paws and spreading digits with which to grasp. They lived in forests of the northern hemisphere from about 60 to 39 million years ago.

Approximately 40 million years ago, at the beginning of the Oligocene period, a burst of evolution and diversification produced the modern families of Carnivora. One subgroup of miacids were ancestors of the arctoids, including modern bears, seals, dogs, raccoons, pandas, badgers, skunks, weasels, and their relatives. The other subgroup of miacids gave rise to the aeluroids, a lineage including the cats, hyenas, genets, civets, and mongooses.

Although all members of these lineages show to some degree the defining features of a carnivoran — the shearing carnassial teeth and specialized hinge-like jaw joint — various species

developed further adaptations, frequently in parallel between the different families. For example, the cheek teeth of weasels (arctoids in the family Mustelidae) show a highly modified dentition for extreme carnivory similar in many ways to that of the felids. Hyenas (aeluroids in the family Hyaenidae) are similar postcranially to wild dogs (arctoids in the family Canidae) because of similar adaptations for hunting in packs and running down their prey. The cats are actually rather unusual in the more limited range of adaptations to be found within the family.

The phyletic relationships (the pattern of evolutionary relationships) among the families of Carnivora are still debated, although this broad division between aeluroids and arctoids is generally accepted. The modern aeluroids all possess a unique arrangement of the auditory bulla with its dividing septum, and share some similarities in the blood vessel arrangement feeding the head and the base of the brain. Within the aeluroids, felids share a surprising number of features with hyenas: similar number and structure of their teeth, for example, with hyenas' teeth additionally enlarged for crushing bone. These felids and hyenids shared a more recent common ancestor and their specializations evolved after their split from their common ancestor.

▲ C.R. Knight's painting of *Smilodon fatalis* is the image universally evoked by the words "sabertooth cat." His painting reflects painstaking study of the skeleton of this great cat of the Pleistocene (2 million–10,000 years ago), but its actual coat color — plain, spotted, or striped — will never be known.

CATS IN COMMUNITIES: PAST AND PRESENT

BLAIRE VAN VALKENBURGH

The evolution of any predatory mammal is likely to be strongly influenced by its prey, its competitors, and its own predators. For large carnivores, their potential competitors and predators are other predatory species that live in the same area. In present-day savanna communities, competition among large carnivores appears especially intense, and battles over the ownership of carcasses are frequently observed: hunting dogs steal from cheetahs, spotted hyenas steal from hunting dogs, and lions steal from hyenas. The battles can be bloody, and occasionally serious injury or death results. Because interactions, both competitive and predatory, among coexisting carnivores appear to be critical aspects of their biology, it is of interest to examine big cats within an ecological context, that is, as part of an assemblage of species.

In all past and present communities, felids have played the role of specialized meat-eaters. Unlike the dog family, Canidae, or the bear family, Ursidae, the cats have never evolved into more omnivorous or frugivorous forms. Moreover, felids usually ambush their prey, relying on stealth and surprise for their kills, rather than exhausting their prey in long-distance pursuits. However, there are exceptions; although they lack the stamina of a hunting dog or wolf, the cheetah runs farther and faster than other large cats to capture its prey. Interestingly, a cheetah-like cat evolved in parallel in North America less than a million years ago but was extinct by the close of the Pleistocene (10,000 years ago). This North American version of the cheetah, *Miracinonyx trumani*, was very similar to its Old World counterpart in having relatively long, slender limbs, a flexible spine, and a small head. However, it appears to have been more closely related to the living puma than to the cheetah.

In all modern and many fossil mammalian communities, the largest species of pure carnivore is a felid. For example, the lion dominates in Africa, the tiger in Asia, and the jaguar in South America. This pattern of large cat dominance has been true in both the Old and New Worlds for about the last eight million years. Prior to that time, a variety of predators assumed the large body size roles, including, among others, members of the now extinct families Nimravidae and Amphicyonidae. Although there are numerous similarities in the number and diversity of carnivore species present in both fossil and modern carnivore assemblages, there is one notable and intriguing difference: the present-day absence of sabertooth cats. During the past 40 million years of mammalian history, there have usually been sabertooth carnivores present in one form or another, as creodonts, or nimravids, or, most recently, felids. Often there were two distinct types of sabertoothed felid present, distinguished by the shape of their enlarged upper canine teeth. For example, the well-known sabertooth cat of the Rancho La Brea tarpits, *Smilodon fatalis*, was a dirk-toothed sabertooth cat with extremely long, narrow upper canine teeth that bore finely serrated edges. It coexisted with both the Pleistocene lion (*Panthera atrox*) and the scimitar-toothed sabertooth cat (*Homotherium serum*) whose upper canines were shorter but broader with coarse serrations, rather like

those on a steak knife. Presumably, these two different kinds of sabertooth cats did not kill and consume prey in the same way. Although both appear to have hunted from ambush, the homothere had relatively long front limbs and more gracile proportions, reminiscent of living hyenas. Thus, the homothere may have pursued prey over greater distances than did *Smilodon*. Notably, a cave in Texas includes the fossilized bones and teeth of more than 34 adult and juvenile homotheres alongside those of hundreds of juvenile mammoths. Apparently, the cave served as a den site for the sabertooth cats, and the mammoth remains represent portions of kills brought to the young. It is extremely unusual for modern elephants to fall prey to any predator, but this may have been less true in the past, as the Texas cave site suggests. Like the scimitar-toothed *Homotherium*, the dirk-toothed sabertooth cats probably took large prey and may have acted as important providers of carcasses to other scavenging species of the Old World, such as hyenas and early hominids. Because of the enormous length and fragility of their upper canines, it appears that sabertooth cats such as *Smilodon* were careful feeders, avoiding any contact with bone that might fracture the canines. Consequently, dirk-toothed cats probably left behind large portions of a carcass and thereby favored the evolution of scavenging in a number of species, including hominids.

The final extinction of the sabertooth cats occurred about 10,000 years ago worldwide, at the end of the last glaciation, and seems to have resulted from the extinction of their presumed prey, the large ungulates and proboscideans of the Pleistocene. Although their extinction no doubt made the world somewhat safer for our own species, it sadly limits our understanding of the diversity of adaptations and behavior among the big cats.

▼ Lions (*Panthera leo*) and jackals (*Canis mesomelas*) are members of a modern carnivore community in Africa. Fossil and modern assemblages of carnivores are remarkably similar in the number and diversity of species present. A notable exception is the modern absence of sabertooth cats.

J. Bracegirdle/Planet Earth Pictures

A DEFINITION OF THE FAMILY FELIDAE

To understand the evolutionary history of cats, and the wildly different hypotheses that have been offered for that history, we must also consider those "sabertoothed cats" that aren't true cats at all. So first we should define "true cats."

All modern species of cats share a great many physical and genetic similarities because they are all descended from a single remote ancestral species whose features they have inherited. Some of these features were evolutionary novelties in that ancestral felid's line, and thus specially characterize its descendants. One such felid feature is the much-shortened face with large, forward-facing eyes, which permits the visual fields of the two eyes to overlap substantially and thus grants stereoscopic vision over much of their field of vision. This arrangement is typical for many predators, especially ambush or stalking predators: they must be sensitive to the slightest movement that might be a prey item, before the potential victim can sense their presence and flee. Once the prey is spotted, the cat must be able to judge its distance and position accurately, which means the depth perception that stereoscopic vision provides is necessary.

Compared with most other carnivorans, felids have a much reduced number of teeth. The carnassial pair — the distinctive set of one upper and one lower tooth forming blades that cut against one another like scissor blades — is the main set of cheek teeth remaining. A specialized hinge-like joint between the lower jaw and the skull permits jaw movement in one plane only, preventing any side-to-side motion of the jaw (such as that seen in a cow chewing its cud) and thus keeping the carnassials cutting against one another. Molars behind this pair have been almost entirely lost, and premolars in front have been reduced in both number and size. The canines are large and long, for grasping prey and delivering the killing bite. The front row of teeth between the canines, the small neat incisors, are unusual in true cats in that they lie in a very straight line across, rather than in the gently curved semicircle typical of other mammals.

Cats also share common features, inherited from that distant ancestor, that are far more difficult to examine in a live cat, even with the most compliant house cat. A very significant one is the structure of the auditory bulla, a bony chamber that is filled with air and houses the ear ossicles of the middle ear. The bulla is a part of the skull, lying between the eardrum at the base of the outer ear canal and the labyrinth of coils and nerve cells that translate the vibrations of the eardrum, transmitted by the ear ossicles, into signals the brain can interpret as sounds. In cats and their near relatives among the carnivorans (viverrids, herpestids, and hyenids), the auditory bulla is a thin-walled, inflated chamber surrounding a relatively large

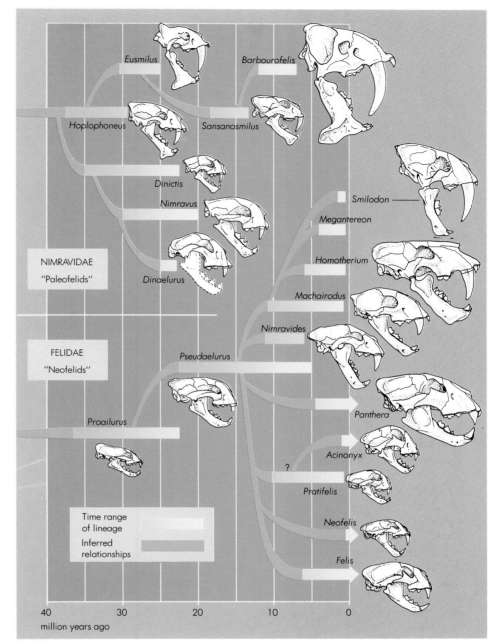

space, and divided by a bony partition. It is this latter feature in aeluroids that is very unusual: the single, nearly complete partition is bilaminar, being composed of one layer from each of the two bones constituting the bulla, the ectotympanic and the entotympanic bones. Felids possess a further specialization in this region: they have almost completely lost the internal-most branch of the carotid artery, which in other mammals enters the skull next to the bulla or middle ear.

Felids also share many other features that are more widely distributed within either the Carnivora or even among the mammals in general. Because these features are not unique to the felids or to the aeluroids, they are not useful for determining evolutionary relationships among these particular groups. One such feature that is frequently cited as distinctively felid is the

▲ The phylogeny of cats and cat-like carnivorans as proposed by the author. The Felidae, true cats or neofelids, include the living cat species as well as the now-extinct sabertooth cats, such as *Smilodon*. The last of the modern sabertooths became extinct only 10,000 years ago. The Nimravidae are paleofelids, long extinct, and possibly not closely related to the Felidae.

MOLECULAR EVOLUTION OF CATS

STEPHEN J. O'BRIEN

A new approach to resolving the taxonomic and evolutionary relationships of cats has emerged recently through the application of the methods and principles of molecular evolution. This methodology compares the rate of change of the genes by directly examining the DNA sequences and protein gene products of different species. Molecular evolution takes into consideration the accumulation of mutational differences over time between species evolving apart. The longer two populations of species have been separated, the greater the DNA sequence divergence in homologous genes. It is possible to calibrate the extent of these differences with the time that has elapsed since the species shared a common ancestor. The paleontologists tell us that the two carnivore families Felidae and Canidae diverged from a common ancestor about 50 million years ago because the "missing link" fossils that share characteristics of the two families are approximately this age. By measuring the quantitative differences that occur in genes and DNA sequences of cats and dogs, we have developed a good quantitative estimate of the amount of mutational change that occurred in these groups over the past 40 million years. This calibration, termed the "molecular clock," is not the perfect evolutionary timepiece, but it has helped resolve a number of controversies in evolutionary studies.

Several molecular metrics have been applied to estimate relationships between cat species, using blood and skin cell cultures as the biological materials. Remember that the Felidae is a very difficult group, mostly because there are many species that have split from each other relatively recently. Five different methods have been applied to samples from living cat species. Three of these, allozyme genetic distance, 2DE genetic distance, and albumin immunological distance, measure differences in protein (gene product) sequences. Two methods, DNA–DNA hybridization and DNA sequence analysis compare the specific DNA sequence code of different cat species.

The results are neither perfect nor complete, but they have converged on several conclusions and on a "best" phylogenetic tree based on concordance of the various molecular tests. The molecules, when calibrated and interpreted along with certain fossil remains, describe a scenario that is summarized in the figure at right. The major conclusion derived from the molecular topology was the resolution of felid evolution into three major lineages. The earliest branch occurred approximately 12 million years ago and led to the small South American cats (ocelot, margay, oncilla, Geoffroy's cat, and others). The second branching occurred about 8 to 10 million years ago and included the close relatives of the domestic cat (wild cats, jungle cat, sand cat, black-footed cat) and Pallas' cat. About 4 to 6 million years ago a gradual divergence of middle-sized and large cats began; the most recent (1.8–3.8 million years ago) produced a split of the lynxes and the large cats.

One dramatic surprise revealed by the molecular methods was the placement of the morphologically specialized cheetah in the midst of the mid-sized cat radiation. Earlier taxonomists had largely agreed that the cheetah's adaptive specializations for high-speed sprinting merited separate generic status and likely indicated an early divergence from the felid evolutionary tree. The molecules did not agree.

Re-examination of other non-molecular characters of the Felidae in the context of the molecular trees has not only reinforced certain patterns but has also shed light on the evolutionary processes that occurred in this group. For example, the chromosomes of all the major cat groups (that is, large cats, domestic cat relatives, and South American small cats) look identical within the clusters but distinct from other groups. Further, many of the anatomical similarities between cat species that have confounded the experts are now beginning to make more sense. We certainly do not have all the answers yet but the recent advances in our understanding of molecular evolution of genes may make the genomes of cats and other mammals — the sum of their genetic information is estimated at more than three billion base pairs — the focus of the most extensive evolutionary excavation in history.

▼ Recent molecular analyses reveal that modern cats evolved in three distinct lines. The largest, the pantherine line led to 24 of the 37 species of living cats, including golden cats, serval, puma, lynxes, cheetah, and all big cats. Another line led to the seven species of small South American cats, and a third line to six species, including the domestic cat and its close relatives.

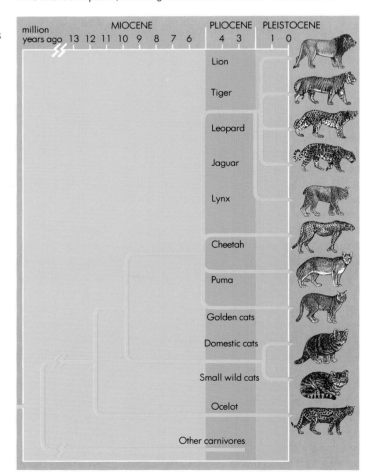

million years ago	MIOCENE								PLIOCENE		PLEISTOCENE	
	13	12	11	10	9	8	7	6	4	3	1	0

Lion

Tiger

Leopard

Jaguar

Lynx

Cheetah

Puma

Golden cats

Domestic cats

Small wild cats

Ocelot

Other carnivores

C.R. Knight/American Museum of Natural History

retractibility of a felid's claws within a fur-covered sheath. All felids retract their claws to some degree (even the cheetah although it is frequently, and erroneously, said not to — it merely lacks the fleshy sheath to cover the retracted claws). But retractile claws covered by a fleshy sheath are also typical of viverrids (such as civets and genets), which are all arboreal in habit, and retractibility, with or without a fleshy sheath, occurs in several climbing species of canids (foxes), mustelids (fisher and marten), and procyonids (ringtails). Early carnivoran ancestors apparently had retractile claws, and their retention in felids is not unusual, probably reflecting a retention of some degree of arboreality.

Similarly, the digitigrade stance of felids (the support of weight on the toes and the ends of the metacarpals and metatarsals) is widespread within the Carnivora, indicating it is a condition that arose early in the evolution of the order and not good evidence for relationships among cat-like carnivorans specifically; nor is it useful for defining the family Felidae.

FOSSIL NEOFELIDS AND PALEOFELIDS
The North American and European fossil record includes a rich diversity of sabertoothed cats and other early cat-like carnivorans. There seemed to be two main radiations, with the earliest, the paleofelids (the Nimravidae or false sabertoothed "cats") occurring primarily during the Oligocene (37–24 million years ago), and the second, the

neofelids (the Felidae or true cats, including the true sabertoothed cats), ranging from the Miocene (25–4 million years ago) to the Recent. Thus these two radiations also appeared to be roughly separated in time, with just a small amount of overlap, as if the neofelids arose from the paleofelids. Indeed, one influential hypothesis from the turn of the century (Hypothesis 1), held that the modern cats, including *Panthera* and *Felis* and their immediate ancestors, for example, *Pseudaelurus*, arose from the least specialized paleofelids, *Dinictis* and *Nimravus*. The extreme sabertoothed paleofelids, *Hoplophoneus* and *Eusmilus*, were thought to be ancestral to the neofelid sabertooths of the Pliocene (5–2 million years ago) and Pleistocene (2 million–10,000 years ago) — such as *Smilodon* and *Machairodus*.

T.A. Wiewandt/DRK Photo

▲ An artist's rendition of *Dinictis*, a sabertooth cat, pursuing *Protoceras*, a small, deer-like ungulate. Species of *Dinictis* and *Protoceras* occurred in North America during the Oligocene (37 to 24 million years ago). *Dinictis* are nimravids, an ancient carnivore group of animals, cat-like in appearance but not closely related to modern cats or the great Pleistocene sabertooth cats.

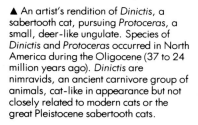

◄ Skeleton of *Dinictis*. The skull shows its long, thin, and curved upper canines. These saber teeth were well-adapted for penetrating skin but not bone.

19

Problems were soon found with this scheme, although satisfactory alternatives have not been proposed until very recently. The details of sabertooth specializations were actually quite different between the paleofelid and neofelid lines: the paleofelids (but not the neofelids) developed a large descending flange on the lower jaw next to the blade-like canines from the upper jaw. The ascending process at the back of the jaw, known as the coronoid process, was much reduced in paleofelids and less so in sabertoothed neofelids. The dentition itself differed in several significant details. Ultimately most significant of all, the ear regions were very different: none of the paleofelids possessed the complete, bilaminar septum and dual ossification of the bulla typical of neofelids and indeed of all other aeluroids.

The picture is further complicated by evidence that at least two types of sabertoothed forms are present within the neofelids: *Megantereon* and *Smilodon* have smooth-edged canines, heavier skulls, and shorter, more robust limbs, while *Homotherium* and *Machairodus* have serrated edges on their canines and are in general more lightly built. The geological range of paleofelids has now been much extended by the discovery of *Sansanosmilus* in the Miocene of Europe and the Near East, and *Barbourofelis* in the later Miocene of North America. That these two genera are clearly nimravids demonstrates the distinction between the families, even though they are now known to overlap in time.

Actually, any hypothesis that sabertoothed "cats" evolved more than once is not as inherently

► C.R. Knight's painting of *Hoplophoneus*, a carnivoran of the North American Oligocene. *Hoplophoneus*, was a sabertooth paleofelid that flourished 37 to 24 million years ago.

► *Thylacoleo* is a marsupial "lion" of the Australian Pleistocene. The largest marsupial carnivore, it had very long canine-like incisors — saber teeth — and preyed on wombats and other big marsupial herbivores. Although cat-like in appearance and probably behavior, its closest living relatives are the phalangers, small arboreal fruit-eating marsupials.

C.R. Knight/American Museum of Natural History

Frank Knight/Museum of Victoria

far-fetched as it might appear at first. Cats are eutherians, examples of the so-called placental mammals. Twice within the other major branch of the Mammalia, the marsupials (commonly called pouched mammals), cat-like carnivores have independently evolved, in each case showing some of the striking features seen in the paleofelids (nimravids) and sabertoothed felids. From the Australian Pleistocene, *Thylacoleo* (the marsupial lion) had large blade-like shearing teeth functioning like carnassials, modified much as are nimravids' carnassials. The role of the saber-like canines was shared in *Thylacoleo* between large, stabbing incisors and a giant, slashing claw on each

thumb. The canines themselves were tiny pegs. The enlarged incisors and reduced canines are features inherited from *Thylacoleo*'s immediate ancestors — more typical herbivorous diprotodonts. Thus the marsupial lion belongs to the same order as the kangaroos and wallabies, and also shares with these forms fusion of the second and third digits on the hind foot.

Even more striking is the similarity of the Pliocene, South American marsupial genus *Thylacosmilus* to the nimravids. All five species of *Thylacosmilus* have recurved, saber-like upper canines parallel to a descending bony flange on the lower jaw. Just as in eutherian sabertoothed cats,

Thylacosmilus had an enlarged surface on the back of the skull for the insertion of powerful neck musculature, and short robust limbs typical of ambush predators with powerful gripping forelimbs. A unique feature in some species is that the roots of the canines remained open throughout their life, permitting continued growth of the thin-enameled sabers, much as a rodent's incisors continue to grow from the base as their tips wear down from gnawing. Thus, although this sabertoothed marsupial has some different features, its impressive similarity to the nimravids demonstrates that the sabertoothed adaptation can certainly evolve more than once.

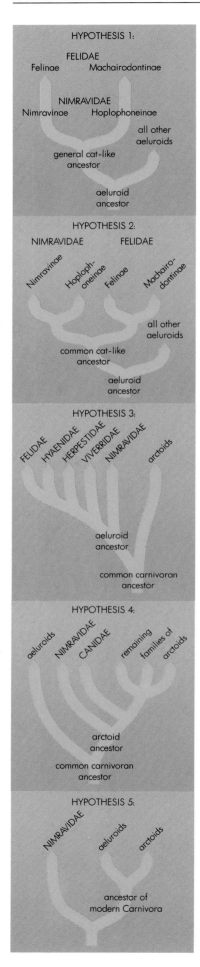

HYPOTHESIS 1:

FELIDAE
Felinae   Machairodontinae

NIMRAVIDAE
Nimravinae   Hoplophoneinae

all other
aeluroids

general cat-like
ancestor

aeluroid
ancestor

HYPOTHESIS 2:

NIMRAVIDAE   FELIDAE

Nimravinae   Hoploph-   Felinae   Machairo-
             oneinae   dontinae

all other
aeluroids

common cat-like
ancestor

aeluroid
ancestor

HYPOTHESIS 3:

FELIDAE HYAENIDAE HERPESTIDAE VIVERRIDAE NIMRAVIDAE   arctoids

aeluroid
ancestor

common carnivoran
ancestor

HYPOTHESIS 4:

aeluroids NIMRAVIDAE CANIDAE remaining families of arctoids

arctoid
ancestor

common carnivoran
ancestor

HYPOTHESIS 5:

NIMRAVIDAE aeluroids arctoids

ancestor of
modern Carnivora

Alternative hypotheses have abounded for the relationships among the various subgroups of paleofelids and neofelids. The figures at left show most of the hypotheses of felid–nimravid relationships that have been proposed in the scientific literature. At one extreme is the theory (Hypothesis 1) mentioned earlier, that the saber-toothed neofelids evolved from sabertoothed paleofelids, and more "normal" neofelids from non-sabertoothed paleofelids. This proposal is no longer accepted by any serious paleontologist because of the many specializations uniting the paleofelids (within the family Nimravidae) to the exclusion of the neofelids (in the family Felidae) and vice versa, effectively refuting the idea that individual nimravids were ancestors of particular lines of felids.

Hypothesis 2 is still promulgated by a few scientists, although it has the drawback of being a poor compromise: the families are certainly both cat-like in general morphology, but the specific features that create this similarity are not valid evidence for this relationship, for one of three possible reasons. First, some features, such as retractile claws, are much more widely distributed, and thus not evidence for this specific relationship. The second reason is the restricted distribution of the parallel adaptations noted earlier. Both lineages show some sabertoothed members, but not all members possess the feature, so it cannot be used to unite the entirety of both lineages.

The third category of feature that argues against Hypothesis 2 comprises specializations that are significantly different in detail in the two families, but in every case either unique to the Nimravidae (for example, a peculiar double layer comprising all of the non-septate, or undivided, partial auditory bulla), or shared between the Felidae and other aeluroids (for example, the complete bilaminar septum in the aeluroid bulla) or even between Felidae and almost all other non-miacid carnivorans (for example, a completely ossified bulla). Thus, Hypothesis 2, in spite of its intuitive appeal as a compromise, actually contradicts all the relevant evidence for aeluroid relationships without being supported by any evidence for a special nimravid–felid relationship.

Hypotheses 3, 4, and 5 all hinge on different interpretations of the actual anatomy represented by the fossils of nimravids, early felids, miacids, and other carnivorans. One might think that paleontologists can "read the story of evolution" directly from the fossil record. There are two levels at which this is not true: first, if by evolution one means the processes by which organisms evolved and diversified, these are hypotheses based on modern biology as well as the diversity throughout time implied by fossils. Such hypotheses may be found to be supported or contradicted by the fossil evidence, but never *proven* conclusively (and often cannot even be conclusively disproven:

a contradiction may mean we've misinterpreted the anatomy or geological context of the fossils). The discussion presented here of cat evolution has not dealt with evolutionary processes and does not need to in order to understand the history of cats. It is clear from the fossil record that great changes in morphology and diversity have occurred over time, but we are not equipped here to review what might have driven those changes. The other level, then, at which evolution can be studied is to decipher the particular course of morphological change, diversification, and extinction, during one group's history — that is, the phylogeny of a group of organisms.

It is not a straightforward problem to decide among the five hypotheses presented if the evidence is contradictory or in dispute. My review up to this point has included various assertions about the anatomy of fossil as well as living cats. One problem is that this anatomy of fossil vertebrate forms is inferred from pieces of skeleton — no other parts of the anatomy in the vast majority of cases — that are usually incomplete, often crushed, distorted, or flattened, and frequently of dubious association with other parts of the skeleton. So our first difficulty is the extreme incompleteness of the study material. The next problem is that scientists differ in what they believe can be inferred about the soft anatomy from the skeletal remains. For example, a foramen (a hole in a bone for blood vessels and nerves) can be interpreted as being for different arteries or veins in many cases, especially if there are no living animals with a closely similar condition. Thus, competent individuals can come to different conclusions about the evidence itself even when dealing with the very same specimens.

The final crowning difficulty is fundamental to comparative anatomy itself: our identification of two structures as "the same" is itself a hypothesis, based on similarity in detail of tissue composition, shape, relationship to surrounding structures, and development from the embryo. Thus deer antlers are taken to be "the same" — all *antlers* — but they are recognized as not the same as the pronghorns of the North American pronghorn antelope, nor equivalent to the horns of various types of cows throughout the world, because of great differences in structure and relationship to the bones of the skull. Structures between two animals differ in their degree of similarity, and the challenge is to decide what was the condition of the structure in the common ancestor of the two, or if that ancestor had anything comparable at all.

Even as we sort out each character, we cannot consider it in isolation. In the case of the nimravids and felids, we have established general agreement that the common ancestral form back to which both can be traced did not have saber-like canines — whether this ancestor is nimravid (Hypothesis 1), something in between (Hypothesis 2), some

◄ Rancho La Brea tar pit in May 1915. The excavation of southern California's Rancho La Brea, one of the world's richest Pleistocene fossil sites, yielded an unrivaled collection of sabertooth cats (*Smilodon fatalis*), dire wolves, and coyotes. Also recovered were human artifacts. These artifacts are evidence of the co-existence of sabertooth cats and the first Americans.

George C. Page Museum

older aeluroid (Hypothesis 3), or an even older carnivoran (Hypothesis 4 or 5). The sabertoothed feature arose within these groups, probably more than once. But we decided this more on the number and complexity of other features uniting felids, or uniting nimravids, than solely on the differences in saber morphology. Thus we juggle numerous hypotheses about characters as we try to decide among phylogenetic hypotheses.

The evidence for Hypothesis 3 hinges on the interpretation of a flange of bone in the ear region of a single specimen of *Dinictis*. If that flange is a partial, bilaminar septum, then nimravids might have had a partial development of the aeluroid bulla, and have been an early branch off that lineage. Numerous specimens, however, are fairly well preserved and yet show no sign of even a partial septum, and other scientists studying the specimen upon which this is based do not think the flange of bone bilaminar. Thus, this hypothesis must be considered still tentative at best.

Hypothesis 4 arose from a reconsideration of the miacids, especially their dentition. A feature of the carnassial in nimravids is similar to the arctoid carnassial. This combined with a re-interpretation of a couple of postcranial features suggested that the Nimravidae might be an early branch off the arctoid side of the tree instead. Many paleontologists are not inclined to give the characters cited much weight, however: the postcranial characters are not as widely distributed within the arctoids as the authors believed, leaving the absence of one cusp on a tooth as the primary evidence.

Finally, the structure of the auditory bulla supports an even more distant relationship. The wall of the bulla itself in nimravids is incomplete,

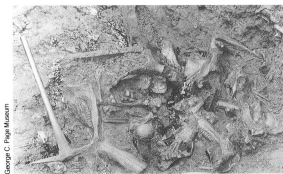

George C. Page Museum

◄ A Rancho La Brea tar pit, photographed in January 1914. The mass of bones at a depth of 3.3 meters (11 feet) includes a sloth pelvis and skull, the lower jaw of a camel, and a sabertooth cat skull. The cat skull appears in the lower right half of the photo.

so the chamber was not entirely encapsulated in bone. The portion that was ossified shows on its smooth, finished edge that it is a sandwich of two very thin sheets of bone with a layer of spongy bone between. This is very unusual and not shared with any other carnivorans. What may be taken to unite the remaining families of Carnivora is the completely ossified bulla composed of two bones, the entotympanic and ectotympanic. The two problems with this hypothesis are the placement of the miacids, which completely lack any ossification of the auditory bulla beyond just the ring supporting the tympanic membrane, and the observation that one group of the extinct amphicyonid carnivores did not have a complete ossification of their bulla. Perhaps the bulla in the Carnivora ossified several times in different lineages and cannot be used to exclude the nimravids from the arctoid or aeluroid lineage.

The only appropriate conclusion is that the contest is still open between the last three hypotheses, and awaits additional fossils and further anatomical studies. The fossil cats are not going to give up their secrets easily.

▶ A detail from Mark Hallett's recreation of a late spring afternoon 20,000 years ago, in the area that is now downtown Los Angeles, California. The sabertooth cat is feeding on a horse known as *Equus occidentalis* and dire wolves hover to steal the prey. A coyote lurks in the background. Coyotes are still common California residents.

Mark Hallett/George C. Page Museum

SABERTOOTH CATS

F. HEALD AND C. SHAW

Asphalt deposits which formed between 38,000 and 4,000 years ago at Rancho La Brea, Los Angeles, California, have preserved millions of late Pleistocene and Holocene plant and animal remains. Approximately one million fossil bones representing large mammals were recovered by the Natural History Museum of Los Angeles County between 1913 and 1931, and are now conserved at the George C. Page Museum of La Brea Discoveries. Of this collection, approximately 162,000 skeletal elements (representing more than 1,200 individual animals) belong to an extinct species of sabertooth cat, *Smilodon fatalis*. The Page Museum maintains the largest and most complete collection of *S. fatalis* remains.

Smilodon was about the same size and weight as a modern African lion, however, the body proportions were different from those of any large living felid. *Smilodon* possessed shorter, stouter (and therefore, more powerful) lower limbs, a comparatively longer neck and shorter lower-back, and a bobtail. The skull and teeth of *Smilodon* were unique. Powerful muscles which elevated and depressed the skull, and closed the lower jaw, were attached to enlarged bony crests on the top and back of the skull. Large paired ridges, adjacent to deep grooves on the palate, buttressed the upper canine teeth from anteroposterior stress. The face was well supplied with tiny (pilomotor) muscles that moved the vibrissae (whiskers) and the lips up and away from the dental battery. The front teeth (incisors and incisiform lower canines) were sharply pointed and interlocked when the mouth was closed. The curved, saber-like upper canines were long, laterally flattened, and serrated on the front and back surfaces, while the meat-shearing carnassials were proportionately the longest of all felids, living or extinct. In addition, the adult teeth of *Smilodon* replaced the milk teeth in a different pattern (and probably at a different rate) from that of all modern cats. Studies of the tongue bones (hyoids) of *Smilodon* indicate that, like lions, this species could roar. *Smilodon* also possessed retractile claws, which were an important weapon for grasping and holding prey. However, the arrangement of these claws was different from all other modern cats. Whereas lions possess a symmetric arrangement, with the largest claw on the central digit of the paw and the adjacent claws progressively smaller, the largest claw on the *Smilodon* paw was located on the first digit (thumb) and the other claws were progressively smaller.

Just over 5,000 bones in the collection at the Page Museum, representing virtually every part of the skeleton, exhibit some kind of pathologic condition (93 percent) or developmental abnormality (7 percent). They fall into five general categories: chronic stress, traumatic injury, dental disease, wounds, and developmental abnormalities. Injuries caused by chronic hyperextension or hyperflexion of muscle and ligament attachments, and lateral torsion of skeletal parts, were the most common afflictions. These often led to degenerative osteoarthritis of the limbs and spinal column, and spondylosis and fusion of the spinal column. Mild to severe traumatic injuries were quite common, and appear in the form of healed fractures, dislocations, and compression injuries to the limbs and spinal column. There are many examples of dental disease including impaction and periodontal infection, and facial asymmetry caused by the early loss of the enlarged upper canine. Wounds and perforations which affected many bones in the shoulder region and along the spinal column, causing osteomyelitis, are reminiscent of infected bite wounds. Parts of some skeletal elements developed abnormally or not at all, causing deformities such as scoliosis and mild spina bifida. As severe as many of these afflictions were, no bones in this collection represent immediately fatal injuries — the animals succumbed to the asphalt traps at Rancho La Brea. Thus the number and kind of maladies reflected in the bones constitute a morbidity report (that is, the rate of disease) on the local sabertooth cat population.

The skeletal structure of *Smilodon* suggests that an extended chase was not employed in prey capture, and the robust front limbs indicate that they hunted prey that greatly exceeded their own weight. Indeed, the shortened lower limbs and lower back, and the lack of a long tail, a balancing organ in prey pursuit, suggest that this species used ambush and stalking techniques to capture prey — that is, to immobilize it with the powerful front limbs and claws before inflicting a lethal bite. There is circumstantial evidence that sabertooth cats may have preferred a diet of slightly more large, thick-skinned animals, such as juvenile elephants. Certain injuries to the neck, back, and chest, and to specific chronically stressed muscle attachments, reinforce these hypotheses and suggest there was a violent, powerful contact with heavy prey at the end of a pounce or short pursuit. Certain muscle groups were most commonly injured at the time of the highest stress, which occurred when the cat was in an outstretched posture, struggling with its prey. At this instant, the upper arms were abducted (elbows out) and flexed at the elbow, and the forepaw in a position of pronation (grasp). The highest stress in the hind limbs occurred when the legs were alternately flexed and extended during the final attack, which ended in physical contact with the prey. Severe impact injuries and chronic reinjuries to the anterior chest, transmitted through the ribs to the spinal column, attest to the frequent violent impact that *Smilodon* inflicted upon its prey. In addition, compression injuries to the vertebrae of the neck, thorax, and lower back are further evidence of high-energy impact during prey capture. In summary, this species relied on stealth and ambush to acquire its food, using surprise and a short rapid pursuit, followed by a violent impact and a lethal bite.

The relative body proportions of *Smilodon* and African lions are similar to modern felids that typically inhabit dense forests. However, lions compete successfully for food on the African savanna, and Rancho La Brea during the late Pleistocene was a brush-covered plain with scattered woodlands. In addition, lions form prides and cooperatively hunt animals that exceed their own body weight. It has been suggested that the success of lions in low-structured habitats is due to their social evolution. In the collection of pathologic bones from Rancho La

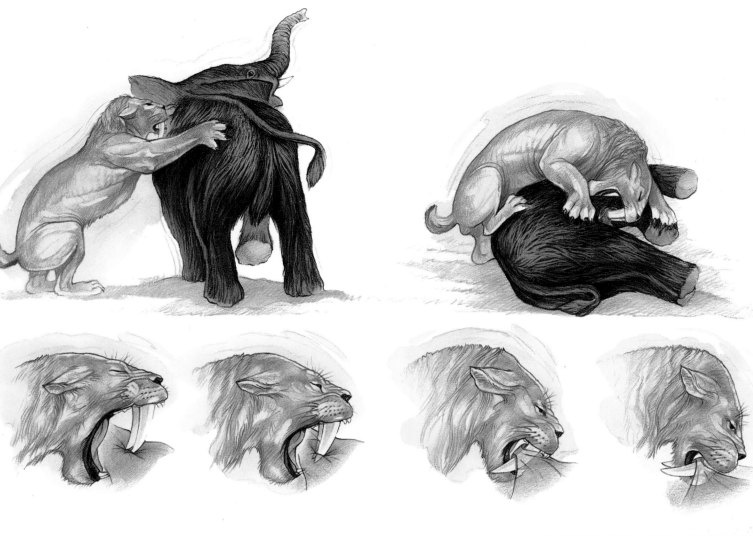

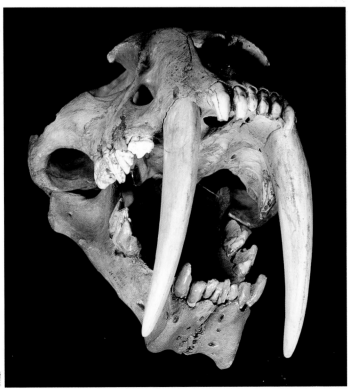

▲ A reconstruction of *Smilodon* attacking and pulling down a young mammoth. Modern big cats use their canines to crush neck vertebrae and strangle their prey. Saber teeth would have broken if *Smilodon* had used them in this way. Instead, *Smilodon* pierced vulnerable fleshy areas such as the abdomen and generally eviscerated their prey.

► The skull of a *Smilodon fatalis* from Rancho La Brea. This sabertooth cat's skull is similar in size to that of a male African lion but, its saber teeth are 6 inches (152 millimeters) in length, whereas the canines of an African lion are 2.3 inches (60 millimeters).

Brea, there are many impressive examples of crippling bony lesions — so severe that the animal would have been incapacitated for many months — yet most of the bones exhibit extensive healing. Support (perhaps better stated as "tolerance") within this species appears to have allowed the survival of an animal with truly amazing injuries. African lions will allow incapacitated members of the pride to obtain food from pride kills, and will afford some protection to injured pride members. The survival of some severely injured individuals of *Smilodon* clearly implies some sort of group social existence, perhaps not unlike that of an African lion pride.

African lions are sometimes injured by others in the pride while feeding at pride kills, and in fights between males for pride dominance. Many of the bone lesions found in the shoulder region and along the spinal column of *Smilodon* are reminiscent of bite wounds, and may have resulted from similar interactions.

THE LIVING CATS

FIONA C. SUNQUIST

Discovering the diversity of forms within the Felidae, characterizing and naming species, arranging these species into a natural system of categories, and advancing an understanding of evolutionary relationship among them are subjects of ongoing study and debate among specialists. We have followed the classification of the species of cats as presented in Honacki et al (1982) and an individual cat can be identified from the drawing and characters given in each account. Because most species originate as geographical isolates, we can expect that a certain number of such isolated populations are on the borderline between subspecies and species, and, indeed, the status of some species is debated among specialists. African conservation biologist Jonathan Kingdon reminds us that "a species is the realization of a unique possibility of existence." In order to explain speciation, the origin of reproductive isolation between populations must be resolved. This information is simply not known for many of the cat populations that are in question. In my view, the taxonomy of the Felidae, based on morphological analysis, has advanced about as far as it can with the specimens now available in museums. Advances in our understanding will come with detailed studies of behavior, ecology, and population genetics.

The use of biochemical methods is a basis for further clarifying relationships and for advancing our understanding of the evolutionary relationships of the cats. Based on the taxonomy prepared by Honacki et al (1982), Wozencraft (1989) grouped the cats into subfamilies, leaving the cheetah in an undetermined or *incertae sedis* position. These relationships are charted here. Using biochemical tools, Stephen O'Brien and his colleagues have proposed that the Felidae be viewed as three distinct lineages: the small cat lineage of South America; the wild cat lineage from which the domestic cat was derived; and the Panthera lineage that includes members from both subfamilies. The order of the listings of the cats in the chart below is organized to demonstrate these lineages. Ernst Mayr taught that the two great aspects of organic nature are life processes and diversity. Our understanding of the nature and extent of the diversity we see in the cats and the evolutionary relationships among them is far from complete.

John Seidensticker

FAMILY FELIDAE

LINEAGE		US FISH AND WILDLIFE SERVICE LISTING	IUCN LISTING
PANTHERA	**INCERTAE SEDIS (UNDETERMINED TAXONOMY)**		
	cheetah *Acinonyx jubatus*	Endangered	Vulnerable (1 subspecies endangered)
	SUBFAMILY PANTHERINAE		
	lion *Panthera leo*	Endangered (1 subspecies only)	Endangered (1 subspecies only)
	tiger *Panthera tigris*	Endangered	Endangered
	leopard *Panthera pardus*	Endangered	Vulnerable (2 subspecies endangered)
	jaguar *Panthera onca*	Endangered	Vulnerable
	snow leopard *Panthera uncia*	Endangered	Endangered
	clouded leopard *Neofelis nebulosa*	Endangered	Vulnerable
	marbled cat *Felis marmorata*	Endangered	
	North American lynx *Lynx canadensis*		
	bobcat *Lynx rufus*	Endangered (1 subspecies only)	
	Eurasian lynx *Lynx lynx*		
	Spanish lynx *Lynx pardinus*	Endangered	Vulnerable
	caracal *Lynx caracal*		
OCELOT	**SUBFAMILY FELINAE**		
	serval *Felis serval*	Endangered (1 subspecies only)	
	African golden cat *Felis aurata*		
	Asian golden cat *Felis temmincki*	Endangered	
	leopard cat *Felis bengalensis*	Endangered (1 subspecies only)	
	fishing cat *Felis viverrina*		
	flat-headed cat *Felis planiceps*	Endangered	
	rusty-spotted cat *Felis rubiginosa*		
	bay cat or Bornean red cat *Felix badia*		Rare
	Iriomote cat *Felis iriomotensis*	Endangered	Endangered
	jaguarundi *Felis yagouaroundi*	Endangered (4 subspecies only)	
	puma, mountain lion, cougar *Felis concolor*	Endangered (3 subspecies only)	Endangered (2 subspecies only)
	ocelot *Felis pardalis*	Endangered	Vulnerable
	margay *Felis wiedii*	Endangered	Vulnerable
	oncilla *Felis tigrina*	Endangered	Vulnerable
	kodkod *Felis guigna*		
	Geoffroy's cat *Felis geoffroyi*		
	Andean mountain cat *Felis jacobita*	Endangered	Rare
DOMESTIC CAT	pampas cat *Felis colocolo*		
	wild cat *Felis silvestris* (includes *F.s. libyca*)		Vulnerable
	Pallas' cat *Felis manul*		
	jungle cat *Felis chaus*		
	black-footed cat *Felis nigripes*	Endangered	
	sand cat *Felis margarita*	Endangered (1 subspecies only)	Endangered (1 subspecies only)
	Chinese desert cat *Felis bieti*		

SUBFAMILY FELINAE
Felis concolor
Puma, mountain lion or cougar

APPEARANCE The puma and the African lion are the only two plain-colored big cats. However, the puma is generally much lighter in build, has a smaller head, and males do not have a mane. The puma's coat can be red-brown, blue-gray, or almost any color in between. The reddish coat color generally seems to be more common in tropical areas, while the gray coat tends to predominate in northern areas. The puma has small ears, a long neck, a slim, elongated body, and a long tail.

SIZE The puma is generally about the size of a leopard, but weights and measurements vary greatly across this cat's broad geographical range. The largest animals are found in the extreme northern and southern parts of its range. Males weigh 67–103 kilograms (148–227 pounds) while females are smaller and lighter at 36–60 kilograms (79.5–132.5 pounds). Males measure 105–195 centimeters (41.25–76.75 inches) head and body length, with a tail of 66–78 centimeters (26–30.75 inches), and females measure 96–151 centimeters (37.75–59.5 inches) head and body, with a tail of 53–81 centimeters (20.75–32 inches).

HABITAT Pumas can live in coniferous forest, tropical forest, swamp, grassland, and brush country. They are found at elevations that range from sea level to 4,500 meters (14,765 feet).

DISTRIBUTION The puma is the most widely distributed of any of the American cats. Its current range includes Canada, North America — west of the Great Plains, southern Florida, Mexico and Central America, and South America.

REPRODUCTION Two to three cubs are born after a 90–95 day gestation period. The cubs are born with a spotted coat but the spots fade and usually disappear as the young become adult. Cubs nurse for three or more months, but begin to eat meat as early as six weeks of age. Young pumas become independent when they are about two years old, and littermates may stay together for a few months after leaving their mother.

SOCIAL SYSTEM Solitary. Females may share overlapping ranges, and male ranges may overlap several female ranges, but there is usually little overlap between resident males. Young and transient animals may move through the established ranges of residents but are not allowed to stay long.

DIET In general, deer are the most important part of the puma's diet. Other prey includes beaver, porcupine, hare, raccoon, opossum, and feral hog. The kill is often dragged to a secluded spot and after the cat has eaten its fill it may cover the carcass with vegetation. Large prey like elk can provide food for a week or more.

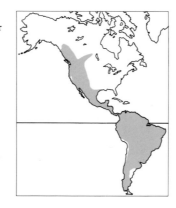

INCERTAE SEDIS (Undetermined taxonomy)
Acinonyx jubatus
Cheetah

APPEARANCE Even if you did not know that the slender, long-legged cheetah was the world's fastest land mammal, this cat looks like a runner. Its slim but muscled frame looks almost gaunt, and its deep-chested, narrow-waisted body has the pared down look of a sprinter. The cheetahs small head has a short muzzle with high-set eyes, wide nostrils, and small rounded ears. The claws are exposed even when completely retracted, and help give the cat more traction during fast turns and rapid acceleration. The fur is short and coarse, tawny yellow, marked with round black spots.

SIZE The cheetah is a lightweight compared with other big cats; adults weigh only 39–65 kilograms (86–143 pounds). The cheetahs head and body is 112–135 centimeters (44–53 inches) with a long tail that measures 66–84 centimeters (26–33 inches).

HABITAT The cheetah's running, rather than stalk-and-ambush, hunting style confines it to open areas where there is enough cover for stalking. It is found in more open habitats, from semidesert to open grassland and thick bush.

DISTRIBUTION Africa and the Middle East.

REPRODUCTION After a gestation period of 90–95 days, females can give birth to as many as eight, but more usually three to five cubs. The young weigh 150–300 grams (5.25–10.5 ounces) at birth and begin to follow their mother when they are about six weeks old. Cubs are weaned by the time they are six months old and leave their mother at about 13 to 20 months of age. Siblings may remain together for several months longer.

SOCIAL SYSTEM Cheetahs have one of the most unusual spacing systems of all the felids. Adult females do not seem to be territorial, but avoid each other. Several related and unrelated females may share large home ranges that overlap each other. Adult male littermates sometimes remain together as a group to defend a small territory, and unrelated males sometimes join together in small groups. In contrast with other cats, female ranges may be five or more times larger than male ranges.

DIET Hunting by day, the cheetah chases mammals weighing less than 40 kilograms (88 pounds), pursuing animals such as gazelles, impala, wildebeest calves, and hares. Prey is stalked to within about ten meters, then chased. Chases last an average of 20 seconds, and rarely more than a minute. About half the chases are successful.

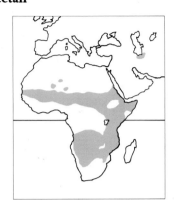

SUBFAMILY PANTHERINAE
Panthera leo
Lion

APPEARANCE Possibly the best known of all the big cats, the lion is well known for its habit of living in prides or groups. Adult lions usually have a plain unspotted coat, light brown to dark ochre in color. Cubs are marked with spots which sometimes persist on the legs and belly until they are fully grown. Male lions have a brown mane, which tends to grow darker and fuller as the animal ages. The tail has a black tuft at the end. "White" lions occasionally occur in the Transvaal region of southern Africa, but these are not true albinos.

SIZE Males stand 123 centimeters (48.5 inches) at the shoulder and measure 170–250 centimeters (67–98.5 inches) head and body, with a tail of 90–105 centimeters (35.5–41.25 inches). Male weights range from 150–250 kilograms (330–550 pounds). Females are smaller, usually standing 107 centimeters (42.25 inches) at the shoulder and measuring 140–175 centimeters (55–69 inches) head and body, with a tail of 70–100 centimeters (27.5–39.25 inches). Females weigh 120–182 kilograms (265–400 pounds).

HABITAT Lions are generally found in open habitats — grassy plains, savannas, arid woodlands, and semidesert.

DISTRIBUTION Across Africa south of the Sahara, south to Botswana. A small population consisting of a few hundred Asian lions still survive in the Gir forest of western India.

REPRODUCTION Lions have no fixed breeding season. Females in a pride will often come into estrus and give birth in synchrony. One to four cubs, each weighing about 1.5 kilograms (3.25 pounds) are born after a 110 day gestation. Cubs can suckle from any female in the pride, and young usually remain with their mother for two years.

SOCIAL SYSTEM Lions live in prides that range in size from 3 to 30 individuals. Pride size varies according to the area and prey availability. A group of related lionesses and their cubs form the stable core of a pride. Daughters are usually recruited into the pride but males leave as they become mature. One to seven males associate with the group of females. Male tenure with a pride can be as brief as a few months or as long as six years, but eventually the pride males are driven off by another group of males.

DIET Lions feed on a variety of large and medium-sized prey, including giraffe, buffalo, zebra, antelope, wildebeest, and warthog. Lions will also eat carrion and smaller prey.

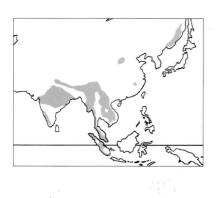

SUBFAMILY PANTHERINAE
Panthera tigris
Tiger

APPEARANCE Being the only felid with stripes, the tiger is probably the most easily recognized big cat. Its coat varies from dark orange to reddish ochre, and the belly, neck, and insides of the limbs are creamy white. The Siberian tiger generally has the palest coat while the tiger in Indochina is much darker. A series of dark brown or black stripes run vertically across the body.

SIZE The tiger is the largest of the living cats, and Siberian tigers may weigh as much as 320 kilograms (705 pounds). In India males more commonly weigh 200–270 kilograms (440–595 pounds), while females weigh 125–160 kilograms (275–355 pounds). Head and body length varies from 140–280 centimeters (55–110 inches), and tail length is 60–95 centimeters (23.5–37.5 inches).

HABITAT Tigers can live in a variety of habitat types and climatic conditions, but they require sufficient cover, year-round access to water, and a steady supply of large prey. They live in snow-covered taiga, tropical evergreen forest, mangrove swamps, and dry deciduous forest.

DISTRIBUTION Tigers are found in India, Nepal, Bhutan, Bangladesh, Burma, Thailand, Vietnam, USSR, and perhaps China.

REPRODUCTION Tigers mate at any time of the year, but most frequently from November to April. Two to three young are born after a gestation period of 104–106 days. The young nurse until they are about six months old and male cubs grow faster than females. The young leave their natal range when their mother has a new litter, or usually when they are about two years old.

SOCIAL SYSTEM Solitary. Females may have exclusive territories, or several female ranges may overlap. Home range size is strongly influenced by prey density, and female ranges as small as 16 square kilometers (6.2 square miles) and as large as 1,000 square kilometers (386 square miles) have been recorded. Male ranges are usually larger, and one male may overlap the ranges of several females. Despite the fact that these cats usually hunt by themselves, tigers are not asocial. Females spend a large portion of their lives accompanied by dependent young, and adults may come together to share a kill.

DIET Tigers feed on whatever large prey they can catch. Their diet includes deer, pigs, gaur, and buffalo. They readily kill domestic livestock and are known to include man in their diet.

SUBFAMILY PANTHERINAE
Panthera onca
Jaguar

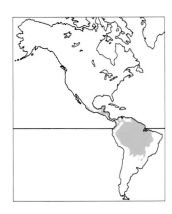

APPEARANCE The jaguar is a powerful, deep-chested, stocky cat with a large, rounded head and short, sturdy limbs. Its size and spotted coat make it look much like a heavyset leopard, however there are minor differences between their spot patterns. The jaguar's fur varies from pale gold to a rich rusty red, and is patterned with a series of dark rosettes that enclose one or two smaller spots. The rosettes on a leopard's coat do not have smaller spots inside them. Along the middle of the jaguar's back, a row of black spots sometimes merge into a solid line. All-black (melanistic) jaguars are not uncommon, and in these black animals the spots sometimes show through the darker background of the fur.

SIZE The stocky build of the jaguar makes it look larger than it really is. The largest jaguars come from the Pantanal region of Brazil where males weighing 136 kilograms (300 pounds) have been documented, but elsewhere jaguars weigh much less. Throughout much of the jaguar's range males commonly weigh about 55 kilograms (121.5 pounds) while the smaller females average 36 kilograms (79.5 pounds). The jaguar's head and body length measures 112–185 centimeters (45–72.75 inches), and the tail length is between 45 and 75 centimeters (17.75 and 29.5 inches).

HABITAT Jaguars are often found in association with well-watered areas, such as the swampy grasslands of the Brazilian Pantanal. In other areas jaguars frequently use riverine forest alongside streams, rivers, and lakes. They may also live in more arid areas, but only where watercourses penetrate this drier habitat.

DISTRIBUTION The jaguar's range has been substantially reduced in the last 100 years. Its present range includes southcentral Mexico, through Central America, and into South America as far south as northern Argentina.

REPRODUCTION One to four young are born after a gestation period of 93–105 days. The young weigh about 700–900 grams (24.5–32 ounces) at birth and remain with their mother for about two years.

SOCIAL SYSTEM Solitary. Home range size and land tenure system vary in response to prey density, habitat, and human disturbance. Female ranges as small as 10 square kilometers (4 square miles) and as large as 168 square kilometers (65 square miles) have been recorded, while male ranges are usually larger, varying from 28–152 square kilometers (11–59 square miles).

DIET The jaguar will feed on almost anything that is available, including lizards, snakes, capybara, caiman, small mammals, deer, fish, turtles, and cattle. The jaguar's powerful jaws and robust canine teeth enable the cat to kill livestock weighing three or four times its own weight, often with a bite to the back of the skull, rather than the more common neck or throat bite employed by the other large cats.

SUBFAMILY PANTHERINAE
Panthera pardus
Leopard

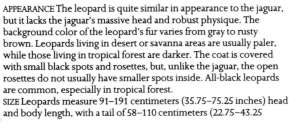

APPEARANCE The leopard is quite similar in appearance to the jaguar, but it lacks the jaguar's massive head and robust physique. The background color of the leopard's fur varies from gray to rusty brown. Leopards living in desert or savanna areas are usually paler, while those living in tropical forest are darker. The coat is covered with small black spots and rosettes, but, unlike the jaguar, the open rosettes do not usually have smaller spots inside. All-black leopards are common, especially in tropical forest.

SIZE Leopards measure 91–191 centimeters (35.75–75.25 inches) head and body length, with a tail of 58–110 centimeters (22.75–43.25 inches). Males weigh 37–90 kilograms (81.51–98.5 pounds), whereas females usually weigh about a third less, 28–60 kilograms (61.75–132.5 pounds).

HABITAT Leopards are great generalists in terms of habitat use. They seem to be able to live in almost any area that has sufficient food and cover. They are found in lowland rainforest, wooded savanna, scrub, arid rocky mountains, deserts, and agricultural and grazing land.

DISTRIBUTION The leopard has one of the widest distributions of any of the felids. It is found throughout much of Africa, except the Sahara, and in parts of Israel, the Middle East, Pakistan, India, Southeast Asia, as well as throughout China and Siberia.

REPRODUCTION In the northern part of its range the leopard mates in January and February, and elsewhere breeding occurs throughout the year. After a gestation period of 90–105 days, two or three young are born in a secluded den. The cubs weigh about 0.5 kilograms (1 pound) at birth, and open their eyes when they are 10 days old. The young remain with their mother until they are 15–24 months old.

SOCIAL SYSTEM The leopard is a solitary cat. Males and females usually maintain territories, which may be 8–63 square kilometers (3–24.5 square miles) in size. A male's territory often overlaps the territory of more than one female.

DIET Leopards feed on a wide variety of prey. They will eat almost anything from insects and rodents to large ungulates, and are known to kill prey weighing several times their own weight. Commonly they prey on animals such as gazelle, deer, pig, and monkey.

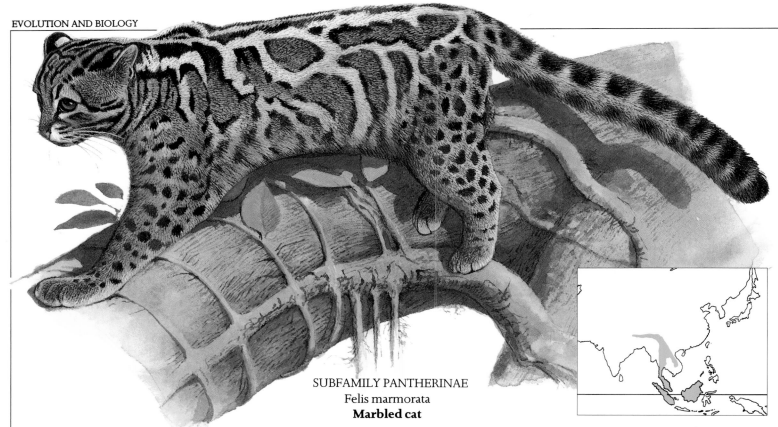

SUBFAMILY PANTHERINAE
Felis marmorata
Marbled cat

APPEARANCE In coat color and markings the marbled cat looks somewhat like a small clouded leopard. However, the marbled cat has much thicker, softer fur and well developed underfur. The background color of the marbled cat's coat can be dark brownish gray, yellowish gray or red-brown. The fur is marked with large dark blotches, stripes, and spots. In proportion to its body, the marbled cat has one of the longest tails of any of the felids.

SIZE Although its thick fur and long tail make it look larger, the marbled cat is the size of an average domestic cat, weighing only 2–5 kilograms (4.5–11 pounds). Head and body length varies from 45–61 centimeters (17.75–24 inches), and tail length from 35–55 centimeters (13.75–21.75 inches).

HABITAT The marbled cat lives only in forested areas, where it is believed to be highly arboreal.

DISTRIBUTION The marbled cat is found in northern India, Nepal, Sikkim, and Assam. It is also distributed through Indochina, Malaysia, Sumatra, and Borneo.

REPRODUCTION Nothing known.

SOCIAL SYSTEM Solitary.

DIET Birds are thought to form a major part of this cat's unknown diet; they are also thought to take squirrels, rats, and frogs.

SUBFAMILY PANTHERINAE
Neofelis nebulosa
Clouded leopard

APPEARANCE One of the most unusually marked cats, the clouded leopard's coat is patterned with large dark, cloud-shaped markings. On the shoulders and back the markings are darker towards the rear, suggesting that this might be the way stripes evolved from spots. The lower parts of the legs, the head and shoulders, and the belly are covered with large dark spots. The clouded leopard has short powerful legs, a very long tail, and, relatively, the longest canine teeth of any living cat.

SIZE These cats can weigh as much as 22 kilograms (48.5 pounds) and measure 93 centimeters (36.5 inches) head and body, with a tail 76 centimeters (30 inches) long.

HABITAT Rarely seen in the wild, there is some controversy as to whether the clouded leopard is an arboreal species — strongly tied to dense tropical evergreen forest — or a terrestrial hunter who uses roads and trails in logged forests. The answer is probably somewhere in between, in that the clouded leopard can hunt both in trees and on the ground. They can also live in drier forests if there is enough suitably sized prey.

DISTRIBUTION The clouded leopard ranges from countries of the Himalayas, southern China, and Taiwan to peninsula Malaysia, Sumatra, and the island of Borneo.

REPRODUCTION The gestation period is believed to be between 86–93 days. The females can give birth to as many as five young, but the most common litter size is two. The young suckle until they are five months old, and males seem to develop faster than females.

SOCIAL SYSTEM Nothing known.

DIET Hunting both on the ground and in the trees, the clouded leopard is thought to feed on birds, monkey, pig, cattle, goat, deer, and porcupine.

SUBFAMILY PANTHERINAE
Panthera uncia
Snow leopard

APPEARANCE The exotic-looking snow leopard has gray-green eyes, and long, thick, smoke-gray fur patterned with large dark rosettes and spots. The head is small with a high forehead, and the ears are short and rounded. The snow leopard has comparatively short legs and large broad paws.

SIZE Slightly smaller than the common leopard, snow leopards weigh 25–75 kilograms (55–165 pounds). This cat has an exceptionally long thick tail, which can be 80–100 centimeters (31.5–39.25 inches) long, almost as long as the head and body, which measures 100–130 centimeters (39.25–51.25 inches).

HABITAT This cat is found in steep and rugged terrain at high elevations. Snow leopards have been recorded in high rocky areas, alpine meadows, alpine steppe scrub, and high altitude forests. They generally live above the tree line at elevations of 2,700–6,000 meters (8,900–19,700 feet). During winter the snow leopard may descend to lower elevations, but in summer it moves back up the mountain to the steepest and most remote terrain.

DISTRIBUTION The snow leopard lives in the mountainous regions of Central Asia. It is rare and very patchily distributed within this large geographical area but can be found in parts of the USSR, Mongolia, China, Nepal, Bhutan, India, Pakistan, and possibly Afghanistan.

REPRODUCTION Births occur from April to June, and two or three cubs are born after a gestation period of 90–103 days. The cubs eat their first solid food when they are about two months old, and a month later begin to follow their mother when she goes hunting. The cubs probably leave their natal range at about two years.

SOCIAL SYSTEM Solitary. Pairs have been seen hunting together but it is not known if they were a male and female or mother and young. Males and females probably have overlapping ranges.

DIET The snow leopard preys mainly on blue sheep and marmots, though it is also known to feed on musk deer, ibex, markhor, pika, hare, and birds. These cats also eat willow twigs and other vegetation, and are known to kill domestic goats and sheep.

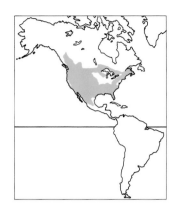

SUBFAMILY PANTHERINAE
Lynx rufus
Bobcat

APPEARANCE Bobcats are very similar in appearance to lynx, but generally have shorter legs and smaller feet. Bobcat fur is short, soft, and dense and varies greatly in coloration. The background color of the fur can be light gray to reddish brown. The fur along the middle of the back is usually darker, while the underparts are generally white. The pelt may be marked with black or dark brown spots or bars, and the backs of the ears are black with a prominent white spot. The short tail is white underneath with a broad black band on the upper tip and several indistinct dark bands.

SIZE Usually about twice the size of a domestic cat, male bobcats weigh about 10 kilograms (22 pounds) and females about 7 kilograms (15.5 pounds). The head and body length of males is about 72 centimeters (28.25 inches) with a tail length of almost 15 centimeters (6 inches), while females have a head and body length of about 65 centimeters (25.5 inches) with a tail length of almost 14 centimeters (5.5 inches).

HABITAT Bobcats live in a wide variety of habitats including coniferous and hardwood forests, brush, and even deserts.

DISTRIBUTION Snow accumulation seems to be the main factor limiting the northern distribution of the bobcat. Their range extends from southern Canada to central Mexico, but they have been eradicated from some midwestern and eastern states in the United States.

REPRODUCTION After a gestation period of about 62 days, females give birth to two to four kittens. The young nurse for about two months, and remain with the female until the spring following their birth.

SOCIAL SYSTEM Solitary. Adult females typically occupy home ranges that do not overlap with those of other adult females. Male ranges may or may not overlap those of other males.

DIET Cottontail rabbit, snowshoe hare, and jackrabbit are the most common food of bobcats. However, they also feed on rodents, opossums, birds, snakes, and deer.

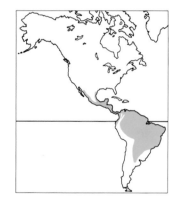

SUBFAMILY FELINAE
Felis yagouaroundi
Jaguarundi

APPEARANCE A very unusual-looking felid, the jaguarundi's long-bodied, low-slung build is reminiscent of a marten. Some people have compared it to a weasel or an otter. This cat has a long slender body, short legs, and a very long tail. Its head is small and flattened and it has short, round ears. Jaguarundi are also one of the few unspotted cats, having almost uniform-colored fur that is either red-brown or gray.

SIZE About the size of a large domestic cat, jaguarundi weigh 3–6 kilograms (6.5–13.25 pounds) with a head and body length of 51–77 centimeters (20–30.25 inches), and a tail length of 28–51 centimeters (11–20 inches).

HABITAT This cat can live in a variety of habitats from arid thorn forests to dense second-growth forest and swampy grasslands. Generally, they seem to be able to live in more open areas than many of the other neotropical felids. These cats can swim well and are often found in riverine habitats.

DISTRIBUTION The jaguarundi's range extends from southern Texas through Mexico, Central America, and into South America east of the Andes to northern Argentina.

REPRODUCTION Commonly two, but occasionally three kittens are born after a 72–75 day gestation period. The young are born spotted but the markings soon fade. The kittens begin to eat solid food when they are about six weeks old.

SOCIAL SYSTEM Solitary.

DIET Hunting mainly on the ground during the day, jaguarundi feed on the most abundant and easily caught food in the area. They eat small mammals, arthropods, birds, opossums, and fruit, as well as rabbits, armadillos, and monkeys.

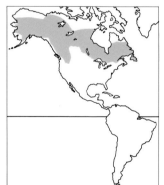

SUBFAMILY PANTHERINAE
Lynx canadensis
North American lynx

APPEARANCE The lynx has long thick fur which is usually yellowish brown in color and may be patterned with dark spots. The tail is short and has several dark rings and a dark tip. This tall cat has especially long hind legs which give it the appearance of being tilted forwards. Lynx also have very large, densely furred feet, which may measure as much as 10 centimeters (4 inches) across. These "snowshoe" feet prevent the animal from sinking into deep snow. The ears are tipped with black tufts of hair and there is usually a flaring ruff of fur around the animal's neck.

SIZE Long legs and thick fur make this cat look much larger than it really is. Males commonly weigh about 10 kilograms (22 pounds) while females are slightly smaller at about 8.5 kilograms (18.75 pounds). They measure 80–100 centimeters (31.5–39.25 inches) head and body length, with a short 5–13 centimeter (2–5 inch) tail.

HABITAT Lynx are found mainly in boreal forests but they can live in farmland if it is interspersed with heavily wooded areas.

DISTRIBUTION Canada and Alaska.

REPRODUCTION Two to four young are born after a nine week gestation period. Kittens are usually weaned at three months of age. Litter size and growth and development of the young are directly related to food availability. Females may breed in their first year when food is abundant.

SOCIAL SYSTEM Usually solitary, but adult females with kittens have been known to hunt cooperatively. Home ranges are usually 16–20 square kilometers (6.25–7.75 square miles), in size but may vary from 12–243 square kilometers (4.5–94 square miles). Home ranges of males are generally larger than females.

DIET North American lynx feed almost exclusively on snowshoe hares, but they also eat mice, voles, red squirrels, flying squirrels, grouse, and ptarmigan. They occasionally kill deer and caribou fawns and may scavenge from deer or moose carcasses. An exception to this regime occurs on Newfoundland Island where lynx prey extensively on caribou fawns.

SUBFAMILY PANTHERINAE
Lynx caracal
Caracal

APPEARANCE The long-legged caracal has a slender body and a short tail. The caracal's hind legs are longer than the forelegs, and this gives a standing caracal the appearance of being tilted forwards. The fur is short and unspotted, usually reddish brown in color on the back and sides, but white on the chin, throat, and belly. The black-backed ears are topped with a long (4.5 centimeter/1.75 inch) tuft of black hair. All-black (or melanistic) caracals have been recorded.
SIZE About the size of a springer spaniel, caracal are the heaviest of the small African cats. They may weigh as much as 20 kilograms (44 pounds), but males typically weigh about 15 kilograms (33 pounds) and females average 11 kilograms (24.25 pounds). Head and body length is usually 60–105 centimeters (23.5–41.25 inches) and the tail measures about 20–35 centimeters (7.75–13.75 inches).
HABITAT The caracal lives in dry woodlands, savanna, acacia scrub, arid hilly steppe, and dry mountain areas. It does not live in true desert or dense tropical forest.
DISTRIBUTION Northern, central, and southern Africa, through parts of the Middle East, Saudi Arabia, USSR, Afghanistan, Pakistan, and northwest and central India.
REPRODUCTION One to three young are born after a gestation period of about 79 days. The young stay with their mother for about a year.
SOCIAL SYSTEM Solitary.
DIET Caracal hunt mainly at night, feeding on birds, rodents, hyraxes, dik-dik, and antelope fawns. They are capable of taking quite large prey, like impala and mountain reedbuck.

SUBFAMILY FELINAE
Felis serval
Serval

APPEARANCE The serval is a tall, long-legged cat. It has a small, slim head dominated by a pair of very large ears and a short tail that reaches only to the animal's hocks. The background color of the serval's coat is tawny gold, and the fur is marked with round black dots which may be as small as a freckle or as large as a quarter.
SIZE Although serval usually weigh about 8–18 kilograms (17.5–39.75 pounds), they stand 60 centimeters (23.5 inches) high at the shoulder. They measure 67–100 centimeters (26.5–39.25 inches) head and body, with a tail of 24–45 centimeters (9.5–17.75 inches).
HABITAT Servals prefer well watered grasslands and are confined to areas near water. They do not live in densely forested areas.
DISTRIBUTION This cat is found only in Africa, where it is widely distributed and often quite abundant in countries south of the Sahara. Historically, it was also found in the Atlas region of North Africa but it has not been seen there for more than 20 years.
REPRODUCTION One to three kittens are born after a gestation period of about 74 days. The den is usually in dense vegetation or an abandoned burrow dug by another animal. The young begin to eat solid food when they are about a month old and acquire their permanent canine teeth when they are six months old. The young leave their natal area when they are about a year old.
SOCIAL SYSTEM Solitary. In Kenya females maintained exclusive territories which were at least 9 square kilometers (3.5 square miles) while males overlapped two or more females. Ranges are maintained by frequent scent marking.
DIET Hunting almost exclusively on the ground, servals are highly specialized rodent catchers. They use their large ears to locate rodent prey in tall grass. Servals also catch and eat frogs, lizards, mole rats, small birds, and insects.

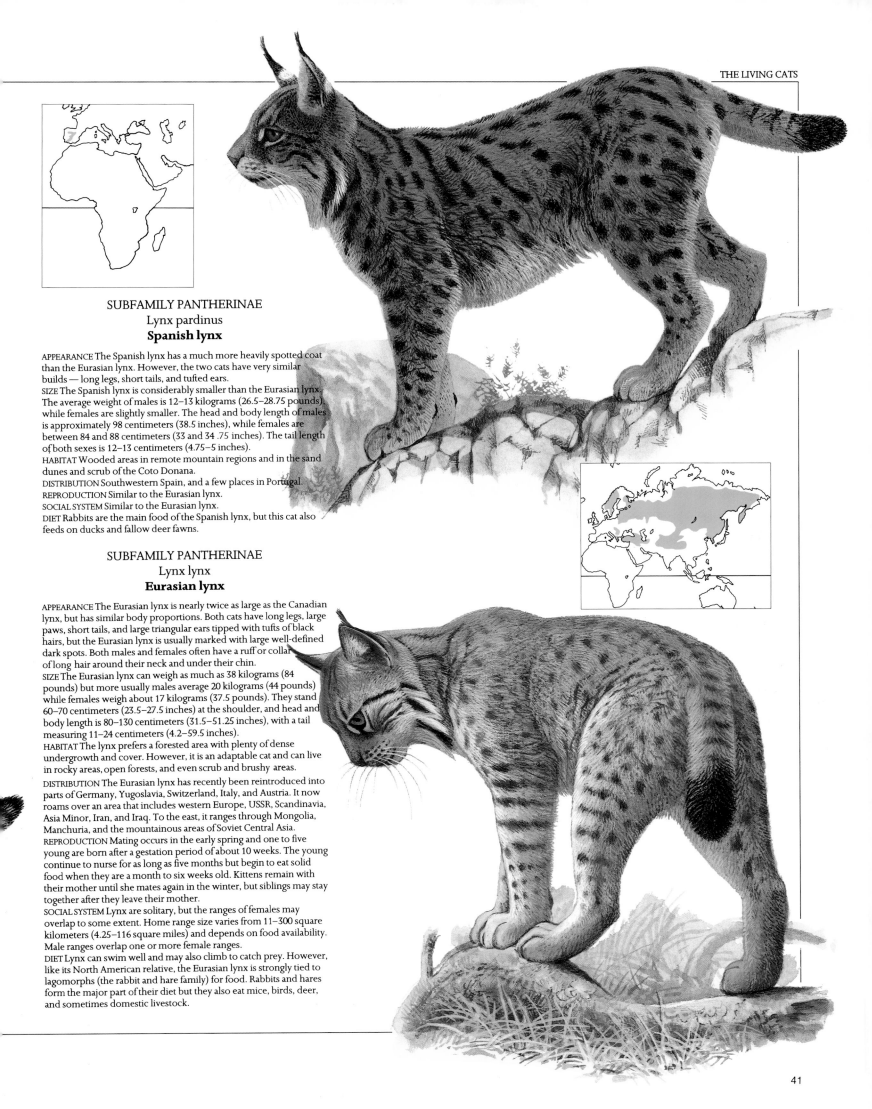

SUBFAMILY PANTHERINAE
Lynx pardinus
Spanish lynx

APPEARANCE The Spanish lynx has a much more heavily spotted coat than the Eurasian lynx. However, the two cats have very similar builds — long legs, short tails, and tufted ears.
SIZE The Spanish lynx is considerably smaller than the Eurasian lynx. The average weight of males is 12–13 kilograms (26.5–28.75 pounds), while females are slightly smaller. The head and body length of males is approximately 98 centimeters (38.5 inches), while females are between 84 and 88 centimeters (33 and 34 .75 inches). The tail length of both sexes is 12–13 centimeters (4.75–5 inches).
HABITAT Wooded areas in remote mountain regions and in the sand dunes and scrub of the Coto Donana.
DISTRIBUTION Southwestern Spain, and a few places in Portugal.
REPRODUCTION Similar to the Eurasian lynx.
SOCIAL SYSTEM Similar to the Eurasian lynx.
DIET Rabbits are the main food of the Spanish lynx, but this cat also feeds on ducks and fallow deer fawns.

SUBFAMILY PANTHERINAE
Lynx lynx
Eurasian lynx

APPEARANCE The Eurasian lynx is nearly twice as large as the Canadian lynx, but has similar body proportions. Both cats have long legs, large paws, short tails, and large triangular ears tipped with tufts of black hairs, but the Eurasian lynx is usually marked with large well-defined dark spots. Both males and females often have a ruff or collar of long hair around their neck and under their chin.
SIZE The Eurasian lynx can weigh as much as 38 kilograms (84 pounds) but more usually males average 20 kilograms (44 pounds) while females weigh about 17 kilograms (37.5 pounds). They stand 60–70 centimeters (23.5–27.5 inches) at the shoulder, and head and body length is 80–130 centimeters (31.5–51.25 inches), with a tail measuring 11–24 centimeters (4.2–59.5 inches).
HABITAT The lynx prefers a forested area with plenty of dense undergrowth and cover. However, it is an adaptable cat and can live in rocky areas, open forests, and even scrub and brushy areas.
DISTRIBUTION The Eurasian lynx has recently been reintroduced into parts of Germany, Yugoslavia, Switzerland, Italy, and Austria. It now roams over an area that includes western Europe, USSR, Scandinavia, Asia Minor, Iran, and Iraq. To the east, it ranges through Mongolia, Manchuria, and the mountainous areas of Soviet Central Asia.
REPRODUCTION Mating occurs in the early spring and one to five young are born after a gestation period of about 10 weeks. The young continue to nurse for as long as five months but begin to eat solid food when they are a month to six weeks old. Kittens remain with their mother until she mates again in the winter, but siblings may stay together after they leave their mother.
SOCIAL SYSTEM Lynx are solitary, but the ranges of females may overlap to some extent. Home range size varies from 11–300 square kilometers (4.25–116 square miles) and depends on food availability. Male ranges overlap one or more female ranges.
DIET Lynx can swim well and may also climb to catch prey. However, like its North American relative, the Eurasian lynx is strongly tied to lagomorphs (the rabbit and hare family) for food. Rabbits and hares form the major part of their diet but they also eat mice, birds, deer, and sometimes domestic livestock.

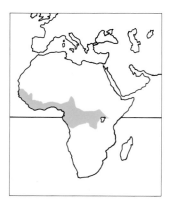

SUBFAMILY FELINAE
Felis aurata
African golden cat

APPEARANCE The African golden cat has a rounded face, small ears, and a short tail. It has one of the most variable coat colorings of any member of the cat family. Its fur can vary from orange to gray, and the various color phases can be either plain and unspotted, partially spotted, or completely covered with spots. Melanistic or all-black individuals have been recorded.

SIZE The African golden cat is about twice the size of a large house cat. This cat weighs between 5 and 12 kilograms (11 and 26.5 pounds), with a head and body length of 61–101 centimeters (24–39.75 inches). It has a comparatively short tail, 16–37 centimeters (6.25–14.5 inches), which measures about one-third of the head and body.

HABITAT The African golden cat is locally known as the "leopard's brother" because the two cats are often found in the same area. Their preferred habitat is moist forest, but they also live in dense secondary vegetation and along watercourses that extend into drier, more open countryside. They can live in mountainous areas, and have been found in alpine moorland.

DISTRIBUTION The golden cat is found throughout West Africa and Central Africa. It may be locally common in some parts of Uganda and the Tai and Azagny national parks of the Ivory Coast.

REPRODUCTION There are no records of a den ever being found in the wild and since there are only a handful of them in zoos, African golden cats are rarely bred in captivity. They give birth to one or two young which develop rapidly. By the time they are six months old the young have permanent canine teeth, and are roughly as large as their mother. Male kittens grow faster than females.

SOCIAL SYSTEM This is undoubtedly a solitary species. Males and females probably maintain their territories with a combination of scent marks, scrapes, and feces.

DIET The golden cat hunts on the ground at dusk and dawn and during the night. It feeds on rodents, hyrax, monkeys, and duikers. It probably also eats birds when the opportunity arises.

SUBFAMILY FELINAE
Felis temmincki
Asian golden cat

APPEARANCE Like the golden cat of Africa, the Asian golden cat may have either a plain unmarked coat or be marked with spots and stripes. The background color of the coat varies from golden brown to dark brown, red, or gray. This cat has a white patch on the underside of the last part of its tail. Melanistic or all-black Asian golden cats are not uncommon.

SIZE Somewhat larger than its African relative, the Asian golden cat usually weighs 12–15 kilograms (26.5–33 pounds) and measures 50–60 centimeters (19.75–23.5 inches) head and body, with a tail of 35–40 centimeters (13.75–15.75 inches).

HABITAT The Asian golden cat lives in deciduous forests, tropical rainforests, and occasionally more open habitats.

DISTRIBUTION Through Southeast Asia from Nepal, east to Burma, China, Thailand, Malaysia, and Sumatra.

REPRODUCTION One to two young are born after a 75 day gestation.

SOCIAL SYSTEM Nothing known.

DIET This cat is believed to hunt mainly on the ground although it can also climb well. It feeds on hares, small deer, birds, and lizards, and sometimes takes domestic poultry and livestock.

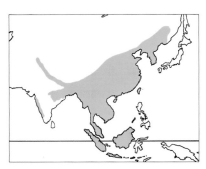

SUBFAMILY FELINAE
Felis bengalensis
Leopard cat

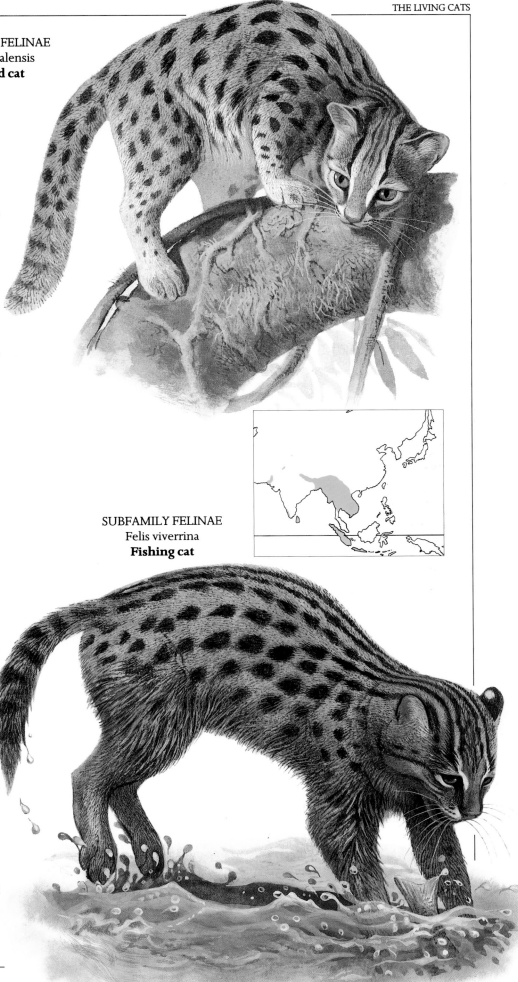

APPEARANCE The leopard cat is about the size of a tall domestic cat, with a small head and narrow muzzle. It has long rounded ears which have a white spot on the back, and a spotted coat which may vary in color and markings. The background color of the coat is generally pale brown — but can range from bright reddish to gray — and the underparts are white. The coat is marked with dark spots which may form bands and blotches. There are usually four longitudinal black bands running from the forehead to behind the neck.

SIZE The leopard cat weighs between 3 and 7 kilograms (6.5 and 15.5 pounds). Its head and body measures 44–107 centimeters (17.25–42.25 inches), and its tail length is 23–44 centimeters (9–17.25 inches).

HABITAT The leopard cat seems to thrive in a variety of habitats, from the dense tropical forests of Sumatra to the pine forests of Manchuria. It also lives in scrub, semidesert, secondary vegetation, and agricultural areas. The leopard cat is not intolerant of human activity.

DISTRIBUTION The leopard cat is found in Pakistan, India, the southern Himalayas, Bangladesh, Vietnam, Thailand, Burma, Malaysia, Indonesia, and part of mainland China.

REPRODUCTION After a gestation period of 65–72 days, one to four, but most commonly two to three young are born in a den. The den may be a hollow tree, a small cave, or a hole beneath the roots of a fallen tree. Kittens open their eyes when they are about 10 days old and reach sexual maturity at 18 months.

SOCIAL SYSTEM Solitary, nothing known.

DIET Leopard cats are primarily nocturnal and hunt both on the ground and in trees. They can also swim very well. This cat is reported to feed on hares, rodents, reptiles, birds, and fish.

SUBFAMILY FELINAE
Felis viverrina
Fishing cat

APPEARANCE The fishing cat is a large, robust-looking felid. It has a deep-chested body and comparatively short legs. The front toes are partially webbed and the claws protrude slightly, even when fully retracted. Small rounded ears are set well back on the large, broad head. The fur is short and coarse, with a gray or olive-brown background, covered with small black spots. The markings sometimes run in longitudinal lines or rows.

SIZE A large male fishing cat may weigh 11–12 kilograms (24.25–26.5 pounds), while females are smaller at about 6–7 kilograms (13.25–15.5 pounds). Head and body length is 65–86 centimeters (25.5–33.75 inches). The tail is unusually thick and muscular near the base, and is less than one-third of the animal's head and body length.

HABITAT This powerful-looking cat is usually associated with areas of thick cover near water, in marshes, mangroves, and densely vegetated areas along rivers and streams.

DISTRIBUTION The fishing cat has a discontinuous distribution in Asia. It is found in southwest India, Sri Lanka, countries of the southern Himalayas, Bangladesh, Vietnam, Thailand, Burma, China, and the islands of Sumatra and Java. Despite this broad geographical range, the fishing cat's real distrubution is quite limited as the species is strongly tied to areas of suitable wetland habitat.

REPRODUCTION Two to three young are born after a 63 day gestation period. The young suckle until they are about six months old, and reach adult size when they are about eight and a half months old.

SOCIAL SYSTEM Nothing known. Probably solitary, but reports from zoos indicate these cats are unusually tolerant of one another, to the extent that several adults can be kept in the same enclosure.

DIET This cat's powerful build and strong swimming ability enable it to take a wide range of prey. They are said to be able to kill calves and dogs, but a more usual diet probably includes birds, small mammals, snakes, snails, and fish. In the wild, fishing cats have been seen crouching on rocks and sandbanks, using a paw to scoop out fish. They have also been observed to seize fish with their mouth.

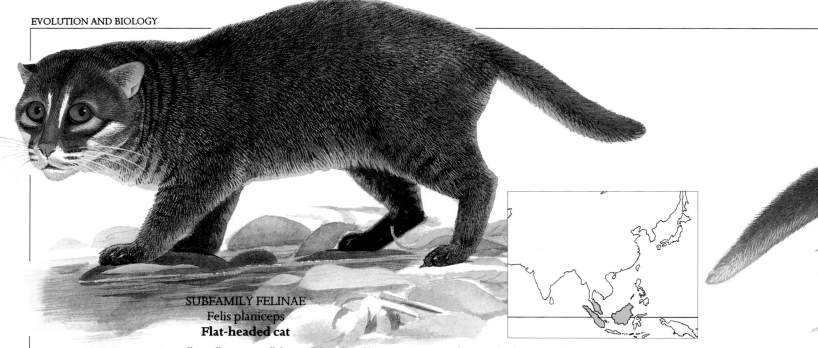

SUBFAMILY FELINAE
Felis planiceps
Flat-headed cat

APPEARANCE Unusually small ears, set well down on the sides of the head, are not the only odd features of the rather different-looking flat-headed cat. It also has a long sloping forehead, comparatively large eyes, and partially retractile claws. Its thick soft fur has a silvery tinge and varies in color from a rich rusty red to dark brown. There are no spots or stripes except on the belly.
SIZE About the size of a domestic cat, this cat weighs 1.6–2.1 kilograms (3.5–4.5 pounds), has a head and body length of 41–50 centimeters (16.25–19.75 inches), and a tail 13–15 centimeters (5–6 inches).

HABITAT Along riverbanks in forested areas. Recently discovered to live in palm oil plantations in Malaysia.
DISTRIBUTION Peninsula Malaysia, Borneo, Sumatra, Thailand, and Indonesia.
REPRODUCTION Nothing known.
SOCIAL SYSTEM Nothing known.
DIET The flat-headed cat is thought to be nocturnal and to hunt for frogs and fish along riverbanks. The recent discovery of this cat in a palm oil plantation in Malaysia indicates that it probably eats rodents.

SUBFAMILY FELINAE
Felis rubiginosa
Rusty-spotted cat

APPEARANCE The rusty-spotted cat has short, brownish-gray fur with a reddish tinge. Cats from Sri Lanka are more russet colored. The back and flanks are marked with lines of elongated brown blotches, and there are large, dark spots and blotches on the paler belly.
SIZE This is a tiny felid, only about half the size of a domestic cat, weighing only about 1 kilogram (2.2 pounds). Head and body length is 35–48 centimeters (13.75–19 inches), and the tail measures 15–25 centimeters (6–9.75 inches).
HABITAT In Sri Lanka, the rusty-spotted cat is found from sea level to 2,100 meters (6,890 feet) in humid forest, low scrub, and the arid

coastal belts. In India, it lives in moist deciduous forest, scrub forest, grassland, and arid scrub.
DISTRIBUTION Mainly Sri Lanka and southern India, but the cat is also recorded in Gujarat and Jammu (northern India).
REPRODUCTION One to two young are born after a 67 day gestation period. The young lack the rusty spotting that is present in adults.
SOCIAL SYSTEM Nothing known. Probably solitary.
DIET This cat is thought to be primarily nocturnal, resting in dense cover during the day. Captive rusty-spotted cats are accomplished climbers, so they may spend part of their time hunting in trees. Their diet consists mainly of birds and small mammals, along with insects, reptiles, and frogs. They are known to kill domestic chickens when the opportunity arises.

SUBFAMILY FELINAE
Felis badia
Bay cat or Bornean red cat

APPEARANCE Everything that is known about this cat is based on a single specimen collected in 1874, and about six skins in museums. There are no descriptions of live animals. The museum specimens are bright chestnut on the back and sides, paler on the belly, with some faint spots on the legs and underparts. The tail is long and tapering with a whitish streak along the last part of the underside.
SIZE The head and body length is 50–60 centimeters (19.75–23.5 inches), and the tail is 35–40 centimeters (13.75–15.75 inches).
HABITAT The bay cat is said to inhabit dense forest and large areas of rocky limestone situated on the edge of the jungle.
DISTRIBUTION The island of Borneo.
REPRODUCTION Nothing known.
SOCIAL SYSTEM Nothing known.
DIET Said to feed on small mammals, birds, monkeys, and carrion.

SUBFAMILY FELINAE
Felis iriomotensis
Iriomote cat

APPEARANCE The Iriomote cat's dark brown coat is marked with rows of darker spots which are arranged in rows that run the length of the body. Five to seven dark lines run along the back of the neck to the shoulders.
SIZE Similar in size to a short-legged domestic cat, the Iriomote cat weighs 3–4.5 kilograms (6.5–10 pounds) and measures 50–60 centimeters (19.75–23.5 inches) head and body, with a tail of 20–30 centimeters (8–11.75 inches).
HABITAT The island of Iriomote consists mostly of broadleafed evergreen forest with dense mangrove along the estuaries. There is a narrow coastal strip of agricultural land. The cats are found in all habitats on the island including the cultivated areas and beaches.
DISTRIBUTION Only on Iriomote Island, an island of 292 square kilometers (113 square miles) off the east coast of Taiwan.
REPRODUCTION Mating has been recorded in February, March, and September/October. Males fight, and both sexes meow and howl like domestic cats. After a gestation period of about two months the female gives birth to two to four kittens in a rock crevice or hollow tree.

SOCIAL SYSTEM Solitary. Each cat occupies a range of 2–3 square kilometers (0.8–1.2 square miles) that overlaps with the ranges of other cats.
DIET The Iriomote cat is known to eat fruit bats, birds, box turtles, rats, skinks, amphibians, crabs, and fish. They hunt both during the day and at night in trees and on the ground. They also swim well and probably hunt fish and crabs in the water.

SUBFAMILY FELINAE
Felis pardalis
Ocelot

APPEARANCE Ocelots have short, close fur marked with both solid and open dark spots that sometimes run in lines along the body. The tail is ringed with black or has black bars on the upper surface. The ears are rounded with a prominent white spot on the back. Both ocelot and margay have very similar coat patterns and are quite difficult to tell apart. Ocelots are generally bigger than margay, and have shorter tails, and slightly smaller eyes.

SIZE Ocelots are medium-sized cats, roughly twice the size of a margay. Males weigh 9–13 kilograms (19.75–28.75 pounds) while females are slightly smaller at 7–10 kilograms (15.5–22 pounds). Males measure approximately 85–100 centimeters (33.5–39.25 inches) head and body length with a tail of 30–41 centimeters (11.75–16.25 inches); females generally have a head and body length of 66–82 centimeters (26–32.25 inches) and a tail of 26–38 centimeters (10.25–15 inches).

HABITAT Found in a broad range of tropical and subtropical habitats including tropical evergreen forest, dry deciduous forest, dry scrub, and seasonally flooded savannas.

DISTRIBUTION Although their recent fossil record extends through much of the southern United States, ocelots are currently found from southern Texas, through parts of Mexico and Central America, into South America as far as Argentina. Populations have generally declined due to hunting and habitat destruction.

REPRODUCTION One or sometimes two kittens are born after a gestation period of 79–82 days. The young begin to follow their mother when they are about two months old but remain dependant on her for several more months. Young ocelots disperse from their natal range when they are about two years old.

SOCIAL SYSTEM Solitary, with breeding females normally occupying non-overlapping territories which measure 0.8–15 square kilometers (0.3–5.8 square miles). Males have larger territories which overlap several breeding females.

DIET Hunting in dense cover, mainly at night, ocelots feed primarily on rodents and mammals weighing less than 1 kilogram (2.25 pounds). They occasionally kill larger prey such as an agouti and they also eat birds, fish, snakes, lizards, and land crabs.

SUBFAMILY FELINAE
Felis tigrina
Oncilla

APPEARANCE One of the world's smallest spotted cats, the oncilla has thick, soft fur marked with black or brown spots and rosettes. It is a daintily built cat, with a small narrow head and large ears.

SIZE A diminutive version of the margay and ocelot, the oncilla weighs only 1.75–2.75 kilograms (3.75–6 pounds). Its head and body measure about 40–55 centimeters (15.75–21.75 inches) with a tail of 25–40 centimeters (9.75–15.75 inches).

HABITAT This is strictly a forest cat, inhabiting cloud forest and humid lowland forest, from sea level to 1000 meters (3280 feet).

DISTRIBUTION The oncilla is found in Central and South America, from Costa Rica southward to northern Argentina. It is rare in most parts of its range, and is probably becoming rarer as deforestation for coffee plantations has destroyed large areas of cloud forest.

REPRODUCTION Nothing is known of the habits of these cats in the wild, but captive studies have shown that usually one but sometimes two young are born after a gestation period of 74 to 76 days. The young develop rather slowly.

SOCIAL SYSTEM Solitary.

DIET The oncilla is nocturnal and thought to hunt mainly on the ground. The limited information on its food habits suggests that it eats rodents and small birds.

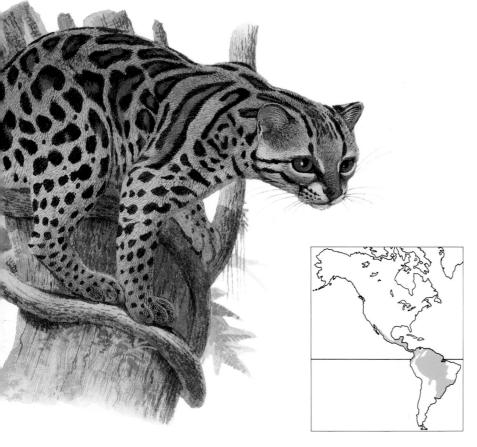

SUBFAMILY FELINAE
Felis wiedii
Margay

APPEARANCE The margay's soft, thick fur is marked with dark brown or black, pale-centered open spots and streaks. The margay's coat color and markings are very similar to both the larger ocelot and the much smaller oncilla, but the margay has a short rounded head with larger eyes and a longer tail than either of the other two species.

SIZE Margay are medium-sized felids that weigh 2.5–4 kilograms (5.5–8.75 pounds). Head and body lengths vary from 47–79 centimeters (18.5–31 inches), and the tail is 33–50 centimeters (13–19.75 inches) long, which is as much as 70 percent of the animal's head and body.

HABITAT The highly arboreal margay is always found in forested habitats, and has even been recorded living in coffee or cocoa plantations. They can live in a variety of natural forest types, but are usually associated with humid, tropical, evergreen forest and montane forest.

DISTRIBUTION The margay is found from Mexico through Central America and South America east of the Andes to Argentina. The margay is thinly distributed but widespread throughout this area.

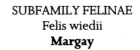

REPRODUCTION In captivity, margay give birth to a single young after a gestation period of about 81 days. The young begin to eat solid food when they are about two months old, and are nearly adult size by the time they are eight to ten months of age.

SOCIAL SYSTEM These solitary cats are thought to live at low densities, but little is known of their social lives.

DIET Margay are anatomically adapted for arboreal hunting but they also hunt on the ground. They are capable of spectacular acrobatic feats and use some of these skills when catching prey in trees. Hunting at night, they catch and eat rodents, birds, reptiles, and insects.

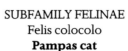

SUBFAMILY FELINAE
Felis colocolo
Pampas cat

APPEARANCE The pampas cat looks like a heavyset house cat. It has a rather broad face, and more pointed ears than other South American cats. Its fur is long but the color, pattern, and texture vary widely. The fur can be dark with red-gray spots, pale silvery gray and almost unpatterned, except for brown bands on the legs and tail, or anything in between. When the cat is frightened or nervous, the long mane-like hairs on its back stand erect, giving it a more formidable appearance.

SIZE About the size of a large house cat, the pampas cat weighs 3.2–6.4 kilograms (7–14 pounds) and measures 60–70 centimeters (23.5–27.5 inches) head and body length. The tail is about 30 centimeters (11.75 inches) long.

HABITAT In Argentina the pampas cat is known to live in open grasslands but in other parts of its range it is found in cloud forest and other humid forests. It seems to prefer high altitude habitats.

DISTRIBUTION Parts of Argentina, Chile, Uruguay, Paraguay, Brazil, Peru, and Ecuador.

REPRODUCTION Nothing known.

SOCIAL SYSTEM Nothing known, probably solitary.

DIET The pampas cat is thought to be nocturnal and probably feeds on ground-nesting birds, and rodents such as wild guinea pigs.

SUBFAMILY FELINAE
Felis jacobita
Andean mountain cat

APPEARANCE The Andean mountain cat has a long, soft, silvery-gray coat which is marked with dark brown spots and stripes. It has a long, bushy tail which is marked with seven dark rings.

SIZE About the size of a large house cat, the Andean mountain cat weighs about 4 kilograms (8.75 pounds). Its head and body measures 57–64 centimeters (22.5–25.25 inches) with a tail of 41–48 centimeters (16.25–19 inches).

HABITAT This cat is confined to the rocky, treeless zone of the high Andes mountains. The area is windy, arid, and very cold. Only a few Andean mountain cats have ever been collected from the wild; most were obtained above 3,000 meters (9,840 feet), and one, in Peru, was collected at 5,100 meters (16,730 feet).

DISTRIBUTION This cat has a very restricted distribution and is confined to a small area of the high Andes in Peru, Bolivia, Chile, and Argentina.

REPRODUCTION Nothing known.

SOCIAL SYSTEM Nothing known, probably solitary.

DIET Probably small mammals, lizards, and birds.

SUBFAMILY FELINAE
Felis geoffroyi
Geoffroy's cat

APPEARANCE Geoffroy's cat is a small, lightly built, spotted cat. The coat color is highly variable, being brilliant ochre in the northern parts of its range, silvery gray in the south, and elsewhere it is intermediate shades between the two extremes. The coat is spotted with round black dots which may merge to form indistinct stripes. All black Geoffroy's cats are not uncommon.

SIZE About the size of a domestic cat, Geoffroy's cat weighs from 2–6 kilograms (4.5–13.25 pounds), with males being heavier than females. Head and body length varies from 45–70 centimeters (17.75–27.5 inches), tail is 24–36 centimeters (9.5–14.25 inches).

HABITAT Geoffroy's cat is a versatile little predator, able to survive in a variety of habitats including scrub woodlands, open bush, rocky terrain, and riverine forest.

DISTRIBUTION The Bolivian Andes and mountains of northwest Argentina, through parts of Uruguay, Paraguay, Brazil, and Chile.

REPRODUCTION Two or three young are born after a gestation period of about 71 days. The den is usually a root cavity, rock crevice, or clump of bushes, and, in comparison with the domestic cat, young Geoffroy's cats develop quite slowly.

SOCIAL SYSTEM Solitary. The home range of a single male was estimated to be less than 1.8 square kilometers (0.7 square miles).

DIET Active primarily at night, the Geoffroy's cat hunts both on the ground and in the trees. It can climb and swim well, and preys on small mammals such as rats, mice, guinea pigs, and agouti, as well as birds.

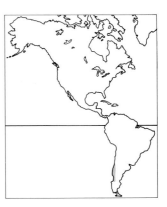

SUBFAMILY FELINAE
Felis guigna
Kodkod

APPEARANCE The kodkod's fur is a buff or gray-brown, and heavily marked with small round spots. The spots sometimes form streaks on the shoulders, and the tail is marked with a series of black rings. All-black (melanistic) kodkods are quite common.

SIZE About the size of a small domestic cat, the kodkod is probably tied in a close race with the oncilla for the smallest cat in the western hemisphere. Kodkods weigh 2.1–2.5 kilograms (4.5–5.5 pounds), with a head and body length of 39–51 centimeters (15.25–20 inches) and a tail length of 19–25 centimeters (7.5–9.75 inches).

HABITAT The kodkod is found in coniferous forest, wooded areas, and semi-open habitats.

DISTRIBUTION This cat is very rare in the wild and is currently threatened by serious habitat destruction. It has an extremely restricted geographical distribution, being confined to a small area of Chile and Argentina.

REPRODUCTION Nothing known.

SOCIAL SYSTEM Nothing known, probably solitary.

DIET Probably feeds on small mammals and birds.

SUBFAMILY FELINAE
Felis silvestris (includes F. s. libyca)
Wild cat

APPEARANCE The wild cats of Europe, Asia, and Africa look very much like a larger version of the domestic tabby cat. However, there can be enormous variation in coat color and markings, and in fur length. In general, the paler forms of the species live in drier areas while the more spotted and striped forms are found in humid areas. In Africa and Asia this cat usually has short, close fur, but in northern Europe and the USSR the fur can be long and thick. This is part of the reason why European wild cats appear to be much more heavily built than the tall, slim African wild cat. Scientists are fairly certain that today's domestic cats are descended from the African wild cat.

SIZE Slightly larger than a domestic cat, wild cats usually weigh between 3 and 8 kilograms (6.5 and 17.5 pounds), with a head and body length of 50–75 centimeters (19.75–29.5 inches) and a tail of 21–35 centimeters (8.25–13.75 inches).

HABITAT The wild cat can live in a wide range of habitats. In northern Europe it inhabits deciduous and coniferous forests; in Africa and Asia it can be found in almost any type of habitat from open rocky ground to scrubby brush and agricultural croplands.

DISTRIBUTION This cat has a broad geographical distribution, which includes parts of Europe, Africa, Saudi Arabia, Iran, Iraq, Pakistan, Afghanistan, the USSR, and India.

REPRODUCTION After a gestation period of about 65 days, the female gives birth to two or three kittens in a secluded den. The young suckle for about a month and begin to accompany their mother on hunting trips when they are three months old. The young are independent by the time they are six months old, but littermates may continue to travel together.

SOCIAL SYSTEM Solitary, both males and females maintain territories.

DIET Primarily a rodent catcher, the wild cat is a highly adaptable predator. In India it is known to hunt desert gerbil, rat, hare, dove, gray partridge, peacock, and sparrow. In the Namib Desert of Africa the wild cat lives almost entirely on small mammals and insects, and in Europe its diet consists mainly of rodents, supplemented with rabbit, hare, and birds.

SUBFAMILY FELINAE
Felis manul
Pallas' cat

APPEARANCE Pallas' cat is a very distinctive, fluffy-looking cat. It has a heavy body, short stout legs, a broad head, and very long dense fur. The ears are short and blunt, and set well down on the sides of the head. The grayish to reddish colored fur is longer and more dense than that of any other wild cat and the fur on the underparts of its body is nearly twice as long as that on the back and sides. Each hair is tipped with white, giving the cat a frosted appearance. Two dark stripes run obliquely across each cheek, and there are sometimes faint stripes on the hindquarters and limbs.

SIZE The dense fluffy coat of the Pallas' cat makes the animal look larger and heavier than it really is. This cat usually weighs a mere 2.5–3.5 kilograms (5.5–7.75 pounds) and measures 50–65 centimeters (19.75–25.5 inches) head and body, with a 21–31 centimeter (8.25–12.25 inch) tail.

HABITAT This cat lives in deserts, steppes, and treeless rocky mountainsides, and may be found at elevations as high as 4,000 meters (13,120 feet). Its well-furred body provides insulation in the cold snowy winters that are common throughout most of its range.

DISTRIBUTION Pallas' cat is found from the Caspian Sea and Iran, to southeastern Siberia and China.

REPRODUCTION Three to four young are born after a 66 day gestation.

SOCIAL SYSTEM Solitary, nothing known.

DIET Pallas' cats are known to climb cliffs and rocks with ease. They are thought to hunt mainly by sight, and the position of their ears may be an adaptation to stalking prey in areas of little cover. These cats are believed to eat marmots, pikas, small mammals, ground squirrels, hares, and birds.

SUBFAMILY FELINAE
Felis chaus
Jungle cat

APPEARANCE The jungle cat has a plain, unspotted coat that can be sandy brown, reddish or gray. Adults occasionally retain some of their striped kitten markings as four or five faint stripes on the outside of their forelegs. Two or three black bands may encircle the short, black-tipped tail. The jungle cat has a long slim face, and tall rounded ears topped with a tuft of black hair. All-black jungle cats occur regularly in Pakistan and India.

SIZE The jungle cat varies in size and weight depending on where it lives. In general they are larger in Soviet Central Asia, where they can weigh as much as 16 kilograms (35.25 pounds). Further south, in India or Thailand, jungle cats are more likely to weigh 4–8 kilograms (8.75–17.5 pounds) and be the size of a large domestic cat.

HABITAT The jungle cat is at home in a wide variety of habitats — from wet reed beds to arid scrub jungle, agricultural croplands, and dense forest.

DISTRIBUTION The jungle cat has one of the widest distributions of all the small cats and is found on three continents. In Africa it occurs only in Egypt, while in Europe and Asia its distribution spans more than 25 countries — Israel, Jordan, and Syria in the east, north to the Caspian Sea and Afghanistan, and east through India, Nepal, Sri Lanka, Thailand and southwestern China, and into Indochina.

REPRODUCTION Two to four kittens are born after a 63 day gestation period. The den may be the disused burrow of another animal, a hollow tree, an agricultural field, or a dense reed bed. The young suckle until they are three months old, and are able to stalk and kill their own prey by the time they are six months old.

SOCIAL SYSTEM Solitary, nothing known.

DIET This cat hunts on the ground, but it has been seen making high vertical leaps in pursuit of birds. It feeds mainly on small rodents and birds, but will tackle larger prey such as chital fawns. Jungle cats will also eat lizards, frogs, beetles, snakes, and fish.

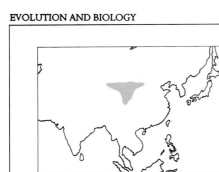

SUBFAMILY FELINAE
Felis bieti
Chinese desert cat

APPEARANCE The Chinese desert cat has yellowish gray fur that is somewhat darker on the back. There may or may not be brownish markings on the flanks, cheeks, and outside of the haunches. There is a short pencil of hair on the tip of each ear and the tail has a black tip and is marked with three or four dark rings. Like the sand cat, this cat has hairy tufts growing between the pads of its feet.

SIZE Larger than a domestic cat, the Chinese desert cat has a head and body length of 68–84 centimeters (26.75–33 inches), with a 29–35 centimeter (11.5–13.75 inch) long tail.

HABITAT Contrary to its name, the Chinese desert cat does not live in desert but is more commonly found in steppe and forest, or brush-covered mountains. This cat lives in the same sort of areas inhabited by the giant panda and golden snub-nose monkey.

DISTRIBUTION The Chinese desert cat has a very restricted range in China. It is found from the eastern Tibetan plateau in central Sichuan northward to Inner Mongolia. This cat is hunted for its skin, and pelts frequently turn up in local markets.

REPRODUCTION Nothing known.

SOCIAL SYSTEM Nothing known.

DIET Nothing known.

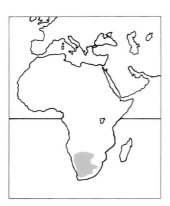

SUBFAMILY FELINAE
Felis nigripes
Black-footed cat

APPEARANCE This tiny cat acquired its name because the pads and underparts of its feet are black. It has tawny-gold fur marked with conspicuous black or brown spots which sometimes merge to form bands or rings. They often flatten their large rounded ears in an "aggressive" posture.

SIZE The black-footed cat is not only the smallest of the African felids but is also one of the smallest cats in the world. Females weigh about 1.5 kilograms (3.25 pounds) while males are slightly heavier at 2–2.5 kilograms (4.5–5.5 pounds). These cats have a short tail that is about half the 36–45 centimeter (14.25–17.75 inch) head and body length.

HABITAT Black-footed cats are found in dry open areas where there is some cover in the form of rocks, scrubby bushes, or grass.

DISTRIBUTION Confined to the arid parts of southern Africa, the black-footed cat is found only in Botswana, Namibia, and South Africa.

REPRODUCTION The black-footed cat has a number of adaptations that enable it to survive and reproduce in a hostile environment. They have a loud "meow" that undoubtedly helps the male and female find each other, a short mating period, long gestation, and rather precocious young. Females usually give birth to two kittens and change dens frequently, probably to avoid attracting predators. They also have a special alarm call which causes the young to scatter and hide when danger threatens.

SOCIAL SYSTEM These small cats are solitary and nocturnal. Their small size makes them very vulnerable to predation and they are well known for taking cover at the least disturbance. They spend the day in termite mound holes or in abandoned aardvark or springhare burrows, only emerging to hunt when it is dark.

DIET Though they will drink if water is available, black-footed cats can get all the moisture they need from their prey. They live in dry, open habitats where they hunt on the ground, making full use of every rock and stone for cover when stalking. They eat mice, gerbils, spiders, and insects, and show great persistence in digging.

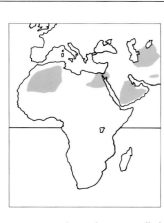

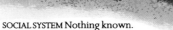

SUBFAMILY FELINAE
Felis margarita
Sand cat

APPEARANCE The sand cat is a small, short-legged cat with a long tail. It has a broad head topped with large ears which are set wide apart and low down on the side of the head. The sand cat's fur is soft and dense, pale sandy brown to light gray in color. The lower muzzle and chest are often white, and there are indistinct dark bars on the limbs. The black-tipped tail has two to six narrow black rings near the end. A dense mat of hairs, 2 centimeters (0.75 inches) long, grows between the pads of the sand cat's feet.

SIZE Standing about 26 centimeters (10.25 inches) high at the shoulder, the sand cat is the size of a small domestic cat. It weighs 2–3 kilograms (4.5–6.5 pounds) and its head and body measures 45–57 centimeters (17.75–22.5 inches) with a tail of 28–35 centimeters (11–13.75 inches).

HABITAT Befitting its name, the sand cat inhabits inhospitable arid regions characterized by rolling sand dunes, flat stony plains, and rocky deserts.

DISTRIBUTION The sand cat lives in parts of the northern Sahara, Egypt, Israel, Arabia, Turkmen, Pakistan, and possibly Iran.

REPRODUCTION Two to four young are born after a gestation period of about 66 days. The female usually gives birth in a burrow, which she may dig herself.

SOCIAL SYSTEM Nothing known.

DIET The sand cat hunts strictly by night. The thick padding on its feet probably helps protect it against hot sand, and the cat uses its large ears and well developed hearing to locate prey. The sand cat feeds on birds, jerboas, small mammals, hares, birds, reptiles, and locusts. There is no free-standing water throughout much of the sand cat's range and it is able to get all the moisture it needs from its prey.

SUBFAMILY FELINAE
Felis silvestris catus
Domestic cat

ORIGIN The domestic cat is probably descended from the African subspecies of wild cat. Some authorities have argued in favor of some hybridization between domestic cats and the European subspecies of wild cat, jungle cat, and Pallas' cat.

APPEARANCE Only within the last century have domestic cats been bred internationally for specific characteristics. There are long- and short-hair domestic cat breeds in a wide variety of colors and in combinations of patterns and colors including a solid body color with contrasting darker mask, ears, tail and paws; tabby; spotted; tortoiseshell and calico. Eye color varies with the breed, and in some breeds eye color "harmonizes" with coat color — blue, yellowish, golden, orange, hazel etc. The Manx and Cymrix breeds are tailless.

SIZE Adults are usually 40–60 centimeters (15.75–23.5 inches) in head and body length with a tail length of 25–35 centimeters (9.75–13.75 inches), and a medium weight of 3–4 kilograms (6.5–8.75 pounds).

DISTRIBUTION Found worldwide, including remote islands, in human settlements and often leading a wild (feral) existence.

REPRODUCTION The female can be in estrus three or four times a year; estrus may last from 20 to 30 days. The gestation period is about nine weeks (63 to 66 days) for most breeds but up to ten weeks for Siamese. Litters are usually three to five with a maximum of six kittens. Kittens usually take their first solid food at four weeks and are sexually mature in 10 months.

SOCIAL SYSTEM When not strictly confined by their owners or when feral, females tend to live singly or in small groups with a few other females, some of which are often daughters from previous litters. In these groups, litters from different females may be reared in the same nest as mixed or communal litters. Some groups include an adult male but many males tend to live more solitary lives. Males usually do not form a close bond with females. Males typically use larger home ranges than females; a male's range may overlap those of several female groups and usually overlaps with the ranges of other males. Males do not usually bring food to lactating females or kittens.

DIET Feral cats are versatile, generalist predators that exploit a wide range of prey and switch readily from one prey to another. Feral cats on continents are chiefly predators of small mammals, especially of young lagomorphs and of microtine rodents. Where cats have been introduced to islands, they live on a few species of introduced mammals and birds, especially breeding seabirds. The extinctions of some island endemic species of birds have been attributed to them.

HOW CATS WORK

RICHARD A. KILTIE

It is not unusual to find textbook statements describing felids as the most specialized of mammalian carnivores. But it is also not unusual for house cats to be dissected in introductory anatomy labs for premedical students. If cats are so specialized, how could their bodies provide helpful introductions to human anatomy?

Actually, felids are specialized in the sense that they are rather uniform in their hunting mode and specific in the parts of prey they consume. They can be stereotyped as stealthy, solitary hunters who stalk prey and attack in a brief rush. Successful attacks generally depend on apprehension with the forepaws and a bite to the prey's neck or throat. They primarily consume the soft parts of prey, and unlike most other terrestrial carnivorans, rarely supplement their diets with plant matter.

It is not difficult to find exceptions to these generalizations, but the fact remains that most of the distinguishing anatomical features of cats can be related to this typical predatory behavior. Otherwise, their structural attributes are sufficiently unspecialized so as to serve as convenient subjects for an introduction to mammalian anatomy. In many respects, they are more generalized anatomically than humans are.

Belinda Wright

THE BODY OF THE CAT

The vertebral column of the cat must support the body while allowing flexibility in movement. The vertebral column of the trunk region (between the fore- and hind limbs) can be modelled as a taut bow, with the belly muscles providing the tension that keeps the column arched; this is a good arrangement for resisting the compressive forces caused by the tissues slung beneath the column. The neck is more like a cantilevered beam, with neck muscles and ligaments providing the tensile forces that keep the head elevated. The tail is like a much more flexible beam at the other end of the trunk. There is no really good functional explanation for cat tails, and in fact some species have almost dispensed with them completely.

Much energy expenditure is required to swing the legs. As would be expected, longer legs allow greater speed because more ground is covered per step, but longer legs also involve greater weight and hence greater energetic cost. This problem can be reduced to some extent by reducing, as much

as possible, the weight of the tissues farthest from where the legs join the rest of the body (the distal portions). Hence in running animals (both predators and prey) we find fusion or loss of some foot bones and muscles. At the same time the effective length of the limb is increased by elevating parts of the feet off the ground. Cats and most other carnivorans elevate the metacarpals ("hands") or metatarsals ("feet") while keeping most of the phalanges ("fingers" and "toes") on the ground. This stance is called digitigrade (as opposed to the plantigrade stance found in humans and bears). Hoofed mammals raise the phalanges above the ground as well, but this makes manipulation of items with the paws impossible and hence would not be desirable for most carnivorans. The bones of the first digits (comparable to human thumbs) on cat forefeet are not so elongated and do not normally touch the ground. The first digits of the hind feet (comparable to human "big toes") are completely absent and the metatarsals just small lumps.

▼ A female tiger *(Panthera tigris)* intently eyes an axis deer in the distance. These magnificent animals must search for, stalk, and kill other large mammals to survive. A female tiger must kill about every five days, and when feeding cubs she must kill even more frequently. On average, a tiger will make only one kill in every 10 hunts.

Step-length in carnivorans is also increased by the positioning of the scapula, or shoulder blade, on the side of the body rather than on the back (as in humans), so that it can swing along with the leg. The clavicle, or collar bone, is very reduced in comparison to what is found, say, in humans because a human-like clavicle would stabilize the scapula rather than let it swing. Flexibility of the spine also helps lengthen the stride of carnivorans (refer to article titled Cheetah Speed, page 140).

A study of the body proportions of large felids has shown that in comparison to the total length of the vertebral column, jaguars and clouded leopards have the shortest forelimbs and shortest lumbar portion of the vertebral column (the part between the hip and the rib cage); and cheetahs have the longest limbs and lumbar portion of the column. These differences can be attributed to an emphasis on limb strength for forest-dwelling species (that consume large prey relative to their own size), as opposed to an emphasis on speed for cheetahs that hunt in open environments.

Interestingly, lions also hunt in open environments, but their body proportions are similar to the forest-dwelling species. Perhaps the fact that they hunt in groups has made cheetah-like adaptations unnecessary.

FEEDING ANATOMY OF THE CAT

Animals that primarily consume tissue of other animals generally have simple digestive systems because animal tissue is rich and needs less extensive digestion than other foods, such as vegetable tissue. Since most cats are purely carnivorous, their digestive systems are even simpler than those of carnivoran species that consume a proportion of vegetable matter. Compared to dogs, for example, cats have a smaller cecum (an outpocketing of the gut at the juncture of the small and large intestine that is useful in digesting vegetation) and a shorter "large" intestine. In addition, cats, unlike dogs, appear to be unable to tolerate low levels of nitrogen (protein) in their diets.

► Two cheetahs *(Acinonyx jubatus)* climbing a candelabra tree in East Africa. All of the big cats will climb into trees to rest and sleep if the trees are easily ascended, but most cats are primarily terrestrial and will hunt almost entirely on the ground. The young of big cats will climb more readily than will older, bigger individuals.

A NATURAL JACKKNIFE

The neck bite that characterizes felid predation requires that prey be well controlled. This control is provided by the paws with their sharp claws. If the claws were arranged in permanent protraction as in dogs, they would be subject to sharpness-reducing wear. The "retractile" claws of cats are elevated above the ground most of the time, and hence protected from such wear. Retraction of the claws is a passive effect of spring-like elastic ligaments. It makes sense that muscular contraction, which is energetically expensive, should be used only to protract the claws because they need to be protracted for comparatively brief periods. As R. F. Ewer has emphasized, it would probably make more sense to call them "protractile" claws. They are almost a natural jackknife.

Retractile claws have also been described in some viverrid species (civets and genets), but the anatomical mechanism is apparently universal among cats. Cheetahs are often described as having nonretractile claws, but W. Gonyea and R. Ashworth have recently maintained that cheetah digital anatomy allows for claw retraction by the same mechanism as in other cats. Cheetah claws just stick out beyond the fur even when retracted. The flat-headed cat is also reported to have semi-retractile claws.

The sharpness of retractile claws allows most cats to climb well. Conceivably, these retractile claws might have arisen in the evolutionary ancestors of cats primarily to allow arboreality, and the prey-controlling benefits of these claws may have come to be used later.

Cat claws are also extremely effective in refinishing living-room furniture. However, their effectiveness in this respect may be downright maladaptive, depending on how angry the owners of the redone furniture become and just how fond of the cat they really are!

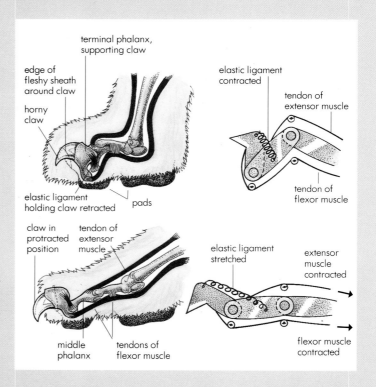

▲ The protrusion mechanism of retractile felid claws. When the claws are retracted (above), the spring ligament is contracted and the dorsal and ventral muscles are relaxed. This is the normal state of the claws when cats are at rest. In use (below), the dorsal and ventral muscles contract, and the spring ligament stretches to protrude the claws beyond the sheath. Many carnivores, including all cats, possess retractile claws that function similarly. Among the cats, cheetahs are mistakenly believed to have non-retractile claws, but cheetahs only lack the sheaths that cover the retracted claws of other cats.

Zefa-BAUER

▲ A female puma *(Felis concolor)* suckling her infants. Small cats generally produce a litter once a year while bigger cats, such as this puma, tend to bear young every other year. Big cats spend more time teaching their young to safely kill prey, which is usually large and potentially dangerous, than do small cats that feed on small animals.

THE REPRODUCTIVE SYSTEM

There is little that is unusual in the reproductive systems of cats. Males have permanently scrotal testes, and like other carnivorans (except hyenas), male cats have a bone in the penis (the baculum). It is however comparatively smaller than the bacula of dogs (for example), and blood-filled erectile tissue is therefore thought to play a correspondingly greater role in intromission (as in humans, who lack a baculum altogether). The penis tip (the glans) is covered with backward-directed spines whose function is uncertain although they may help maintain copulation or provide stimulation for the female.

There are as many as six pairs of mammary glands in cats, depending on the typical litter size. The milk of domestic cats contains 50 grams (1.75 ounces) of sugar, 92 grams (3.25 ounces) of protein, 35 grams (1.25 ounces) of fat and 11 grams (0.5 ounce) of salts per liter (2 pints). In contrast, human milk contains much less protein (11 grams/ 0.5 ounce) and more sugar (75 grams/2.75 ounces) per liter (2 pints). This difference seems to reflect differences in growth rates and eventual feeding habits between cats and people.

All cats have a tendency to mark and inspect certain areas, apparently as a part of scent communication. Substances that can leave scents include urine, feces, and products of certain glands, especially the anal sacs found in nearly all carnivorans. Ducts from these glands open close to the anus on either side. Males can direct urine backwards to coat specific objects. Scent-producing organs may not be as elaborate in cats as in many other carnivorans because visual and vocal signals are more important.

THE SKULL

On the whole, much more work has been done with skeletal features of cats than with other anatomical components because bones are easier to store. Skulls have been especially well studied because they are more compact than many postcranial skeletal elements and because so much of a species' biology and evolutionary history is summarized in its skull. Certainly, many of the features that enable us to distinguish cats from other carnivorans are associated with the head.

The late L. B. Radinsky investigated variation in carnivoran skull shape. He found that what most distinguished skulls of the Felidae were relatively large openings for the eyes and relatively short skulls. In comparison to canids (such as dogs) and most viverrids (such as civets or genets), cats also had a greater cross-sectional area of the jaws, larger jaw muscles, and shorter sets of cheek teeth (premolars and molars). Large eye openings were thought to indicate greater dependence on visual sensory information among cats, for hunting and capturing prey, than among other carnivorans.

Many biologists have noted that cats seem to show less interspecific morphological variation than other carnivorans, but Radinsky was the first to test this suggestion objectively. He found that for skull features linked to bite strength, cats were indeed less variable than other carnivorans. Why should there be a lack of size-independent, bite-force variation among cats? The answer could be related to their comparative uniformity in hunting and feeding style. With respect to head breadth and relative eye size, though, cats are as variable as the other carnivoran groups.

Within the Carnivora, bears show the greatest absolute range in body size among species (30–800 kilograms/66–1,765 pounds), but cats show the greatest relative variation in body size (1.5–300 kilograms/3–660 pounds, or 1:200). The way that skull size and shape varies with average adult size seems to be the same in cats as in most other groups. That is, the larger the total body size, the greater the tendency of the head to decrease in proportion to the rest of the body. The anterior portion of the skull (occupied by the jaws and associated muscles) is proportionately larger in large species than in small species, and correspondingly, the relative brain volume is comparatively smaller in larger species (at least in felids, viverrids, and canids). The size of the openings in the skull for the eyes is also relatively smaller in larger species than in smaller ones.

Cat dentitions are truly distinctive. The teeth are reduced in number and specialized in operation. Typically, there are 15 teeth on each side of the adult skull. These include, on each side, three upper and three lower incisors, one upper and one lower canine, three upper and two lower premolars and one upper and one lower molar. The upper molar is comparatively small, and sometimes the most anterior premolar is very reduced or does not appear at all. Cat incisors are not unusual, but the canines, of course, are large. As suggested by Paul Leyhausen, the canines can be inserted between the neck vertebrae of prey to kill them very quickly, and cats appear to have the musculo-sensory apparatus necessary to be positioned so precisely. The canines of cats are longer, more rounded, and stronger (relative to skull length) than those of canids.

Jim Brandenburg/DRK Photo

▲ Like this lion's tongue, the tongues of all cats are covered with tiny hook-like papillae that help to scrape every last bit of flesh from the bones of prey.

▼ The skeletons of cats exhibit variation on a common theme. In general, only the relative proportions of the various parts of the skeleton vary from species to species. Characteristics of the skull, such as length and breadth of canine teeth, are influenced by the diet of the particular species while post-cranial traits, such as limb length, vary with the habitat-utilization patterns of the species.

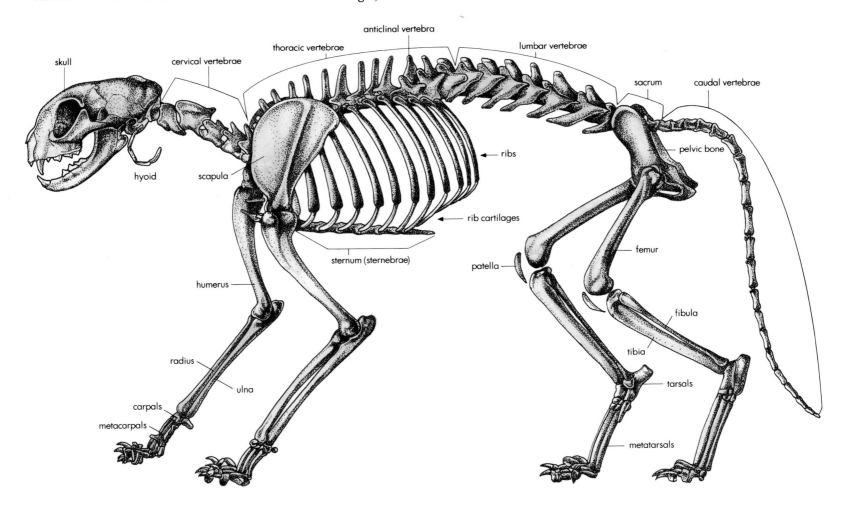

In most terrestrial carnivorans the rearmost upper premolars and the most anterior lower molars are called carnassials. Carnassials have laterally flattened blades that shear past one another when the jaw is closed. The comparative extent of the carnassial blades is related to the degree of emphasis on pure carnivory. Bear "carnassials," for example, have low crowns like ours, which makes them better for crushing than for slicing, and the carnassials have a portion developed as a blade and a portion for crushing. In cats, the carnassial blades are especially elongated, the crushing portions of the teeth are eliminated, and other cheek teeth are either very small or modified as blades as well.

►▲ The teeth of cats are specialized for different functions: their large canines are used to grab and kill prey; the scissor-like molars, or carnassials, are used to tear chunks of meat from a carcass; and the small incisors are used to remove the last bits of meat from the bones of kills. The lion *(Panthera leo)* pictured at right is using its canines to kill a zebra, and the puma *(Felis concolor)* pictured above is shearing pieces of meat from a deer carcass with its carnassials.

In mammals, the hyoid apparatus is a series of skeletal elements that support the larynx and the base of the tongue. They are derivatives of bones that supported the gills of the aquatic vertebrate ancestors of mammals. These elements are of interest because in species of the genus *Panthera* (as opposed to the smaller cats) portions of this apparatus remain cartilaginous throughout life instead of becoming completely bony. This incomplete ossification is thought to help large cats roar.

Many of the soft-tissue features of cat heads can also be related to their feeding habits. For instance, anyone who has a cat knows that cat tongues have bumps, with sharp points directed toward the rear, on the dorsal surface. Presumably these help remove flesh from the bones of prey, and are present in many other carnivorans.

The basic arrangement of the jaw-closing muscles in cats is like that found in other

BODY SIZE AND FEEDING TACTICS

LOUISE EMMONS

The cat species of the world are sharply split by mean body weight into three groups: small, medium, and large. Between the sizes are large gaps where no species occur, but the picture is not as clear as this seems because the "medium-sized" cats (actually large, for example, jaguar, puma, and leopard) vary so much in body size that there are individuals that fill most of the gap between these and the largest cats (lion and tiger).

Field studies of cats and their prey in Africa, India, and in Peruvian rainforest give clues about why cats fall into three size classes. Diets of a cat from each of the lower two size classes, ocelot (small) and jaguar (medium), were studied in Peru. In this rainforest habitat each species took a wide array of prey, so wide that, astonishingly, these two cat species between them ate the entire size range of available mammalian prey. This mammal prey was neatly divided, with 92 percent of ocelot prey consisting of small species of less than 1 kilogram (2 pounds) body weight; and 85 percent of jaguar prey consisting of species weighing over 1 kilogram (2 pounds).

South America has only a few large mammals and no very large ones. In contrast, there are many very large mammal prey species in the savannas and woodlands of Africa and Asia. In these areas, one member of the largest size class of cats (lions or tigers) is present alongside members of the two smaller classes: only three cats are needed to cover the entire size range of cat prey in the world, from mouse to buffalo (a few species above the usual prey range of living cats, such as rhinos and elephants, always seem to exist in any habitat). Hence the three size classes of cats — but if we delve more deeply, much more complex effects of body size begin to emerge.

The number of prey animals that are present in a habitat can be estimated and multiplied by their average weights to give the biomass, or weight per unit area. Then if the amount of prey eaten by a predator is estimated (the offtake), one can calculate what proportion of the available prey is eaten each year by one or a set of predators. Three studies on different continents (Africa, Asia, and South America), focusing on different big cats (lion/cheetah/leopard, tiger, and jaguar/puma) all arrived at almost exactly the same estimates of 8 to 10 percent annual offtake of the standing crop biomass (weight of all prey alive on the area at a given time) taken by all or the main large predators.

In Peru, the same kind of estimate for ocelots and their chief mammal prey showed that this small cat alone ate 75 percent of its standing crop of prey per year! How can this be?

If we split all of the terrestrial mammals known in the study area into two groups at the 1 kilogram (2 pound) mark — the body weight where jaguars and ocelots mainly split them among themselves — two remarkable facts emerge: the species are divided almost exactly in half, with 34 species below 1 kilogram (2 pounds) and 35 species above; and all species below 1 kilogram (mainly small rodents and opossums) are animals that have high potential reproductive rates, including multiple litters of young each year, females that can breed when less than one year old, and litter sizes that can reach three or more young. With two exceptions, all species above 1 kilogram (2 pounds) have much lower reproductive rates, with one litter or less each year, females that first reproduce at one year old or older, and small litters of only one or two young.

Putting these pieces together, we see that ocelots can eat three-quarters of their standing crop of prey because the prey is multiplying like crazy. If the amount eaten relative to the total prey that could be produced in a year is calculated, the offtake of ocelots comes to 6 percent, which is close to the 8 percent eaten by the big cats.

The small cats of the world that have been studied mainly eat small rodents or rabbits and hares, and the big cats eat larger ungulates (that is, animals with hooves). This basic difference can influence many aspects of a cat's ecology. The prey species of small cats are much smaller than the body size of the cats themselves, and therefore they often need to catch several animals every day (which requires prey that breeds rapidly to survive). On the other hand, the prey of big cats is relatively much larger, and so these big cats may only need to capture prey once or a few times a week. Therefore, the prey species do not need to be rapid-breeding species. The prey species of small cats are mostly nocturnal, while those of big cats are about equally diurnal and nocturnal, and the activity of the cats reflects this. Small cats compete for their prey with many other predators, such as weasels, hawks, owls, and snakes, while big cats have few competitors for their large prey. The prey species of small cats are subject to population cycles that may cause large swings in their own populations, but this is not the case with large cats.

Large and small cats thus seem to need different ecological tactics that may be tightly tied to their body sizes — to the extent that they fall into sets with a size gap between them — from which we can speculate that certain cat species would be too large to have a small cat diet and strategy, and another cat species too small to have an effective large cat strategy.

▼ The cat species of the world can be divided by mean body weight into three groups, and the cats in each seem to have diets and strategies peculiar to, and appropriate for, the size group to which they belong.

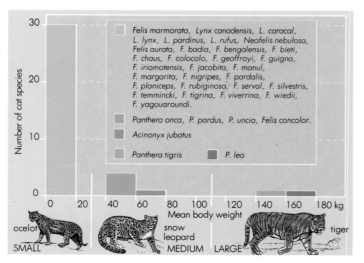

Felis marmorata, Lynx canadensis, L. caracal, L. lynx, L. pardinus, L. rufus, Neofelis nebulosa, Felis aurata, F. badia, F. bengalensis, F. bieti, F. chaus, F. colocolo, F. geoffroyi, F. guigna, F. iriomotensis, F. jacobita, F. manul, F. margarita, F. nigripes, F. pardalis, F. planiceps, F. rubiginosa, F. serval, F. silvestris, F. temmincki, F. tigrina, F. viverrina, F. wiedii, F. yagouaroundi.

Panthera onca, P. pardus, P. uncia, Felis concolor.

Acinonyx jubatus

Panthera tigris   P. leo

carnivorans. Three muscles on each side of the mammalian skull can jointly bring about jaw closure and, to a small extent, side-to-side motion of the jaws. These are the temporalis muscles, which are suited to snapping the jaws shut, and for counteracting forces generated by struggling prey; and the masseter and medial pterygoid muscles, which are jointly suited to controlling side-to-side movements of the jaws. As carnivorans move their jaws side to side less than herbivores do, they have relatively larger temporalis muscles. We also find that the coronoid process, the part of the mandible on which the temporalis muscles attach, is correspondingly enlarged. Because the jaws are moved little from side to side, the jaw joint itself is very well buttressed by the surrounding tissues of the skull and forms a strong hinge.

THE EYES

As already mentioned, cats have unusually large eyes for their skull sizes. Nocturnal species particularly exhibit this characteristic because large eyes with large pupils have better light-gathering abilities. The eyes of house cats are only slightly smaller than those of humans, but cats can open their pupils to a maximum area about three times greater than people can (125 square millimeters/ 0.19 square inches for cats as against 40 square millimeters/0.06 square inches for people). If all else were equal, the large eyes of cats would also produce acute vision because large, detailed images could be projected onto the sensory cells on the retina of the eyes. However, the resolving power of cat eyes is not as great as it might be because of certain other constraints imposed by adaptations for nocturnal vision.

One factor limiting cat visual acuity is the predominance of a type of sensory cell called "rod" cells instead of "cone" cells in the retina. Rods are more sensitive to light than cones, but rods do not permit much discrimination among light wavelengths. Cones require higher light levels to be activated, but they occur in forms which respond to specific ranges of light wavelengths that permit color vision. Contrary to statements frequently found in older literature, cats do have some cone cells, but they are not nearly as abundant as in human retinas (for example). We do not know for sure how many kinds of cone cells cats have, and to what extent, if any, cats actually use color information. There is some evidence that they can only discern the color of relatively close or big objects, but much remains to be learned about color vision in cats, and indeed other carnivorans.

There is another attribute of cat eyes that heightens their sensitivity to light, but limits their visual acuity. This is the presence of a layer of reflective cells surrounding the rods and cones called the *tapetum lucidum*. It is found in many nocturnal mammals and in almost all carnivorans. After light has passed through the sensory cells

Rafi Ben-Shahar/Oxford Scientific Films

once, the tapetum reflects light back through the sensory layer, and hence gives the cells a second chance to respond. This makes the eyes more sensitive, but acuity is reduced because the reflection is not perfect and the image further blurred. The tapetum lucidum is responsible for the "eyeshine" of cats, and other nocturnal carnivorans, when they look into a light at night.

The net effect of these features is that cats can operate quite effectively under conditions that we would consider to be complete darkness. Since most cats must also be active at least occasionally

▲ Cats, like this leopard (*Panthera pardus*), see about as well as humans in daylight. Their night vision, however, is far more acute than ours. Images are intensified by a specialized part of the eye, the *tapetum lucidum*, which reflects light back through the eye and restimulates the receptors of the retina. This produces the characteristic nocturnal "eyeshine" of cats.

COMPETITION AND COEXISTENCE OF CAT SPECIES

A major goal of ecologists has been to understand the natural determinants of species diversity. Usually this question has been addressed in the context of assemblages, or "guilds," of species that earn their livings in basically similar ways in the same geographic region. For a time in the early 1970s there was practically a consensus that there were patterns in the coexistence of species, often manifested in regular size ratios among the species constituting a guild — for example, the largest species being twice as heavy as the next largest, which is twice as heavy as the next largest.

Such patterns were thought to reflect co-evolutionary adjustments to minimize competition for food resources among species, with each species usually taking prey appropriate for its size. More recently, however, a number of ecologists have questioned the evidence that there are patterns among coexisting species and expressed skepticism about the importance of interspecific competition in shaping assemblages of species. They have suggested that such assemblages may be basically random collections of species. Nearly everyone has agreed, though, that if interspecific competition is an important force in nature, it should be most evident among relatively large carnivorous species such as cats.

Jaw length, defined as the distance between the jaw joint and the canines, has been a convenient measure of cat size because it can be determined from the many specimens housed in museums, whereas data from statistically useful samples of body weight or body length are considerably harder to obtain. The data available indicate that cat jaw length is highly correlated with typical prey size.

Cat species occur in most of the world's major terrestrial biomes (major ecological communities), but assemblages of cats that include the greatest number of species occur in or near the tropics. If interspecific competition does limit size similarity among coexisting species, the resulting pattern should be clearest in these multi-species assemblages. When we consider the most widespread assemblages occurring in tropical South America, Africa, and Asia, we can see immediately that regular interspecific size ratios are not maintained — in each of the assemblages there are two species that are identical in jaw size. These include the jaguarundi and margay in South America, the caracal and serval in eastern Africa, and the Asian golden cat and fishing cat in Southeast Asia. When these species are treated as one "morphospecies" (that is, two or more distinct species that are grouped together for statistical analysis), the pattern of size ratios is much more regular.

Perhaps in each assemblage the two species that are identical in jaw size differ in some way other than prey size, so they are not really in competition. That possibility is suggested by the fact that in each of these pairs, one species is spotted and the other has a plainer coat. These coat color differences may be linked to differences in habitats or habits that would imply differences in prey species. Unfortunately, we do not know enough about the ecology of these species, or about the significance of coat color, to say for sure.

Another possibility is that although jaw length is a good indicator of average prey size, it is not good enough. Recently T. Dayan, D. Simberloff, E. Tchernov, and Y. Tom-Tov reported that strikingly regular ratios occur among canine diameters of the cat "species" of Israel when males and females of each species are counted as a separate species. If, as Leyhausen has suggested, there is a very precise relationship between a cat's canine diameter and the size of neck vertebrae that can be quickly separated to kill prey, canine diameter may be a better indicator of prey size than jaw length. Data on canine sizes are not yet available for the South American, African, and Asian assemblages, but they should be illuminating when they are.

▼▲ How can two, or as many as seven, felids survive in the same place? They do so by hunting at different times, or in different places, or on different sized prey. Caracals *(Lynx caracal)* and servals *(Felis serval)* overlap in distribution throughout Africa, and they are almost identical in size. The serval (right), using its fine sense of hearing, feeds primarily on small grassland rodents in riparian habitats. Within the same broad distribution, the caracal (left) feeds on birds and rodents in more open, drier habitats. In this way, they avoid competing with each other for scarce food resources.

in bright light, they need to be capable of greatly restricting light entry through the pupil, so that their light-sensing cells are not overwhelmed. The vertical slit characteristic of the pupils of smaller cats allows more complete limitation of light entry than the round pupil characteristic of species like ourselves. The big cats are reported to have round or oval pupils more like ours. This may reflect a somewhat lesser dependency on nocturnal hunting for them than for small cats.

Another distinctive attribute of felid visual systems is the extreme frontal, as opposed to lateral, positioning of the eyes. Because people also have frontally arranged eyes, it has probably contributed to the human fascination with cats through recorded history. The functional

significance of the arrangement is that it permits stereoscopic vision, which in turn allows accurate judgment of distance from the viewer to an object. Ability to judge distance is especially important to predators like cats, which must rapidly and accurately seize prey.

FELID HEARING
Our knowledge of felid hearing is almost totally limited to that of house cats, which is probably representative of other small cats. The highest frequencies that house cats can hear (60–70 kilohertz) are far higher than the highest for humans (15–20 kilohertz), but their useful frequency range apparently cannot go as low as ours. The range of greatest sensitivity depends on

▲ Stereoscopic, or binocular, vision enables cats, like this lion (Panthera leo), to accurately judge distance. This ability is extremely important for predators that must stealthily approach potential prey to just the right distance before making a final charge to take the prey down.

SPOTS AND STRIPES

Surprisingly little is known with certainty about the "hows" and "whys" of cat coat coloration. Most cats have some type of blotched, spotted, or striped pattern on at least part of the body. Sometimes the spots or stripes are solid and sometimes they are just outlined by solid, spotted, or stippled markings. These marks may grade from one to another on an individual's coat. There may be variation among members of a species (both within and among populations) in the characteristic form and distinctness of the markings and in the hues involved.

Undoubtedly the primary function of the coloration is to make cats cryptic or camouflaged against vegetation or the ground. Because most cats are not capable of sustained pursuit, it is important that they get close to their prey, without being discovered, before making their rush. For the smaller cats and for young of all species, cryptic coloration may also make them less vulnerable to larger predators.

Some cat species can be described as having "plain" coats, in the sense that relatively large stripes or spots are absent. Even for these, the hairs may be finely barred when viewed close-up ("agouti" hairs), and spots or stripes may be on the extremities. Comparatively plain-coated species include the lion, puma, jaguarundi, African golden cat, Asian golden cat, caracal, flat-headed cat, Bornean red cat, Pallas' cat, Chinese desert cat, and jungle cat. Some of these have faint coat markings in some populations but not in others (for example, the African and Asian golden cats). The young of some species may have spots or other markings that disappear with age (for example, the lion, puma, and jaguarundi). In contrast, cheetah cubs start out with a fairly uniform, bluish-grey mane on the back and darker spotting underneath, but then develop complete dorsal spotting at about two and a half months of age.

Why are some cat species strongly spotted or striped and others less so? Why do coat patterns sometimes disappear with age? A common suggestion is that spotted or striped coats confer better camouflage in the dappled shade of forests and that plainer coats are more cryptic in open country. Spotted young are thought to occur in species with plain adults because the young spend time in wooded areas while mothers hunt in the open. There may be some truth to these ideas, but they do not explain everything. Several plain-coated species occur primarily in forests (for example, the African and Asian golden cats, and puma) or occupy forests over a substantial portion of their range (for example, the puma). On the other hand, adult cheetahs prefer open areas and avoid dense forest or thick bush, yet they are strongly spotted. R. L. Eaton has suggested that the coloration of cheetah cubs causes them to be confused for honey badgers (ratels) at a distance; this may be adaptive for the cheetah cubs because honey badgers are very aggressive and perhaps best avoided by even large predators.

The best way to test ideas on relative camouflage of different coat patterns is to measure how well-spotted and plain-coated species match random samples of their typical backgrounds. This would be very difficult to do because most cats are so secretive and because the equipment needed for assessing background matching is not widely available. A start along these lines has been made by D. Godfrey, J. N. Lythgoe, and D. A. Rumball, who used a technique developed for analyzing digitized images from spy satellites to assess how well a tiger and a zebra matched a typical background. The irregular stripes of the tiger matched the irregular lines in its background, but the regular stripes of the zebra did not. It seems that zebra stripes were more for communication with, or display for, other members of the species than for camouflage.

Differences within a species are another perplexing aspect of felid coloration. This refers to mixtures within local species' populations of individuals with strikingly different coats. The most widely cited case of such polymorphism among cats is that found in leopards, especially those in Southeast Asia, where unusually dark (melanistic) individuals co-occur with typically spotted ones. Similar cases of polymorphisms have been reported for jaguar, Asian and African golden cats, jaguarundi, kodkod, and oncilla. It has been suggested that the melanistic leopards and jaguars are as cryptic as normal ones in deep, humid forests. This may well be the case, but because so many cat species reside in forests, one must wonder why more species do not show such variation.

House cats show great variation in coat coloration, and genes for these variants have been identified. The species from which house cats were originally obtained, the European wild cat, is normally tabby, and these cats do not seem to be more prone to unusual coat coloration in the wild than other cat species do. This suggests that in the wild there is strong natural selection against non-tabby coat color mutants. Under conditions of domestication, cat breeders have replaced natural selection with artificial selection favoring the breeds they desire. With sufficient time and facilities, it would probably be possible to develop as many breeds of most other cat species.

▼ The spotted fur that most cats possess provides them with adequate camouflage to stalk prey undetected.

Christian Zuber/Bruce Coleman Ltd

the dimensions of the ear canal and therefore on the size of the head; thus in smaller animals such as house cats the most sensitive frequencies are higher than humans (8–10 kilohertz versus 0.5–5 kilohertz). Cats' refined muscular control of the outer ears (the pinnae) undoubtedly further increases their hearing sensitivity and directionality — which would help them detect movements of potential small prey. It is thought that the expansion of the auditory bullae (the bony portions of the skull surrounding the middle ear cavity) also improves sensitivity to ecologically important sounds, but this remains unproven in cats. We do not know how the hearing range or sensitivity of large cats compares with small cats, or with our own hearing.

THE OLFACTORY SENSES

Even less is known about the olfactory senses of cats. Traditionally, they are considered less sensitive than dogs, but it is not clear that this distinction is justified. In addition to the usual nasal olfactory sensors, cats (and other carnivorans) have a vomeronasal organ, which is an auxiliary olfactory membrane located in paired canals leading from the roof of the mouth on each side, just behind the incisors. The sensory functions of this organ are not thoroughly understood. It seems to be used by males when they make a characteristic "flehmen" grimace in response to female urine; presumably in response to the female's reproductive condition at the time. Humans lack vomeronasal organs.

TEMPERATURE CONTROL

As is the case in other carnivorans, sweat glands are not abundant in cat skin; they are most concentrated in the footpads and in the area around the anus and external genitals. Panting cools the body, and a special arrangement is present to cool the brain. Blood in many tiny vessels loses heat to the air in the tortuous nasal passages and then is carried to a chamber called the *cavernous sinus* at the base of the brain. Here the venous blood arriving from the nasal passages bathes a network of small blood vessels called the *carotid rete,* which carry arterial blood to the brain. The arrangement acts as a heat exchanger: the blood going to the brain passes its heat to the cooler blood from the nose, and so the brain does not receive blood that is too warm for its proper functioning. This effect is especially important during exercise, when body and blood temperature are greatly elevated. Somewhat surprisingly, dogs have a less elaborate carotid rete system than cats.

▼ Male lions *(Panthera leo)* display "flehman," which is a grimacing lip-curl that brings chemical signals of female estrus into the olfactory sensory system of the male. For most cats, vision and hearing are the important senses for hunting while olfactory or chemical communication plays a large role in social behavior between members of the same species.

Jonathan Scott/Planet Earth Pictures

CAT BEHAVIOR

JILL MELLEN

Cats have been described as the perfect killing machine — some species are able to take down prey many times their own body weight. The method of hunting is almost universal among cat species. The hunt begins with the cat carefully and cautiously stalking its prey. This instantly recognizable posture includes the cat's ears flattened and to the side of the head, seemingly unblinking eyes riveted to its goal, and a low crouch with every muscle tense. The cat then begins to move closer and closer with infinite patience, freezing whenever its victim shows any signs of wariness. Next in the hunting sequence is the rush. In a burst of speed, the cat covers the remaining distance between itself and its prey — often visible to the human eye as just a streak of motion. And finally, the sequence ends when the cat pounces and grasps the prey with its paws and delivers a killing bite. Most cats kill by biting the back of the prey's neck, inserting the canine teeth between the neck vertebrae of their victims, and severing the spinal cord. Larger prey are killed by grasping the throat of the intended victim and suffocating it.

This scenario could represent a moment in the life of a tiger, a serval, a bobcat, an ocelot, or our own domestic cat. While the type of prey hunted ranges from a grasshopper to an elk and the kind of habitat utilized varies from a tropical rainforest to a desert steppe, all of the 37 species of cats are remarkably similar both in their behavior and in their appearance.

Anup & Manoj Shah/Animals Animals

Using a multi-faceted approach, scientists have begun to piece together the natural history of some of the world's cats. We can zoom in to examine the nuances of social behavior and maternal care by studying cats in zoos, or zoom out to learn more about habits and movements using radiotelemetry combined with thousands of hours of patient field observations. More can be learned about these elusive creatures by studying their scent marks and by talking with indigenous peoples who have shared their lands with wild cats for millennia. Domestic cats add yet another piece to the puzzle by living among us and allowing us to become a part of their social world. Most of what is known about the sensory abilities and reproductive physiology of felids comes from studies of domestic cats.

Cats are found in many different habitat types. Some have adapted to desert areas. A few, like the cheetah and the lion, have successfully invaded the open savannas. However, most species of cats are found in the temperate or tropical forests of the world. The remarkable climbing ability of most cats has allowed them to utilize the three-dimensional environment of the forests. It is possible to find as many as seven species of cats on the island of Sumatra — more species than inhabit

all of North America. Some cat species are active at night, others at dawn and dusk, and still others, like the cheetah and jaguarundi, are active during daylight hours. Most species of cat are very flexible in their pattern of activity. Their activity cycle is dependent upon the type of prey they pursue, the kind of habitat they live in, the climate, and the amount of human interference with which they must contend.

Cats use urine, feces, and certain glandular secretions to communicate with one another. These smelly "signposts" relay information about sexual status, territorial ownership, and individual recognition. In felids, the most prominent scent-marking behavior is performed by backing up to a tree trunk, boulder, or fence post and spraying urine against it. As a cat patrols the boundaries of its home range, this "olfactory flag" is hoisted every night. Anyone who has had a domestic tom cat spray near his or her home is aware of the potency of this "flag."

Some species of cats also scrape or scratch the ground with their hind feet while urinating. These scrapes probably function as a visual signal, indicating the boundaries of a cat's home range, or in some species their territorial boundaries. Scrapes of two radio-collared male pumas were

▼ Going for the kill, a cheetah (Acinonyx jubatus) puts on its legendary burst of speed to close the gap between the hunter and the hunted. All cats follow a slow, painstaking stalk with a burst of speed to catch prey, but none reaches the 110 kilometer per hour (68 mph) maximum speed of a coursing cheetah.

► A male cheetah (*Acinonyx jubatus*) scent marks a tree within his territory. Cats spray urine and rub scent glands on various environmental substrates, such as the ground, grass stems, low branches, tree trunks and rocks, using chemical communication to relay information about their identity, sex, and reproductive status, and to indicate territorial possession.

▼ Female lions (*Panthera leo*) may copulate hundreds of times with several males before conceiving. Female lions, like many other cats, are believed to require the stimulation of copulation to ovulate and conceive young. Multiple copulations with multiple males may reduce competition between the male lions in a pride.

most common in areas where their home ranges overlapped. Pumas are also known to scrape vegetation into a pile and then urinate on that pile. A urine mark itself is not a deterrent — that is, it doesn't seem to warn off an intruder. Instead it allows use of the same space, but at different times, thereby averting confrontation.

A cat often approaches the urine mark of another, sniffs, and then raises its head with its mouth half open. In small cats (*Felis* species) the upper lip is slightly withdrawn; in large cats (*Panthera* species) the upper lip is withdrawn so that the cat appears to be grimacing. The cat seems almost immobilized, has a staring look, and breathes slowly. This odd behavior is called "flehmen." Cats flehm after sniffing urine, the anogenital region of another cat, birth fluids, or any novel odor.

What is the function of this strange-looking behavior? When a cat flehms, it uses its tongue to bring droplets of whatever substance it is investigating in contact with the opening of a secondary olfactory (sense of smell) system called the vomeronasal organ (VNO). With the exception of marine mammals and humans, virtually all other mammalian species have, and use, their VNO. The vomeronasal organ, or Jacobson's organ as it is sometimes called, allows an animal to examine message-ladened molecules called "pheromones" that are otherwise too heavy to be inhaled and smelled in the conventional sense. The VNO allows its owner to get a second or closer "look" at signposts left by others.

In cats, the opening to the VNO is located on the roof of the mouth right behind a cat's front teeth. Two tiny holes are visible within a slightly raised area and can be seen on your own domestic cat. One of the most common situations in which flehmen occurs is when males "test" the urine of females, presumably to determine whether females are in estrus (ready to mate). Female cats also exhibit a flehmen response, but less often than do the males. Flehmen is widespread, possibly universal among the 37 species of cats.

Felids also use feces to scent mark, but to a considerably lesser degree than urine. Defecation patterns are similar between sexes although they differ from species to species. For example, many species of small cats (*Felis* species) bury their feces while large cats (*Panthera* species) do not. In captivity, some species of felids defecate in their water bowls while others do not. The European wild cat and lynx bury their feces in areas within their territories, but leave feces uncovered on stones or stumps between territories. In feral domestic cats (that is, domestic cats that are not fed or cared for in any way by humans), dominant cats do not bury feces while subordinates do. Interestingly, while many feral domestic cats do not bury their feces, most household cats do.

Another behavior a cat uses to mark its home

range is claw raking. When our domestic cat shows this behavior, we say it is "sharpening its claws." Although this behavior may function to remove loosened claw sheaths, it probably doesn't sharpen a cat's claws at all, but instead serves to leave visual and olfactory traces (from sweat glands in the paws) within the boundaries of its home range — yet another signpost.

Felids also rub various parts of their bodies against objects to scent mark. When our own domestic cat rubs against us, we in effect become one of its signposts. Cats have tail glands, chin and lip glands (used for marking inanimate objects), and glands on their forehead (used in marking conspecifics, that is, members of their own species). Cats often chin and cheek rub against objects which have previously been sprayed with urine. When cheek rubbing, cats also rub saliva onto inanimate objects. Saliva, like urine, is rife with information about its producer. Scientists have found that domestic tom cats can differentiate between the cheek rubbings of a female that is in heat and one that is not. Rates of all scent marking as well as flehmen responses increase in both males and females when a female is coming into estrus and decline as the female actually enters estrus (becomes receptive to the male's mounting attempts).

Many species of cats vehemently rub the back of the neck against inanimate objects. This neck-rubbing behavior is often seen in association with other scent-marking behaviors, but it is unclear as to whether a cat is laying down a scent or actually anointing itself with a foreign scent. Cats frequently neck rub against urine, vomit, and catnip. Additionally, this behavior is frequently

Jonathan Scott/Planet Earth Pictures

▲ A serval (*Felis serval*) rakes his claws across the bark of a tree. These scrape marks serve as a visual signal for other members of the species, and scent marks deposited from sweat glands on the paws serve as an olfactory signal. Many species of cats also leave scrape and scent marks on the ground.

◀ As these male cheetahs (*Acinonyx jubatus*) are doing, cats often cheek and chin rub against trees previously sprayed with urine. While cheek rubbing, cats also deposit saliva, which, like urine, contains chemical information about the animal that deposited it.

Jonathan Scott/Planet Earth Pictures

▲ Males test for female estrus by sniffing the female's anogenital region. When out of estrus and just as she comes into estrus, the female rebuffs the male with a swipe of her paw and bared teeth. Later, the estrous female is receptive to the male's attention. To initiate copulation, the male approaches the female, grasps her by the nape of her neck, and mounts. In response, the female elevates her hindquarters (called lordosis) and moves her tail aside. Following intromission and ejaculation, the female cries out. She then throws the male off her back, often growling or swiping at him. The female then rolls on her back for from five to thirty seconds while the male watches.

▼ Serval (*Felis serval*) performing "flehmen," a behavior in which the cat withdraws its upper lip and stands immobile with a staring look. Cats flehm to get a better "look" at the scents of other cats. Male cats flehm more often than females; flehmen may help males to determine from a female's urine whether she is ready to mate.

seen when a male and female meet after a separation or when a female is in estrus. It appears to indicate "friendly" intentions.

Cats use combinations and gradations of facial expression, body postures, and vocalizations to communicate with one another. Nowhere is this more pronounced than during aggressive exchanges. Gradations of facial expressions include altering the size of the pupils and, more importantly, changing the position of the ears. While dozing, watching a bird, or surveying its domain, a cat's ears are erect and facing forward; the pupils are usually constricted. In contrast, an aggressive cat — one that is on the offensive — threatens a conspecific by rotating its (still erect) ears so that the backs of the ears face forward, toward the recipient of the threat. Paul Leyhausen, who studied cats in captivity for many years, proposed that "the proportion of the attacking mood is indicated by how much of the back of the ear is visible from the front." The body posture of an aggressive cat includes standing with its back parallel to the ground or with its weight shifted forward to its front legs. The aggressor's tail thrashes from side to side and low growling is often audible.

At the other extreme of this gradation, a submissive cat — one that is on the defensive — flattens its ears out to the side; in the extreme, the ears are almost invisible when viewed from the front. Its pupils are dilated and increase in size as the intensity of the defensive posture increases. This submissive cat may slink away, crouch down, or even roll on its back, hissing intermittently during the altercation.

The position of the ears, the appearance of the pupil, the stance adopted by the cat, and the vocalizations it emits all combine to produce a range of fine-grained signals that a cat uses to communicate with its neighbors, its potential mates, or its rivals. Konrad Lorenz, the father of modern studies of animal behavior, commented that there are few animals that display their "mood" as distinctly as cats. He further stated that the cat's face invariably reveals "what it's up to" and what kind of behavior is likely to occur in the next moment. Why should cats be such "honest communicators"? Most species of animals tend to hide their "intentions" from a rival to give themselves an advantage in an aggressive altercation. Why then should cats signal what they are about to do? Since nearly all cats are able to kill prey as large as themselves, aggression between conspecifics is potentially lethal. The unambiguous signals within a cat's behavioral repertoire probably have evolved to reduce the risk of fatal encounters. Thus, each cat is an honest communicator because it reduces the risk of injury to itself by avoiding fights which escalate.

Many species of cats, both large and small, possess contrasting white patches of fur on the backs of their ears, sometimes called "eye spots." It has been suggested that these white eye spots serve as a signal to the young and make it easier for them to follow their mother in heavy vegetation. However, these eye spots may also function to enhance threat postures. All cat species, with the exception of the jaguarundi, have contrasting color on the backs of their ears. For example, the backs of a lion's ears are black, tigers have white eye spots, and servals have both a white eye spot and a black bar on the backs of their ears.

Markings on the tails of most cat species include rings or contrasting colored tips. These

markings may enhance tail movements or postures. In aggressive encounters, cats often thrash their tails from side to side as a threat. Just like the markings on the backs of the ears, the contrasting markings on the tail probably function to exaggerate or accentuate a threat.

The courtship behavior of the tiny, two-kilogram rusty-spotted cat is almost identical to that of the domestic cat, and the courtship behavior of the domestic cat closely parallels that of the Siberian tiger. For several days prior to the actual copulation, a male follows and attempts to approach a female coming into estrus. Presumably, the male has determined the onset of the female's receptive period by monitoring her scent marks (using both the primary sense of smell and flehmens) and her vocalizations. The resident male spends his time scent marking at an increased rate, and monitoring the female's receptivity.

As the female nears her period of receptivity, the courting male alternates between approaching the female, cheek rubbing, and neck rubbing, all the while orienting towards her. Initially, the female hisses and strikes at him with her paws, sniffs his scent marks, and scent marks too. This sequence is repeated many times for several days.

Once the female is truly in estrus, in other words, receptive to mounts by the male, a courtship sequence begins. This sequence lasts one to five minutes and is repeated as many as 100 times in a single day. Most species of cats remain in estrus for about three days, or longer if the female is not mated.

Males of the *Felis* species maintain a firm grip on the nape of the female's neck throughout the entire mount. If a *Felis* male releases or even relaxes his grip, the female either turns and strikes him with her paw or runs away. In contrast, the males of larger cat species (*Panthera* species) lightly, almost gingerly, pinch the nape of the female at the beginning of a mount, but soon release their grip and instead yowl loudly — called

▼ Female leopard (*Panthera pardus*) and cubs resting in a deep forest lair. Like other cats, female leopards seek out sheltered den sites in which to give birth. Blind and helpless at birth, cubs remain in the den while their mother hunts.

a caterwaul — during the mount. This modified nape bite at the beginning of the mount may be an adaptation by these big cats to avoid potential injury to the females during copulation.

With the possible exception of the lion, all species of cats appear to be induced ovulators. This means that the stimulus of copulation provides a neuronal trigger for a subsequent hormonal sequence, resulting in release of the egg by the ovary. Induced ovulation appears to be an adaptation for solitary cats, as well as other solitary species, to ensure that eggs released have a high probability of being fertilized. There seems no better way to assure fertilization than to couple egg-release with copulation. (This is in contrast to other mammalian species that are spontaneous ovulators. For example, humans are spontaneous ovulators, releasing an egg about every 28 days, even in the absence of males.) Male cats, in fact, have small spines on their penises. Upon withdrawal from the female's vagina, these penile spines provide additional neuronal stimulation for the induction of ovulation and may explain the females' vehement copulatory cry, associated with the end of the copulatory sequence.

With the exception of lions, the male's direct involvement in the production of young ends with copulation. After a female has mated, she and the male return to their pattern of mutual avoidance. Gestation, or length of pregnancy, for cats is closely linked to their size. For the tiny sand cat it is 66 days while for the tiger it is 103 days.

When the female is about to give birth, she finds an appropriate den site for her litter, which averages from one to four young. The cubs or kittens (the young of larger cats are called cubs, the young of smaller cats are kittens) are blind and helpless at birth. Their eyes open at about two weeks of age, but even before then, each youngster in a litter has staked its claim to one of its mother's teats. "Teat ownership" apparently serves to reduce the number of squabbles among littermates. A small mother cat must hunt for herself and return to her den several times a day to nurse her offspring. In big cats, such as leopards, the female will remain away from the young as long as a day and a half at a time.

The youngsters spend their time in and around the den learning about their environment. Through play, cats practice the social skills they'll use as adults. Cats play-fight, wrestling and chasing one another, before they practice the stalking skills they'll use in hunting. Scientists believe cats practice social skills in the safety of their dens, and before their potentially dangerous teeth and claws can be damaging. Later, when their agility and coordination are better developed, they begin the stalking, rushing, and pouncing that we see when our domestic kitten plays with a ball of twine. These are the skills that must be perfected in order to become a successful hunter.

► Like young cats of all kinds, cheetah (*Acinonyx jubatus*) cubs are very playful. Play-fights between siblings involve wrestling, chasing, stalking, and pouncing, and help cats to learn the social and hunting skills they will need to be successful adults.

► Only hunger and the need to hunt keeps most cats from sleeping their lives away. Lions (*Panthera leo*) may rest and sleep for up to 19 hours of every day. With no predators to fear, lions sleep with abandon, often sprawled out in the shade of a stand of trees.

Anup Shah/Jacana

When the young are three to four months of age, the mother cat begins to bring prey to her litter, allowing them to practice the most difficult aspect of the hunting sequence, the killing bite. Much to the chagrin of their owners, domestic cats often bring home headless rodents or freshly killed birds. Some people believe that domestic cats view their owners as youngsters that need to be taught to hunt. This human–cat interaction is not limited to domestic cats. A female Siberian tiger in a zoo brought mice that she had caught in her exhibit into her holding area in the morning, presumably for her human caretakers.

As the youngsters grow older, they begin to accompany their mother on hunting trips, improving and refining their skills as a hunter. At one to two years of age (larger cats stay with their mothers longer than do the smaller cats), the

Gunter Ziesler/Bruce Coleman Ltd.

young cats begin to establish their own home ranges. Male littermates usually move well away from their natal area, while females often establish their home ranges near those of their mother.

One final universality among the 37 species of cats is that behavior or "activity" which occupies the majority of every cat's time — sleeping. The lifestyle of cats has been described as "one of inactivity punctuated by forays in search of food." From our own domestic cat to the regal lion, cats tend to sleep unless hunger dictates that they hunt — many species sleep up to 18 hours per day. During waking hours, all species of cats share similar methods of hunting, scent marking, and socializing. Each of the 37 species is unique in its coat pattern, habitat use, prey choice, and activity cycle. Unfortunately, all are threatened by destruction of their habitat by humans.

VOCAL COMMUNICATION IN CATS

GUSTAV PETERS

All cat species use sound communication at close, medium, and long distances. At close, and less so at medium range, the simultaneous occurrence of visual signals is common in certain behavioral contexts and it is important that combinations of the different signalling modes be considered together. At long distances, the sound signal is usually the only form of communication used at a specific moment, but indirect interaction with other modes such as olfactory signals is probable. The wide range of contexts in which felids use sound communication is largely equivalent in all species. As in many other higher vertebrate groups, the acoustic signal repertoire of cats comprises discrete sound types such as spitting, and ranges of graded signals such as meowing. Only within the latter do sound types show a considerable degree of variability in all three structural dimensions — intensity, duration, and frequency composition — and certain types are linked to each other by transitional forms. The number of acoustic signal types defined in the repertoire of a species is dependent to some extent on the criteria used for classification, and can be no direct yardstick for the communicatory potential of the signal system. The complete acoustic repertoire has not been analyzed for any cat species but about 12 vocalization types is probable for most felids.

All species of the Felidae share a basic set of acoustic signals. In addition, all species are likely to have one or several vocalizations which are peculiar to their own or only certain other species. With the exception of a few specific vocalizations restricted to females in heat, males courting, and either sex during copulation, female and male felids of a species have the same repertoire. Most cat vocalizations are very likely generated by oscillations of the vocal folds during exhalation. There are very few felid vocalizations which regularly include inhalatory sound production. Hissing is a sound which probably can be performed without laryngeal sound generation. With the exception of purring, the exact mechanism of sound production and modification is not established for any felid vocalization. For all species the frequency range of their vocalizations is mainly between 50 and 10,000 hertz. Most sounds and calls of

juveniles and adults cover only a part of that range. Cats can hear much higher frequencies than those present in their own acoustic signals. The loudest intensity measured for any felid call is 114 decibels for the roaring of a male lion.

"Meow" types of calls are common to all cat species even though to the human ear the meow of a lion may sound quite different from the meow of a domestic cat. In the Felidae there is no correlation between the size of a species and the average pitch of its meow-type calls, for example, pumas produce high-pitched, whistle-like calls whereas much smaller species like the black-footed cat or the sand cat have relatively low-pitched meows. Within the same species these calls can vary considerably in intensity, duration, pitch, and tonality, according to their function and the motivation of the vocalizing individual. The major behavioral context of primarily low-intensity meows is mother–kitten interaction at close range; high-intensity forms are used by adult males and females for territorial advertisement and mate attraction.

The acoustic repertoire of felids in agonistic situations is also fairly uniform; it is within such contexts that vocalizations generally occur with visual signals, such as specific body postures and facial expressions. All species spit, hiss, and growl — the sounds in this sequence indicating an increasingly aggressive motivation in the vocalizing individual — the first two are discrete sounds, while the growl is graded and thus well suited to conveying the subtle changes in motivation of the sender. Shriek-like calls may be uttered by a subordinate animal being attacked or even bitten.

In friendly close-contact situations, felids use three different short (less than half a second), low-intensity, noisy sound types as appeasement, reassurance, or greeting signals — gurgling, prusten, and puffing. Each species has only one of these sounds in its repertoire and they are equivalent in function. Puffing sounds like a bout of stifled sneezing, and is only present in the leopard and lion. Prusten is a sound similar to the snorting of a horse and exists in the clouded leopard, snow leopard, tiger, and jaguar. Gurgling is very probably present in all other species

▼ ▶ (Opposite page) A female puma (*Felis concolor*) uttering a meow-type call. (Right) A sound spectrogram of a female puma in estrus uttering a meow-type call. In this spectrogram, the approximate phase of articulation in which this animal is with its call is marked with a pointer. In a sound spectrogram, the increasing darkness of the traces represents increasing intensity of the components of the call.

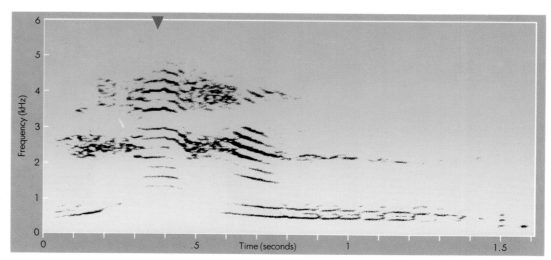

Zefa-BAUER

of Felidae. Its rhythmically pulsed sound can vary between forms similar to the cooing of pigeons and those resembling the sound of bubbling water. It can be directly coupled with a meow to form a coherent vocalization.

The best known, friendly, close-range vocalization of felids is purring. In intraspecific communication, purring is most common between mother cats and their kittens in the nest, or in other situations of undisturbed close contact. Kittens start to purr at a very early age and can even do so while they nurse. Generally in these contexts, purring is an "all is well" signal, the mother's vocalization having a soothing and reassuring effect on the kittens, and the purring of the kittens an "all is well" in return. Because of the close proximity of sender(s) and addressee(s), the very low intensity of purring is sufficient for its signal function, and at the same time reduces the risk of being detected by predators. As a vocalization, purring is peculiar in that it can be produced continuously during both phases of respiration, often going on for minutes on end. Cats can produce certain other vocalizations while purring.

It has been postulated that because the hyoid of the lion, leopard, jaguar, tiger, and snow leopard has a cartilaginous portion, unlike all other species of the Felidae in which it is completely bony, only the latter are able to purr and cannot roar whereas the former can roar but cannot purr. Anecdotally, purring has been reported in many species but verifiable evidence has been presented for only a few. Which felid species actually purr? The question cannot be answered definitively; a correlation between the degree of hyoid ossification and the ability to purr is not proven.

For none of the five felid species named above in which roaring is the alleged mutually exclusive "counterpart" of purring is there reliable evidence of purring. Some of the loud calls termed "roaring" in these species are structurally so different that they cannot be lumped together as the same vocalization type. The common notion of roaring in lions is that of a long, structured call sequence with a species-specific composition in relation to the duration of single calls and intervals between them, and intensity change. Neither tiger nor snow leopard has an equivalent call sequence; moreover, the tiger lacks one call type and the snow leopard two which are components of the roaring sequence of lions. All the component call types of the lion, and an equivalent roaring sequence, are present in leopards and jaguars. The low and intense calls of lions, leopards, jaguars, and tigers are due to the fact that their vocal folds are thick pads compared to the relatively sharp folds of the other species of the Felidae, the snow leopard holding an intermediate position in this respect. The peculiar hyoid structure may also affect certain call characteristics in these five species, but it has no influence on the presence of specific call types in their acoustic repertoires. Therefore the subdivision of the Felidae into "roaring" and "purring" cats and its foundation on a correlation between hyoid structure and vocalization is in need of revision.

Although the roaring of lions is probably one of the most commonly known wild animal vocalizations, various misconceptions about its functions still exist. Lions do not roar to intimidate potential prey. Several lions of a pride will join in communal roaring probably to strengthen their bond, claim their territorial rights towards adjacent prides, or give stray members of the pride information of its whereabouts. Individual lions may roar to re-establish contact with their pride or when searching for other members of their own species. It is likely that when communal roaring takes place within a pride, certain individuals may have specific roles. The functional facets of lion roaring, however, still have to be studied in detail, like many other aspects of vocal communication in the Felidae.

▲ A female African lion (*Panthera leo*) chases wildebeest from a Serengeti waterhole. Despite their tremendous power and adaptive efficiency, cats are more likely to fail than succeed in their attempts to kill.

CATS UP CLOSE

LIONS

J.P. HANBY AND J.D. BYGOTT

The lion (*Panthera leo*) — King of the Beasts! Why? Not only because the lion is big and beautiful, social, vocal and visible: its monarch status is largely due to the fact that lions have been our distant, powerful and terrifying neighbors for so long. In historic times, lions were found throughout Africa, and across the Middle East into India, occupying almost any habitat except the densest forests and the most barren deserts. Humans have lived in awe of these huge predators for thousands of years.

Lions have been immortalized in statuary, heraldry and legend for centuries. They have been pets and possessions of rulers, sometimes revered and sometimes treated very cruelly. Julius Caesar is said to have killed more than 400 lions just to consecrate the opening of his forum. Of course it has been the male lion who has been the focus of attention. It is the male who has guarded libraries, bridges and castles all these years. Head framed by a hairy ruff, standing or crouching or even lying flat out, his stance exudes power — as a symbol, the King of the Beasts has no equal.

Recent research has tried to probe beneath the emperor's symbolic clothes. Wild lions in Africa have been the subjects of numerous studies for more than a quarter century. Indian lions have also been studied but to a lesser extent. Such scientific observations of behavior and ecology have cleared up many myths, and also widened our understanding of lion society and the lion's place in its realm.

Peter Johnson/NHPA

▲ The distinctive mane that adorns a male lion may signal his sex and adult status to females and males alike. It may also protect his head and neck during fierce combat with other males.

▶ Lions risk lethal injury from the flying hooves of zebras every time they attempt to kill one of these striped equids. Even so, zebras are a mainstay in the diet of lions on the East African savanna.

THE SOCIAL SYSTEM OF LIONS

Studies of lions in the wild have rightly brought the female lion into the spotlight. Females are the basis of lion society: they are the hunters, cub rearers, and property owners and defenders. Females can survive on their own, but they only thrive as members of a kin group. As a communal creature, the female lion has few equals.

Sociality is probably the single most exciting facet of lion life and, as compared to other cats, cannot be overemphasized. That great symbol, the imposing male, is a loner by human design only. In reality, in the wild, a male's chances of survival

alone are at best slim, and not helped by its all too visible mane that alerts enemies as well as prey. Also, a lone male's chances of gaining access to, or keeping, females long enough to produce viable cubs are dimmer than his chances of winning a fight all by himself (though the mane would help here, intimidating as well as protecting).

King or queen, a lion needs to be part of a pride. A pride usually comprises about five to six adult females, a set or coalition of adult males, and any cubs. A small pride can be just one female and her cubs, the largest can number up to 40, but the norm is around 15. The essential thing about pride structure is that all the females are related: mothers, daughters, aunts, cousins. Only under very rare circumstances do distantly related or unrelated females team up. In fact, there is no hard evidence at this time, which indicates that unrelated females will accept each other long enough to form an enduring pride, that is, one with generations and a more or less stable range.

Males, on the other hand, do join together even when unrelated as the dangers and lack of opportunities for single males seem to be so great. Unrelated males will form coalitions that last for years. Pairs and trios of males are just as often unrelated as they are related while groups of four or more males are usually related: brothers, half-sibs, cousins, all born in the same pride.

Whether a coalition of "buddies" or a true brotherhood, young male groups need to hunt together or scavenge to survive. Young males are always ousted from their natal pride when their fathers lose out to intruding males. At that age, usually two to four years, they are not yet

Kiltarlity kids
in shinty action

The annual Kiltarlity indoor first shinty competition was completed last week, as youngsters competed for the Charlie Mainland Shield. The winners are in the back row, from left – Andrew Wallace, Laura Gallacher, Lachlan Savage-Lowden (capt), Leanne Mainland (daughter of sponsor), and Iain Lamont. The runners-up are at the front. They are – Stuart Dingwall, Greg Matheson (capt), Rebecca Gallacher and Scott Lamont. A competition was also run for Kirkhill kids, see next week's edition for details.

Picture: Phil Downie

'Fifth man' role gives MacDonald a chance to gain glory with Sc

Highland crash to last day rugby defeat

HIGHLAND Rugby Club went down 42-0 in their final division three match of the season against second-placed Allan Glen's in Glasgow at the weekend.

For the first 20 minutes, the north side conceded three soft tries without reply and, although the scoring slowed down, Allan Glen's were 30 points up at the interval.

The visitors lost stand-off Drew Buxton with a hamstring injury after 15 minutes and full-back Paul Scofield was drafted in to lead a Highland line which was fairly ineffectual when it did get some ball.

Despite some good work by captain for the day, Gordon Fraser, the visiting forwards failed to subdue a big Glasgow pack, who seemed to have trained particularly hard for this clash.

Former skipper Bruce McGregor came on halfway through the first half and he added a bit of steel into the Highland forwards by charging into the rucks with real aggression.

After the break, Highland played much better up front and the Glasgow team only managed two further tries.

Highland had a couple of chances to get points on the board, but could not finish the attacks with Stevie Henry looking pretty sound on his return to the wing after a long injury.

The Glasgow three-quarters were always up in defence and Highland could not break through the tackles and also had problems with passing and handling.

Allan Glen's also lost lock Matt Heeps, who was rucked over and had to get

Curler Ewan Winter olyr

By Charles Bannerman

INVERNESS curler Ewan MacDonald's bid for selection for a second Winter Olympics in Turin next year continues on the west coast of Canada next week when he appears in the World Championships as fifth man in the Scottish team.

It will also allow him the chance to chase a unique family double, as he aims to win an Olympic medal – just as wife Fiona achieved three years ago.

And as a veteran of four previous World Championships, where his medal tally includes the gold in 1999 and also a bronze, he has a unique reserve of experience to offer at this year's event in Victoria, British Columbia.

It was the rink skipped by MacDonald himself which so narrowly failed to reach the latter stages of last year's World Championships in Sweden and this time selection has fallen to skip David Murdoch, along with team-mates Craig Wilson, Neil Murdoch and Euan Byers.

However, it is normal to take a 'fifth man' in reserve on these occasions and with the championships now running to 12 teams – and hence a gruelling 11 game round robin – it is even possible that the Inverness man may be called upon to play a game or two.

Ewan, speaking to the *Highland News Group*, explained: "Again it's fantastic to be going to another World Championships. That's what we play the sport for and that's where you want to be.

"So when I'm out there, depending on how things

▶ This male African lion has vanquished a competitor. In order to breed and see their young survive to adulthood, male lions must control prides of breeding females. Up to five or six related males may form coalitions to take over and maintain a female pride. But the males' tenure is usually short, and takeover and defence often require bloody combat with other male coalitions. Many males die in combat and few survive past 12 years of age.

competent hunters, having been provided for by their mothers and sisters, and they wander widely trying to stay alive. These males, or nomads, have to learn to hunt, a task made simpler only in times of abundant prey such as when the wildebeest calve on the Serengeti Plains. It may also be an advantage to young males to have a small or blond mane when learning to hunt as they are not as conspicuous to prey, and other adult males are less likely to notice, attack, or steal food from them.

Some young males are lucky enough to be evicted along with their sisters with whom they can hunt. And some are lucky enough to be born with many brothers and not evicted until around the age of four by which time they are fully grown and have large manes. Having a big mane goes with being well fed and healthy, and if the big mane is black it seems to have the added advantage of intimidating other males from a distance. A large mane may also alert females and give them clues as to the health and vigor of the males in question. Well-grown young males in large groups can more or less march into a neighboring pride, chase off the resident males, and settle in to live a good life.

Once established with a pride, males are usually able to scrounge food from the females, but they also have pride duties: males have to patrol and mark their territory by spraying urine, rubbing secretions of glands on objects, and roaring. Females also mark and roar and both males and females have to chase or fight off intruders, risking death or disability. Males only defend against other males while females defend against other females as well as strange males.

Lions can mate as often as every 20 minutes or so, on and off for several days, eating little in the meantime. Only about one in five sessions results in a litter of cubs, born about three months after successful fertilization. As in many other animals, including humans, all this sex is not just to procreate. Much of it is to familiarize males and females thoroughly. Also, by being receptive for a substantial length of time, females can mate with one or more males, thus presumably reducing competition between males within a group.

Competition between male groups for access to a pride can be intense — female groups do not go unescorted for long. Membership in a pride is usually gained by a new group of males ousting any resident males and often this involves fights that are sometimes lethal. The larger the group of males the more successful they are. We have known six males who together not only captured a pride as youths, but by subsequently splitting into smaller units later held several different prides at once. We have found that members of large male groups, during their lifetime, sire more offspring per capita than do members of small male groups.

Sometimes adult males will abandon a pride after they have stayed for about two years, in order to find receptive females in a new pride. Even

Mitsuaki Iwago

when abandoned, the females of a pride do not just accept any males. Sometimes they will mate with several different sets of males before settling down to just one. Again, it is the larger groups of males who will usually have the tenacity and win out. If some of the pride's females have little cubs they will often run away from any unfamiliar males thus dividing the pride which then may take

months or years to reunite under the tenure of a specific set of males. Gaining new males is usually a traumatic event for a pride. New males will chase and kill any cubs, subadults, or even adult females if the females do not mate with them.

If their cubs have been killed, the females are generally ready to mate soon after, and so this cub killing or infanticide ensures that any cubs born subsequently will be the offspring of the new males. Courtship and mating between pride females and new males is an especially extended affair. During the months after a takeover, females repeatedly come into estrus without getting pregnant. This not only allows females time to get to know the various males trying to breed with them, but it also allows the males to sort

▶ Male and female lions survive because of their ability to form coalitions and prides. But when a kill is made, a dominance hierarchy based on size and age quickly becomes apparent. Males are first to eat, followed by females, and then juveniles. The youngest cubs are the last to eat, and as a result, cubs may starve when prey is scarce.

Jonathan Scott/Planet Earth Pictures

themselves out. Eventually, after about six months of periodic mating, cubs are born.

Often several females will bear at around the same time. Cubs born into such "synchronized" or "communal" litters have a number of advantages. First, they have a better chance of survival, being suckled and defended by more than one "mother," and second, their fathers, newly in possession of the pride, are likely to be around while the cubs grow up. The adult males now protect instead of persecute. Communal litters also do better in the long term because there is a greater chance that both males and females will have like-sexed littermates, which helps them to survive and establish themselves when they leave their natal pride. Without question, lions in groups do better at all stages of life.

Even in groups though, males have a hard life. They seldom live longer than 12 years in the wild while females sometimes reach 16 or older. Even when an old female loses most of her teeth the pride will wait for her and share with her, as long as she can keep up. When males are old, they are ousted from the pride by younger and stronger males. Exiled males can steal from most other predators but if they have to hunt on their own they fare poorly and often get terrible wounds from kicks and horns. When they lose their teeth or health, or, indeed, when they lose a team-mate they soon die.

HUNTERS OR SCAVENGERS?

Lions are not only the most social of cats, they are also among the largest and most powerful. By reputation they are superlative hunters, yet recent research shows that they are really only moderately successful, killing perhaps once in every five attempts. We also now know that lions will scavenge as much of their food as they can. They are alert to the movements of vultures and to the calls of feeding hyenas, and, where prey and other predators are plentiful, they may scavenge half their total food intake. Males are especially prone to scavenge and they freely scrounge from females as well as from other predators. In between bouts of hunting or scavenging lions usually conserve energy by resting. Wild lions are usually at rest about 19 hours out of 24, but they do have to work, and they mostly do it at night. Indeed, most hunting and social behavior occurs between dusk and dawn. ·

Lions are versatile predators. They can catch animals as small as hares and as large as bull giraffes, but they specialize in medium- to large-sized prey such as zebras and wildebeest. They can sometimes consume as much as 35 kilograms (77 pounds) in one feeding. Each lion needs, on average, about 5 kilograms (11 pounds) of meat per day to stay alive, that is, about 30 medium-sized prey animals a year. If the prey were few and all of one species, lions might make a difference to

Jonathan Scott/Planet Earth Pictures

◄ It is a great advantage for a lion — male or female — to have siblings or other pride mates of the same age. As cubs, they can nurse from their aunts while their mothers hunt. Later in life, pride mates form male coalitions and female prides. Female lions tend to synchronize breeding and birthing to increase the success of their young.

their numbers. But generally, lions are eclectic hunters, opportunistically taking whatever they can catch or scavenge. If one kind of prey becomes scarce, lions switch to another kind. In Africa, there is usually a large variety of prey species wherever lions roam. In all of the areas studied so far, it is the density of resident prey animals that determines the distribution and density of the lion, rather than the other way around.

Lions may not greatly affect the numbers of their prey but they definitely exercise selection and that may affect their prey in other ways. For instance, they tend to take solitary animals, usually young or peripheral males, as well as the very young, old, lame, sick, wounded, and unobservant, thereby influencing the evolution of the prey population. Much remains to be learned about these aspects of lion ecology.

Lions and their prey are further influenced by fellow predators. The realm of lions is grassland and bush, home of many grazers and browsers as well as many other predators such as hyenas, leopards, cheetahs, wild dogs, jackals, and smaller cats. These predators mostly take the small- and medium-sized animals but competition is keen, especially during seasons or years of low prey density. Few predators can afford to specialize totally on a certain type of prey, yet by being fairly general they come into conflict. Resolution of this conflict has resulted in different sizes and life styles

of predators (for example, hunting at different times of day, short denning periods, nomadism or prey following). Although a lion does fairly well in hunting, compared with other predators, in groups lions can bring down animals like buffalo, giraffe, rhinoceros, hippopotamus, and even small elephants. In sharing a large kill, they make use of a resource that would otherwise fall to scavengers.

The development of sociality in lions as compared to the other cats is only partly due to lions in groups being able to capture larger prey than their fellow predators. Studies of feeding efficiency have shown that if food were the only factor, lions should hunt alone or in groups of four or five. Lions consistently hunt in groups larger or smaller than the optimum for feeding. It is as though the cooperative hunting and sharing of prey allows lions to be social, as opposed to them being social in order to hunt cooperatively.

By sticking together, lions obtain many benefits besides shared food. As a group they can better defend, against other lions, ranges that are large enough to provide prey all year round. Furthermore, united females can better protect their cubs from marauding males and intruding females. By forming crèches, females can also provide a larger and more constant supply of food and a fail-safe adoption scheme should one mother die. All these factors improve survival and thereby influence the evolution of sociality.

CONSEQUENCES OF INBREEDING IN LIONS

DAVID E. WILDT

Genes largely dictate health and reproductive success. Forty years of research with farm livestock has proven the harmful effects of father–daughter, mother–son or sibling matings. In comparison to "non-inbred" offspring, inbred offspring generally have problems conceiving, and smaller, less healthy litters result. In 1979, National Zoo (Washington D. C.) scientists discovered that inbred zoo animal populations had high rates of neonatal and juvenile mortality. For the zoo community, this was the first warning of the dire consequences of inbreeding. Mismanaged zoo animals unfortunately may have no choice but to mate with each other, but does inbreeding occur in free-living populations?

One of the most intriguing documentations of lost genetic diversity occurs in cheetahs. This entire species experienced a population bottleneck so profound that the genetic make-up of all cheetahs is remarkably uniform. Cheetahs also ejaculate an extraordinarily high number of structurally abnormal sperm. Unfortunately, because all cheetahs are similar genetically and because all produce abnormal sperm, it is impossible to prove that poor semen quality is the direct result of inbreeding. The lion, on the other hand, has provided us with the first evidence of a relationship between genetic diversity and reproductive characteristics in a wild population.

National Zoo, National Cancer Institute (Frederick, Maryland) and University of Minnesota scientists have compared the genetic and reproductive characteristics of lions on the Serengeti Plains in Tanzania with lions geographically isolated in the Ngorongoro Crater, an extinct volcanic caldera also in Tanzania. The Crater is about 260 square kilometers (100 square miles), and contains the earth's highest density of lions (about 100 animals). Because of the naturally steep walls of the Crater and plentiful prey, there is little incentive for lions to leave; thus, as the population increases, so does the likelihood of inbreeding. Indeed, molecular genetic analysis has revealed that, compared to the Serengeti Plains lions, Crater lions have less genetic diversity. Even though sperm numbers among adult males in the two populations were similar, the Crater lions consistently produced twice as many abnormal sperm. Even more thought provoking was the analysis of a third population, a remnant population (fewer than 250) of Asian lions in India, which experienced a severe population bottleneck in the first quarter of this century. Genetic evaluation of this population revealed a severe incidence of inbreeding, similar to that of the cheetah. These Asian lions produced twice as many abnormal sperm as the lions of the Serengeti Plains. They also produced less vigorous and fewer total sperm, and lower blood levels of the main male sex hormone, testosterone.

This study revealed the sinister impact of inbreeding on sperm health, but it remains unknown whether actual reproductive performance is seriously impaired. Nonetheless, records indicate that female lions mated with Asian males often fail to conceive, or produce only stillborn cubs. In vitro fertilization studies also reveal that abnormal sperm are less

Purdy & Matthews/Survival Anglia

▲ In a small population, the probability of close relatives breeding is very high. As a result, genetic variability in small populations may be greatly reduced. The loss of variability usually leads to increased juvenile mortality, shorter life spans, and greater susceptibility to disease.

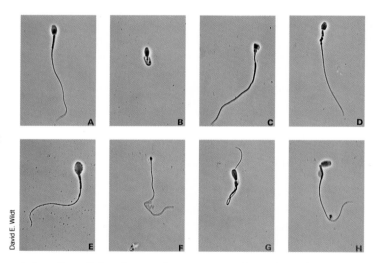

David E. Wildt

▲ One effect of inbreeding may be an increase in the incidence of abnormalities in the sex cells of male mammals. These defects may reduce their fertility. A shows a normal lion sperm cell; B through H picture some of the defects frequently detected in the sperm of inbred male lions.

capable of attaching to and penetrating eggs in a "test-tube" environment. These results illustrate the potential dangers of natural or man-induced population bottlenecks, and should show all of us the need for, and importance of, skillful management of animal populations in zoos.

Frans Lanting/Minden Pictures

What is the limit of pride size? Studies in Serengeti and Ngorongoro indicate that three is the minimum number of adult females that can successfully hold a range and rear cubs (that is, perpetuate themselves). Prides usually have twice that number and more. Large prides tend to split into subprides that share an extended range. Although all members of the pride are seldom together at one time (except when sharing large kills), by mixing and matching, any one female can usually find a relative with whom to hunt, feed, and guard cubs and range. It is worth noting that the only case of unrelated females teaming up even temporarily was in the inhospitable Kalahari Desert, when the females were in a position where they either had to leave their natal ranges or face starvation. It is highly likely that they teamed up to defend kills and a hunting range, rather than for any particular prey catching advantages. Defense of a known range, defense of cubs, and in the case of males defense of their rights to the pride, appear to be more important to lion sociality than cooperative hunting.

THE FUTURE OF LIONS

To see a scrum of lions all bloodied, snarling, and shoving around a carcass might suggest an image of unmannered medieval lords and ladies who can take what they want. But like all royalty, lions have their enemies and their status is not secure. They are still hunted down by men for "sport" and trophies and in the name of livestock protection. Elephants, buffaloes, and rhinoceroses can scare off and even kill lions, as can a determined posse of hyenas. Leopards, jackals, wild dogs, fire and flood are all hazards for small cubs left in dens. Parasites and pests also take their toll — a plague of biting *Stomoxys* flies once decimated the lions of Ngorongoro Crater. Heavy burdens of ticks and worms may weaken lions and hard-earned kills may even be stolen by a relentless army of safari ants!

The lion may lose its old reputation as King of the Beasts in favor of a more democratic and ecological view of the animal kingdom. Even so, lions will remain one of the most popular of beasts — sought after, photographed, and studied.

▲ Male lions, with their showy manes, are not particularly good hunters. In fact, they largely rely on their great size and intimidating behavior to steal kills from female lions and smaller carnivores such as leopards and cheetahs. Groups of hyenas or jackals, however, are able to drive a lone male lion from a kill.

▶ A pride of lions on the floor of Tanzania's Ngorongoro Crater, a volcanic caldera isolated from the great Serengeti plains by steep walls. This 260 square kilometer (100 square mile) area teems with wildlife, but with population interchange virtually absent the genetic diversity of the crater lions is about 40 percent less than that of Serengeti lions.

Mitsuaki Iwago

KIN SELECTION IN LIONS

BRIAN BERTRAM

Most lions spend the main part of their lives in the company of relatives. The long-term studies that have been carried out have made it clear how this comes about. In general, young females remain all their lives in the pride in which they were born, and into which strange females are not accepted. Young males, when ousted as juveniles from their natal pride, usually wander as a group among companions with whom they grew up, before collectively acquiring possession of another pride, and becoming the breeding males there.

Compared with all other cat species, lions are more thoroughly social — they are usually found with companions, they form long-lasting relationships, and they cooperate in hunting, in defending their area and in rearing their young. It appears that this sociability towards companions and the relatedness of those companions is interlinked.

In evolutionary terms, it is easy to see why a mother cat suckles her young: the young survive, and as a result the mother's genes continue into the next and perhaps subsequent generations. They are not in fact just "her" genes that are passed on, but roughly a random sample of 50 percent of them, the other half coming from the other parent. By the same process of reasoning, it is easy to see that a female lion that allows her daughter's cubs to suckle from her is achieving much the same thing but in a diluted form: she is helping to ensure the survival of 50 percent of the genes which are in her daughter, half of which originally came from herself. Just as a mother is related by 50 percent to her own offspring, so a grandmother is related by 25 percent to her granddaughter. And just as natural selection

favors mothers who help their offspring to survive, so it favors grandmothers who help their grandchildren to survive. Genes which may contribute to this helpful behavior are likely to become more frequent in the population over the generations.

Female lions in a pride include mothers, grandmothers, aunts, and sisters. Two full sisters are related by half — just as mother and daughter are — because they each received a random 50 percent of the genetic endowment of each of their parents. A female lion who suckles her sister's cub is doing the same as the grandmother described above — namely, improving the chances of that cub, which shares 25 percent of the same genes, surviving into the next generation. Natural selection is all about favoring genes which, because of their effects, result in there being more of those genes in later generations. That part of natural selection which is brought about through the action of relatives other than the parents is known as kin selection.

Kin selection is likely to have played, and to still play, an important role in the evolution of social organization in lions. It favors the widely found communal suckling, whereby cubs are allowed to obtain milk from lactating lions who are not their own mothers. It seems that female lions favor their own offspring most, which is to be expected because parents and offspring are the closest relatives, but they also contribute to the survival of the cubs of their related companions.

The fact that it seems straightforward and rational for female lions to do this should not detract from the fact that it is highly unusual for animals to divert some of their own resources into

▲ A look at the kin structure of a lion pride, with an arbitrarily selected cub as the "hub." Matrilines hold long-term tenure in a home area while small groups of males, usually related to each other but not to the females, are periodically replaced in the pride.

1 father's brother, 2 father's half-brother, 3 father, 4 aunt, 5 grandmother, 6 mother's half-sister, 7 great aunt, 8 brother, 9 sister, 10 mother, 11 mother's half-sister, 12 half-sister, 13 cousin, 14 cousin, 15 "hub" animal.

Mark Deeble and Victoria Stone

◀ Alert female lions survey their territory from a rocky outcrop in the Serengeti. Prides averaging about 15 related females maintain territories from which they exclude other groups of females. Pride territory size in East Africa varies from 20 to 400 square kilometers (7.5 to 155 square miles) depending on the size of the pride and the availability of prey.

Aiken/Zefa

◀ A single kill seldom feeds all the members of a large lion pride. Consequently, all pride members are rarely together at the same time. Females in groups of two to five go off to hunt by themselves and only periodically join other pride members to feed on large kills, such as this one.

rearing the offspring of other individuals. Most animals do not do so, and would be selected against if they did. It is the fact that recipients of the help — whether that help be milk, food or protection — are relatives who share genes by common descent from a shared ancestor, that enables the helping behavior to be favored in evolution through kin selection.

Of course kin selection does not account entirely for this helpful behavior. A female lion's cubs will do better in later life if they have companions. It is therefore in a female lion's selfish genetic interest to help her cubs' potential companions to survive even if they are not relatives; the fact that they usually are adds to the strength of the selective pressure.

The social system of lions, and aspects of their behavior, become clearer when the workings of kin selection are understood: lions share their food, for example (admittedly with more grace when they are not too hungry). By sharing, they are helping their relatives and so indirectly contributing to the propagation of replicas of the genes they both contain. They are

also helping to ensure that they themselves will continue to have the healthy companions they depend on for successful communal hunting and cooperative defense of territory.

Male lions show remarkable tolerance in allowing their companion males to mate with a female in estrus — one might expect to see frequent and bloody battles. The reasons behind this tolerance are various, including that a convention of prior ownership is respected, that fighting is costly, and that any one mating is statistically most unlikely to result in an extra offspring; but an additional reason is the fact that the rival is usually a close relative. So, although the onlooker male would do better in propagating replicas of his genes if he himself were doing the mating, he is nonetheless achieving some of the same effect in a more diluted form by letting his brother or cousin do it instead.

Needless to say, such calculations are unlikely to go through any lion's mind. But they are weighed up by natural selection, which includes kin selection, in the evolution of the lion's fascinating and unique social system.

ASIAN LIONS

A.J.T. JOHNSINGH AND RAVI CHELLAM

The Asian lion (*Panthera leo persica*) is one of many large mammal species that has declined in number and range over the last couple of centuries due to the activities of man. Numerous lions once roamed the Middle East and eastwards, through to the northern half of India, but when pitted against men with firearms, they proved no match and were exterminated from country after country. The decimation of the Asian lion would have continued to its ultimate conclusion were it not for the Nawab of Junagadh, who in the early part of this century took to protecting the few Asian lions that remained in the malaria infested 5,000 square kilometer (1,930 square mile) Gir Forest in the state of Gujarat, India. Reports indicate that in 1913 the lion population in Gir went down to as low as 20 animals before gradually recovering to about 300 lions, which is the estimated population today.

Genetic studies have tentatively established that the Asian subspecies separated from the African subspecies 200,000 to 55,000 years ago. Certain morphological, osteological, and genetic traits differentiate the Asian lion and the African lion. The most important morphological feature is the presence of the belly fold, which is found in almost all Asian lions, both male and female, but is uncommon among adult African male lions and even rarer among adult females. Asian males show only moderate mane development on top of their heads between their ears, and their ears are always distinctly seen. In contrast, up to a quarter of male African lions have luxuriant manes that cover the top of their heads and hide their ears. Some maneless lions have, however, also been recorded in Africa. Also, about 50 percent of the skulls of Gir lions have paired infraorbital foramen, a feature that is distinctly different from African lions. When the Gir lions decreased in numbers to a mere 20 animals they apparently underwent a genetic bottleneck and as a consequence now exhibit no genetic variation; the African lions, on the other hand, exhibit moderate genetic variation.

Since 1947, when India gained independence, the major conservation efforts to save the lion by the Indian government have been the banning of hunting in 1955 and the creation of the 1,265 square kilometer (488 square mile) Gir Wildlife Sanctuary in 1965. Eventually, in 1975 the area under protection was increased to 1,412 square kilometers (545 square miles) and a core area of 258 square kilometers (100 square miles) was declared a national park and freed of people and livestock. (Around 3,000 semi-nomadic graziers, "maldharis," still live there, with their livestock, in thorn-enclosed settlements called "nesses.")

A study by the Wildlife Institute of India (WII) was launched in 1986 to ascertain prey numbers, lion predation patterns and use of space by lions. Eight lions were radio-collared and monitored for periods ranging from six months to three years and over 3,000 scats and 500 kills were collected. Road transects were run to estimate wild ungulate numbers. In stark contrast to

▼ ▶ Only about 300 Asian lions survive today. This remnant population is restricted to a fragment of forest in northern India, the Gir Forest.

Anup Shah/Planet Earth Pictures

the findings of Paul Joslin almost two decades earlier (when the scats were found to contain mainly livestock), the WII study showed that nearly 70 percent of the scats contained wild prey remains; chital remains were present in 40 percent of them. This shift in the lion's predation pattern is related to a tremendous increase in the wild ungulate population, which presently numbers between 30,000 and 35,000.

Territorial male lions of Gir live in groups which number between two and six. These "male coalitions" actively patrol and defend a territory, within which one or more groups of lionesses live with their young. An unknown number of nomads move through the area. Annual home ranges of males have been estimated to be from 100 to 140 square kilometers (40 to 55 square miles) and those of lionesses from 40 to 80 square kilometers (15 to 30 square miles).

On the Serengeti Plains in Africa, most lion groups have both adult males and females, whereas males in Gir seldom associate with the females unless they are in estrus or on a large kill. In Serengeti abundant large prey, such as buffalo, zebra, and wildebeest, enables a pride to nutritionally support its males. In Gir the prey size is much smaller — the most common prey, the chital, weighs around 50 kilograms (110 pounds). Moreover, the presence of livestock, which is easier to capture, in some parts of Gir enables the males to independently sustain themselves. (Females are located much less frequently on livestock kills.) The forested Gir habitat also affords the males ample stalking cover, which enables them to hunt with a greater degree of success than their counterparts on the Serengeti grasslands.

There is a marked difference in habitat use by male lions and lionesses in Gir. During the dry season lionesses are almost exclusively located in the riverine tracts where wild ungulates come to drink; the males are infrequently seen. During the monsoon season, the males appear to favor relatively dry, open hilltops, which are insect-free because of the breeze. Females normally avoid such open areas.

The government of India is, and has been, aware that it is not advisable to have the entire population of this subspecies in one reserve. The search for an alternate home is under way, but the findings of the WII indicate that for the proposed translocation to succeed it would need at least 500 square kilometers (193 square miles) of suitable habitat, and effective long-term monitoring. An effort to translocate lions from Gir to Chandraprabha Sanctuary, saw the population increase from one male and two females to 11 in eight years before they reportedly disappeared.

Currently the lion population in Gir has reached a density of about one lion per 5 square kilometers (2 miles) of protected area. Largely as a result of this high density, there has been a tremendous increase in the incidence of lions straying into human habitations and conflicting with human interests. Between mid-1988 and early 1990 about 100 people were mauled — more than 15 of them died and some were even eaten by the lions. These lions regularly kill livestock because there is very little wild prey available outside the protected area. Not surprisingly, there is a very high level of resentment towards the lions amongst the local population, a situation that must be resolved. Lions that are found outside the protected area should be captured and given to zoos as there is an acute shortage of purebred Asian lions in captivity, failing which they should be eliminated by shooting. Special conservation-oriented development programs need to be implemented in the villages around Gir. The alienation of the local population would prove to be disastrous to the long-term conservation interests of Gir — the last bastion of Asian lions in the wild.

TIGERS

MEL SUNQUIST AND FIONA C. SUNQUIST

Tigers (*Panthera tigris*) are the largest of the living cats. Siberian tigers weighing 360 kilograms (790 pounds) have been recorded, and a huge male can measure more than four meters (over 13 feet) from the nose to the tip of the tail. While the other races of tigers are somewhat smaller than the Siberian, the latter is nevertheless recognizable as a tiger because the tiger is the only cat with a striped coat.

CATCHING PREY

The tiger is a formidable predator, whose large canines, long, sharp retractile claws, and massive forearms and shoulders enable it to single-handedly overpower prey much bigger than itself.

Tigers are also capable sprinters, but they do not pursue prey very far. Instead, they rely on stalk and ambush techniques.

A stalking tiger uses every available piece of cover. It approaches cautiously, carefully placing

▼ Tigers (*Panthera tigris*) are the largest of the felids, ranging in size from 360 kilograms (790 pounds), for the largest male Siberian tiger recorded, to 72 kilograms (160 pounds) for a female Sumatran tiger. This Bengal tiger is estimated to weigh 230 kilograms (510 pounds).

Belinda Wright/DRK Photo

Belinda Wright/DRK Photo

each foot on the ground. It crouches behind small bushes or rocks, or hugs the edge of a riverbank, all the while remaining focused on the prey. With its striped coat effectively breaking up its outline, the tiger moves slowly forward, patiently closing the distance or waiting for the prey to move closer. Having got to within 10 to 20 meters (about 30 to 60 feet) or less of the prey, the tiger gathers itself up and suddenly rushes its victim, covering the final distance in a few bounds.

The attack is usually from the side or rear so that the first contact is often on the prey's hindquarters. The impact may knock the prey off its feet or unbalance the fleeing animal to the extent that the tiger can get a grip with its claws. Keeping its hind feet on the ground, the tiger tries to bring the prey down or into a position where a

killing bite can be delivered quickly. It is a dangerous moment and even with the advantage of surprise, the tiger risks a debilitating injury. Speed, experience, and concentration are essential — an estimated one stalk in twenty results in a kill.

Tigers use two basic modes of killing. One is a bite to the back of the neck, which severs or damages the spinal cord. The other is a bite aimed at the throat, which either severs or obstructs the larynx and carotid arteries, resulting in death by suffocation. The neck bite is commonly used on small- to medium-sized prey and the throat bite on larger prey (over 100 kilograms/220 pounds). In a study of tigers in Royal Chitwan National Park, Nepal, where individuals were monitored using radio-tracking techniques, it was discovered that when the weight of the prey was more than half

▼ Largest of the obligate predators in their ecological community, tigers are found only where species of large deer and wild pigs are also found. In India, sambar deer form a major portion of the diet of the tiger.

that of the tiger, the tiger used a throat bite to kill — apparently the most effective and safe way to kill large prey.

If a kill is made in the open, the tiger usually drags the carcass into dense cover before beginning to feed (usually on the hindquarters). The tiger also opens the prey's abdominal cavity and removes the entrails; it then drags the eviscerated carcass a short distance and alternately feeds and rests until only pieces of skin and large bones remain. Sometimes the remains of kills are covered with grass. Tigers can eat prodigious amounts of meat and on several occasions individuals have consumed about 25 to 35 kilograms (60 to 80 pounds) of meat in a night's feeding. Small prey are quickly eaten. Larger kills, such as sambar deer, gaur, and domestic cattle provide a single tiger with food for several days, although several tigers can finish even a large carcass in short order. A female tiger accompanied by two large young consumed about 100 kilograms (220 pounds) of meat in just two days. On another

HOW TO GET TIGERS TO PHOTOGRAPH THEMSELVES

CHARLES McDOUGAL

Although tigers are much less nocturnal than formerly supposed, it is not to be denied that they are most in their element during the hours of darkness. For this reason, photographs of tigers taken in daylight somehow seem to miss the point. My friend, Mike Price, and I decided to try to capture images of the tiger at night. We soon discovered that this was not an easy task.

First we had to predict the route our subject would take and then, at a suitable spot, place a trip device in its path, which would trigger a motor-driven camera and flash. We experimented with a variety of mechanisms — ranging from electric beams to crude homemade varieties — and finally settled on the pressure pad as the most reliable under damp jungle conditions. What we wanted was a picture of the tiger walking toward the camera. There was only a fifty-fifty chance it would come from the right direction. And even if it did, there was a 50 percent chance it would overstep the pad with its forefoot and land on it with a hind foot, resulting in an out-of-focus picture. Further, it could have missed the pad completely, the flash might have failed to function, or one of a number of other things might have gone wrong.

As it happened the tiger did not react adversely to the flash, but it did to the noise made by the motor drive — no matter how much we muffled the camera, the tiger might avoid the site for weeks after. Therefore, we had to keep changing the location. Mike and I set up the camera every night for seven months, and the net result was three decent pictures! Working on my own in later years, I tried to improve the technique, sometimes using thorns and sharp stones to channel a tiger's movements to the right spot.

Apart from whatever artistic merit they might possess, camera-trap photographs also have scientific value, and have proved invaluable for the identification of different tigers moving through a particular area.

flash with plastic covering

motor driven camera muffled and camouflaged   6 volt battery   buried cable   buried pressure plate

occasion, a large domestic buffalo and an adult cow were eaten in six days by four tigers — an adult male fed on the kills for four days, he left, and a tigress with two large young fed for two days. These four tigers had consumed an estimated 195 kilograms (430 pounds) of meat; all edible parts of the carcass had been eaten.

Over much of the tiger's broad geographical range, wild pig, wild cattle and several species of deer figure prominently in the diet. All of these are forest/grassland ungulates, which vary in weight from the smallish hog deer at 30 kilograms (65 pounds) to the large gaur at 910 kilograms (2,000 pounds). In Chitwan National Park tigers killed mostly deer and pigs weighing between 45 and 90 kilograms (100 and 200 pounds), although they seemed to prefer the large sambar (180 kilograms/400 pounds), taking this species of deer out of proportion to its abundance. In some parts of southern India, where gaur are locally abundant, tiger predation on this species is common. Some species, such as adult rhinoceroses and elephants, appear to be invulnerable to tiger attack, largely by virtue of their size.

Tigers kill animals from a broad spectrum of age classes, including prime adults. They do not particularly select young or old animals, as is sometimes seen in the pack-hunting canids (or wild dog family). Predation by tigers takes more of a random sample, which reflects their hunting style. Any animal that for whatever reason ends up in a vulnerable position may be attacked. The place where prey are killed, however, does not appear to be random. Some sites, especially near water holes, are repeatedly used to ambush prey, and areas of dense cover along well-used game trails are often repositories for kills. Radio-tagged tigers in Chitwan National Park were often observed to hunt by walking slowly along roads and trails, and at other times they would spend several hours "working over" a small patch of forest. Individual tigers definitely had favorite hunting spots that they visited regularly.

Tigers hunt primarily between dusk and dawn, a time when their major prey are also active. They usually rest between mid-morning and mid-afternoon, although it is not uncommon, particularly for a female tiger with young, to be out hunting during the daytime. They travel

▲ Seldom found far from rivers or other water sources, tigers are surprisingly strong swimmers and they seem to enjoy lounging in water. Tigers live comfortably in the extensive wet mangrove forests at the mouth of the Ganges and other great Asian rivers, at times swimming tidal rivers more than 5 kilometers (3 miles) wide.

► A tiger takes down a sambar. After a careful stalk, a tiger makes a short rush towards its prey, usually approaching from the side or back to avoid hooves and antlers. Grabbing the prey with the forepaws, the tiger then quickly bites the back of the animal's neck or its throat. Death comes as a result of broken vertebrae and suffocation.

Anup Shah/Planet Earth Pictures

► In habitats with limited water supplies, adult tigers may come together to drink and rest during the heat of the day. These congregations may include a female, her cubs, and the local resident male. An older daughter may also join the group but never another adult male.

extensively in search of prey, often covering 8 to 24 kilometers (5 to 15 miles) in the course of an unsuccessful night of hunting. Roads and trails are favored travel paths as movement along these is rapid, and much quieter and easier than stalking through dense cover.

Most of the tiger's time is spent just trying to locate prey, and to do this tigers have to remain on the move. In Chitwan National Park tigers rarely rested in the same location on consecutive days unless they had a large kill. Tigers eat small prey very quickly and kills of these species are only known from identification of their remains in tiger feces. Female tigers made a large kill about once every eight to nine days. This rate translates into 40 to 47 kills per year per tiger. However, a female tiger with two six-month-old young to feed made a large kill every five or six days, which amounted to 61 to 73 kills per year. What impact this level of predation is having on prey populations is not known precisely. In Chitwan, where tiger and prey populations have been monitored for more than 10 years, predation by tigers has not limited prey.

While tigers are known to occasionally socialize at kills, the demands of living in dense cover, where relatively small- to medium-sized prey are scattered and time-consuming to find, have not promoted the development of complex social structures. Under these circumstances the most efficient strategy of exploitation appears to be by a solitary animal employing stalk and ambush techniques. The tiger has few competitors and so can get the maximum from each carcass, thus eliminating the need for group defense of kills or sharing kills. To efficiently operate as a group, tigers would either have to kill more often or take much larger prey, otherwise the energy return per individual would be less than that already available to a solitary hunter. Large animals such as elephants and rhinoceroses are still essentially invulnerable to group-hunting tigers, and even to group-hunting lions. Gaur occur at high densities in a few tiger areas, but these large ungulates are already vulnerable to being taken by a single tiger. Thus, under existing conditions, group hunting by tigers appears to be uneconomical.

The manner in which tigers hunt also appears to promote a social system in which individuals are separated by space or time. In Kanha National Park, India, the ranges of three female tigers overlapped, but each centered its activities in a different area, and only rarely were two females seen in the same area at the same time. In Chitwan National Park there was little overlap in the ranges of seven adjacent females. In three additional cases, adjacent ranges were occupied by a female and her daughter, and for each pair there was essentially no overlap in their ranges. Thus, even closely related individuals established mutually exclusive ranges.

Range of *Panthera tigris*
- P.t. altaica
- P.t. amoyensis
- P.t. corbetti
- P.t. tigris
- P.t. sumatrae
- Historical – 100 yrs ago
- P.t. virgata – extinct
- P.t. sondaica – extinct
- P.t. balica – extinct

REPRODUCTION AND REARING YOUNG

A more-or-less solitary life style appears to offer advantages to both sexes in terms of hunting, mating, reproduction, and care of young. Joint use of areas could result in interference, and reduced hunting success because the prey in an area where another tiger is, or has just been hunting, are probably more alert and not as vulnerable.

The ranges of male tigers in Chitwan and elsewhere also show little overlap, and males, by excluding other males from an area, ensure exclusive access to females for mating. For males the critical resource is females and each male's range usually encompasses the smaller ranges of two or three females. One male in Chitwan quickly expanded his range after the death of a neighboring male and thereby increased to seven the number of females with which he mated.

While the male is not directly involved in helping the female rear young, the exclusion of other males reduces the competition for resources that are needed by females. The exclusion of other males may also lessen the possibility of infanticide. For females, who must kill regularly and predictably to successfully raise offspring, excluding other females ensures access to food, cover, and a secure place to raise young. In Chitwan, 13 females established ranges and each successfully raised young; females not holding ranges did not breed.

The job of raising young falls to the female, who after reaching sexual maturity at about three years of age is usually pregnant or rearing young for the next dozen or so years. Studies in Chitwan and elsewhere indicate that a female tiger will have a new litter every two to two-and-a-half years. This

TIGER SUBSPECIES

SRIYANIE MITHTHAPALA

Different populations of the wide-ranging tiger (*Panthera tigris*) tend to have several characteristic differences; when these characteristics are sufficiently distinct, subspecies are described and named. Vladimir Mazak classified eight subspecies of tigers: the Caspian tiger (*P.t. virgata*); the Bengal tiger (*P.t. tigris*); the Indo-Chinese tiger (*P.t. corbetti*); the Chinese tiger (*P.t. amoyensis*); the Amur or Siberian tiger (*P.t. altaica*); the Sumatran tiger (*P.t. sumatrae*); the Javan tiger (*P.t. sondaica*); and the Bali tiger (*P.t. balica*).

In historical times, the tiger was distributed across most of Asia. The present distribution of the tiger is extremely fragmented and three subspecies — the Caspian, Javan and Bali tigers — are now extinct. According to Mazak, all subspecies can be distinguished by several characteristics that include weight, color, and stripe pattern.

The Amur tiger is the largest subspecies and the Bali tiger the smallest. Although coat color varies among individual animals and between seasons, there is a graduation of color from north to south — the Amur subspecies is the lightest, the Bengal brightest, and the Bali tiger darkest.

All tigers are striped, but not all tigers are striped similarly. The Chinese tiger has the fewest stripes, followed by the Amur tiger, the Bengal and then the Indo-Chinese; the island subspecies have the most stripes. In addition to differences in the number of stripes, the pattern also varies in the island subspecies. The Bali tiger had a single horizontal stripe on its forehead and three short double horizontal stripes on its head; the stripes on its flanks and back were often double looped. A similar complexity was found in the Javan tiger.

The Amur and Sumatran tigers can also be distinguished by the length of their fur. Of all the subspecies, the Amur tiger has the longest fur on its neck, back and belly, while the Sumatran has the longest facial ruff hair.

Certain measurements of bones in the skull reveal differences among the island subspecies. Sandra Harrington found that the Chinese tiger has distinctive skull proportions: with a shorter brain case and more forwardly directed eye sockets. These characteristics of the Chinese tiger indicate that it is the oldest tiger subspecies, and the geographic area in which it is still found places it as the center of origin for the species.

Recent genetic studies have revealed that the Amur, Bengal and Sumatran tigers are biochemically distinct.

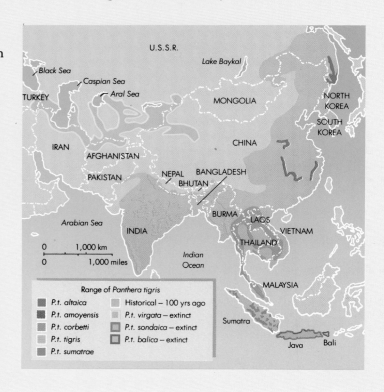

Range of *Panthera tigris*

P.t. altaica · Historical – 100 yrs ago
P.t. amoyensis · P.t. virgata – extinct
P.t. corbetti · P.t. sondaica – extinct
P.t. tigris · P.t. balica – extinct
P.t. sumatrae

Anup Shah/Planet Earth Pictures

time includes a gestation period of about 103 days followed by 18 to 20 months of rearing young. Litter size at birth is rarely known, but two to three young per litter appears common. Young are born blind and helpless and a female tiger will often remain with the young continuously for the first couple of days. Thereafter she will never be far away, leaving only for short periods to drink or hunt. During the first month the female tiger's range will shrink to about a quarter of its normal size. As the young mature the female's range gradually expands, and by the time the young begin to accompany their mother on hunting trips her range will have returned to its former size.

Young are dependent on their mother's milk for the first six to eight weeks of their lives, and after that the female starts to take them to kills. Male cubs grow faster than their female siblings and by one year of age are noticeably larger and more independent, sometimes spending the day away from their mother. By 16 months of age, tigers have fully developed canines, but they are not very efficient at killing even domestic animals. By 18 months of age, male young weigh about

Gérard Lacz/NHPA

▲ Litter size in tigers varies from one to three. Tiger cubs are vulnerable and can die from starvation, disease, and, occasionally, predation by wild dogs, striped hyenas, and humans. A typical female tiger, which dies by the age of 15 years, may produce five litters and see only 10 cubs live to adulthood.

◄ Tiger cubs remain with their mother for nearly two years. Males leave to seek territories far from their birth site but may later return. Some daughters never leave the territory of their mother and may eventually force their mother out. Old females that are driven out in this way succumb to starvation or fatal encounters with other tigers.

A. Visage/Auscape International

Gunter Ziesler/Bruce Coleman Ltd.

▲ The largest of tiger subspecies, and of all cats, the Siberian or Amur tiger inhabits the deciduous and evergreen forests of the Amur River valley in the Soviet Far East. In this habitat, tigers prey upon red deer, wild pigs, and serow, a goat-like antelope related to North American Rocky Mountain goats.

▶ The present distribution of tigers is fragmented, and three subspecies — the Caspian, Javan and Bali tigers — are now extinct. If the remaining five subspecies of tigers are to survive in the wild, new, innovative strategies must be developed that will allow tigers and humans to co-exist in the same areas.

135 kilograms (300 pounds), which is about 45 kilograms (100 pounds) heavier than their sisters. At this age both young make some of their own kills, and while they are still using their mother's range they often spend long periods of time away from her.

The age at which young tigers disperse from their natal or birth range varies from 18 to 30 months, depending largely on when their mother has a new litter. Most young tigers leave their natal range two to three months after a new litter is born, which coincides with the time when the new litter begins to follow the mother. The actual process of dispersal may take a month or more and involve several exploratory trips, but male young typically travel farther than females. The average dispersal distance for 10 subadult males in Chitwan National Park was 33 kilometers (20 miles); for four females the average dispersal distance was less than 10 kilometers (6 miles). This shorter distance for females is due to the tendency of daughters to settle next to their mother's range.

For female tigers a range is a place to rear young, and in Chitwan, where prey abundance is high, the home range sizes of resident females are only about 20 square kilometers (8 square miles). In the Soviet Far East, where prey are much less abundant and make large seasonal movements, female ranges are reported to vary from 100 to 400 square kilometers (40 to 155 square miles) and male ranges may reach 1,000 square kilometers (400 square miles). Male territories in Chitwan are about three times larger than those of females.

Tigers leave scent marks throughout their territories to indicate that the area is occupied. This marking is a passive form of defense, although fights do occur. The scent marks include urine sprayed on bushes and trees, feces and urine left in prominent places, scratch marks on trees, and

scrapes made by raking backwards with the hind feet. Both sexes routinely freshen scent marks, and the frequency of marking is higher in zones where contact with neighboring tigers is likely.

Once a female tiger has managed to establish a territory, she will usually remain there for the rest of her breeding life. Adult female ranges are generally stable and females tend not to expand their range even when a neighbor dies. Most females in Chitwan used essentially the same range for seven years, although two were resident for at least 10 years. Male ranges expand and contract in response to the number of females each male is able to defend. In Chitwan, the average length of a male's tenure was about three-and-a-half years, although one outsized male was able to dominate a major portion of the park for six years.

Over the past 20 years in Chitwan, the number of breeding females has been increased by daughters squeezing in next to their mothers, and the population consists of clusters of related females. The degree of relatedness among female tigers living on the floodplain in Chitwan is now known to be as high as that of female lions in a pride. While this is probably not uncommon, there are limits to the number of tigers that can be compressed into a park. If tigers are to continue to survive in the wild, future management strategies cannot rely solely on squeezing more and more tigers into parks and protected areas. Rather they will have to focus on innovative ways to allow tigers and humans to use the same space.

CHUCHCHI: THE LIFE OF A TIGRESS

CHARLES McDOUGAL

Very occasionally it is possible to document highlights in the life history of a wild animal, and this provides insights that add to our understanding of the species.

We do not know Chuchchi's date of birth, but she was born not later than the spring of 1972, based on the fact that she had her first cubs in June 1975. I was able to monitor the movements and activities of this female tiger from an early age because of a slight deformity in her left rear foot that left a distinctive, identifiable pugmark. She was also tracked by radiotelemetry from 1978 through 1981.

During her lifetime, Chuchchi produced five litters of cubs, and a total of 16 offspring of which no less than 11 survived to dispersal age. Three of her daughters settled locally and themselves reproduced. The first of these, from Chuchchi's 1977 litter, established a territory adjacent to that of her mother following the death of the resident female of that area. A second daughter, born in 1979, acquired the northern half of Chuchchi's 26 square kilometer (10 square mile) territory, and Chuchchi thereafter confined herself to the southern part. Finally, a daughter born in 1982 dispossessed the 14-year-old Chuchchi of the remainder of her territory. Subsequently a transient, Chuchchi was killed in August 1987 at not less than fifteen-and-a-half years of age, during an encounter with a young male tiger, who was the son of an unrelated neighboring female tiger.

In addition to the three males that sired her five known litters, there were four other males in Chuchchi's life, and it is possible that one or more of them fathered additional cubs which did not survive long enough for their existence to be discovered. When, at the beginning of 1981, Chuchchi had her first estrous period after a long interval (during which she had been raising her last litter), a young, recently matured male suddenly arrived on the scene. In a contest for Chuchchi's favors he worsted the resident male in a fight, biting off his tail near the root, and caused him to leave the area. Six months later the usurper was killed by a third male who had also begun to court

Masahiro Iijima Asia Photo

▲ The glimpse we had into Chuchchi's life was essential to the understanding we now have of tiger ecology and behavior.

Chuchchi. He in turn was replaced by a fourth male early in 1982. Truly, Chuchchi was a *femme fatale* of the tiger world.

One day Chuchchi charged out of a patch of thick grass and attacked a domestic elephant grazing nearby. It transpired that she had given birth to cubs in that very cover only a couple of days earlier. The valiant mother had only been trying to protect her young when the unfortunate elephant strayed too close.

Late one monsoon afternoon, I had a close encounter with Chuchchi when we met coming from opposite directions on a knife-edged ridge. As I crested a rise, there she was, crouched, facing me at 15 meters (50 feet). She had heard me coming at the last minute. Our eyes locked for what seemed a very long time. It then dawned on me that one of us would have to retreat, and that she was leaving the first move up to me. Slowly, so as not to alarm her, I turned around and returned the way I had come, resisting the impulse to look over my shoulder.

HOW MANY TIGERS CAN THERE BE?

K. ULLAS KARANTH

How many tigers do you have? This is perhaps the most common question that a park manager is asked. It is also one of the hardest to answer since the secretive habits of tigers make accurate field counts almost impossible. Individually identifying tigers from camera-trap photos or by marking them with radio-collars are reliable but difficult techniques. In India, attempts have been made to individually identify and count tigers from the shape of their tracks. However, the results were unreliable, since the reported number of tigers seemed excessive based on considerations such as availability of sufficient prey, and in light of what we know about the dynamics of wild tiger populations. Therefore, most existing estimates of tiger population size essentially involve subjective judgments of varying accuracy. Rather than total population size then, ecological density, which measures the number of tigers that live in a unit of area (say 100 square kilometers or 100 square miles), is often used to estimate tiger abundance.

Tigers are predators perched atop a complex ecological pyramid, living on herbivorous prey. Therefore, the capacity of the land to produce a regular crop of prey animals is a key determinant of tiger density in an area. Environmental variables such as climate, topography, and soil govern the capacity of the land. Over the extensive range of the tiger prey abundance varies widely, and so do tiger densities. Moreover, the prey has to be of the right size. The economics of energy gain and expenditure involved in catching prey make it impossible for the large-sized tiger to subsist chiefly on small prey species. Though highly productive habitats like rainforests or mangrove swamps can produce large renewable crops of insects, fish, amphibians, reptiles, birds, or even small mammals, they cannot support tigers unless the larger prey also occur there. Tigers that subsist on fish in a mangrove swamp are as improbable as lions that live off grasshoppers in the African savannas!

Tiger prey ranges in size from 30 kilogram (66 pound) pigs to massive gaur, which may weigh 1,000 kilograms (2,200 pounds). Other potentially important prey include deer species such as chital, hog deer, sambar, barasingha, red deer; wild cattle like banteng and buffalo; and livestock. Abundance of these large ungulates depends not only on the quantity of plant food that the land produces, but also on its quality and accessibility. Because large ungulates are primarily grazers or browsers, they attain higher densities in tropical deciduous forests and alluvial grasslands than in rainforests, mangrove swamps, or temperate woodlands. In areas where prey is more abundant, tigers probably need to move over shorter distances to find them, and are likely to exploit smaller home ranges. In consequence, tiger densities tend to correlate strongly with prey abundance. For instance, home range sizes of female tigers vary from 10 to 20 square kilometers (4 to 8 square miles) in southern Asia to 100 to 400 square kilometers (40 to 155 square miles) in Siberia. Forests and grasslands in the Indian subcontinent seem to pack more tigers in a patch of habitat than in an equal-sized area of Indonesian rainforest or Siberian boreal forest. It is for this reason that densities are as high as 3 to 4 tigers per 100 square kilometers (7.8 to 10.4 tigers per 100 square miles) in prime habitats in India and Nepal and as low as 0.2 to 1 tiger per 100 square kilometers (0.5 to 2.6 tigers per 100 square miles) in eastern USSR.

With appropriate habitat management, prey and tiger densities can be increased up to a point. However, the social organization of the tiger includes spacing mechanisms such as defended home ranges and long distance dispersal of subadults, which tend to maintain tiger densities in an area at a level sustainable on available prey.

Habitat structure influences the way that a tiger uses its home range. When grasslands are burnt annually in Nepal's *Terai* region, tigers use the burnt short grass areas less, probably because of an increase in the difficulty of capturing prey. Since tigers prefer to keep cool in dense, moist rest-sites during hot weather, distribution of water and heavy cover within a tiger's range also affect habitat utilization. Such habitat preferences may also influence home-range size, and ultimately, density.

TIGER DENSITIES IN DIFFERENT RESERVES

Location	Habitat Type	Prey Biomass (kilograms per square kilometer/pounds per square mile)	Tiger Density (number per 100 square kilometers/ 100 square miles)	
Royal Chitwan National Park, Nepal	Grassland and forest mosaic	2,581/14,737	2.8–3.7/7.3–9.6	The densities in the table are of adult resident tigers. If transient adult and dependent young animals are included, the estimates get higher. In prime habitats in India and Nepal such overall densities may even reach 7–12 tigers per 100 square kilometers (18–31 tigers per 100 square miles).
Kanha National Park, India	Shorea forest and meadow	1,708/9,753	3.1–4.7/8–12.2	
Udjung Kulon Reserve, Indonesia	Rainforest and meadow	492/2,809	0.75–1/1.9–2.6	
Silhote–Alin Reserve, USSR	Temperate woodland and forest	–	0.2/0.5	

LEOPARDS

JOHN SEIDENSTICKER

Cautious, tough, pragmatic, the adaptable leopard (*Panthera pardus*) is able to live in man's shadow more effectively than any of the other big cats. The geographic distribution of the leopard is enormous, with a historical range that extends through all of sub-Saharan Africa, along the North African coast, through the Middle East, Asia Minor, South and Southeast Asia to the Amur Valley in the Asian Far East. They live on surprisingly small islands including Java (127,000 square kilometers/49,000 square miles), Sri Lanka (65,600 square kilometers/25,300 square miles), Zanzibar (1,500 square kilometers/580 square miles), and even Kangean (750 square kilometers/290 square miles), which is located northeast of Java. Some 27 subspecies, 13 in Africa and 14 in Asia, have been described.

▲ Louis A. Sargent's 1909 painting of leopards attacking a chital depicts beautiful but savage beasts in exotic, far-off lands. Paintings of this kind, however, perpetuate two common misconceptions about leopards: they do not live or hunt in pairs and they do not launch attacks on large prey from trees.

▶ Leopards readily swim rivers when necessary but large bodies of water are a barrier to them. Unlike tigers and jaguars, leopards are not dependent on water. Leopards live in the Kalahari Desert without free-standing water, getting the moisture they need to survive from the prey they kill.

THE ADAPTABILITY OF THE LEOPARD

Just how adept leopards are at living in the forest–village interface became apparent in Nepal when scientists radio-tracked a leopard into a village one night. The leopard appeared to be trying to capture a goat from the herd kept in a village shed. Daylight came before the leopard could make a kill or retreat from the village. Caught away from any lane of escape, the cat spent the day in a woodpile amidst the hustle and bustle of daily village life. No one in the village — not even the dogs — knew it was there. The following night, it escaped. Leopards live in the suburbs of Nairobi and other African cities, much as coyotes live in the suburbs of Los Angeles, or foxes and raccoons live in the middle of Washington, D.C.

With this kind of demonstrated adaptability, leopards were perceived by cat researchers as survivors. Other great cats of Asia — the lion, tiger, cheetah, and snow leopard — suffered great losses from hunting and habitat destruction. We thought leopards would slip by these problems, much as the leopard slipped in and out of the village. Further assurances came when leopards near some African wildlife reserves were declared locally "over abundant." We are not so sure about that now. Throughout much of its range, the leopard is threatened or endangered. This enigma sparks the questions: what is it about leopards, about their morphology, their behavior, and other traits that make them so adaptable? And why, if they are so adaptable, are they not faring well in some areas?

Adult male leopards weigh on average 60 kilograms (132 pounds) while females weigh 40 kilograms (88 pounds). The general size of leopards seems to remain relatively constant across much of its geographic range, although there is an extraordinary variation in the size of some leopard subspecies, rather like the variation found in tigers, pumas, and jaguars.

Leopard tail length is more than half the head and body length, which averages 140 centimeters (55 inches) for males and 120 centimeters (47 inches) for females. Shoulder height averages 65 centimeters (25 inches) for adult males and 50 centimeters (20 inches) for adult females. The average head width of males (16 centimeters/6.25 inches) is significantly wider than that of females (13 centimeters/5 inches). A study of the comparative morphology of the skulls of cats showed that the relative size of the canines in relation to the size of the muzzle and lower jawbone in leopards is similar to that of other *Panthera* cats. In other words, the dimensions of the leopard's skull and canines relative to body size were not as unusual, for example, as the very large canines of the clouded leopard.

Depending on where in its range a leopard is found, the base color of its coat varies from a beautiful golden color to a pale yellow. Leopards tend to have black spots on the limbs, flank, hindquarters, and head, with rosettes on the remainder of the body. Black or melanistic leopards occur throughout the leopard's range, although they appear to be more common in some areas than others. In melanistic leopards the spots and rosettes are apparent but indistinct.

From a morphological perspective then, there really isn't anything remarkable or extraordinarily specialized about the leopard in comparison to the other great cats: no specialization for speed as in the cheetah, or great size as in the lion and tiger, or extra-large canines and adaptations for living in trees like those of the clouded leopard, or thick coat for very cold temperatures as in the snow leopard, or stout legs and powerful canines like those of the jaguar. And that is the point — leopards hold the central ground amongst the big cats. We know the importance of body size as a defining trait in life history strategies from studies of many groups of mammals (refer to the article on "Body Size and Feeding Tactics," page 62). The leopard is smaller than the largest members of the genus by a factor of about four, and larger than the clouded leopard by the same factor of four. As we

Keith Scholey/Planet Earth Pictures

▲ Leopards pull carcasses into trees to avoid losing their kills to scavenging competitors like lions, hyenas, and wild dogs. In some cases, a leopard may have several kills of various ages stored in the same tree. Some anthropologists believe that tree-stored kills provided food for human ancestors living on the African savanna.

▶ On average, leopards are about one-fourth the size of tigers and lions. Tigers and lions will kill leopards when the opportunity arises, but leopards survive alongside these competitors by hunting during different times of the day and avoiding the areas frequented by them.

Sumatra and Borneo. The existence of cover to lie up in and from which to stalk prey is a very important habitat component. Yet, I have watched leopards move through relatively open fields. At these times they must make use of bushes, grass clumps, and small depressions both to stalk prey and to move from one large patch of cover to another. These are open areas a tiger would not usually traverse. In the Kalahari, leopards stalk prey over very long distances (275 meters/300 yards on average) using this approach technique. The ability to use broken cover is pivotal to their wide distribution and habitat tolerance.

The leopard is a solitary hunter that hunts mostly on the ground; it specializes in capturing by stealth animals that are both as large or even larger than itself and animals that are much smaller. The behavioral sequence leopards use — search, stalk, sprint, take-down, and killing bite to the throat — is similar to that used by the other *Panthera* cats, although the sprint seems especially explosive compared to the sprint of the tiger or lion. Leopards do have one post-killing behavior that is different from the other big cats: they sometimes store their prey in trees. A leopard may even have more than one kill in the same tree at a time. John Cavallo found that tree-stored leopard kills in the Serengeti lasted on average at least four times longer than same-size kills stored on the ground. Storing kills in trees facilitates the leopard's success amidst great pressure from scavengers and competing predators.

Depending on what is available, leopards catch and eat monkeys, pangolins, axis deer, and village goats, calves, and dogs. Over a seven-week period, an adult female I radio-tracked in the Royal Chitwan National Park in Nepal killed one domestic water buffalo calf, three axis deer, one barking deer, and one hog deer. She usually remained with each kill for the night. Nights between kills ranged from two to seven with an average of four. Thus, she killed once every five or six days. In this natural riverside habitat of tall grass and forest, her ungulate prey were in the 20 to 50 kilogram (45 to 110 pound) range. She appeared to be selecting prey in this size class. When hunting axis deer she killed the smaller yearlings or fawns; when she hunted sambar she killed fawns; the smaller hog deer were apparently taken without regard to age or sex. The park was adjacent to fields and livestock grazing areas in the scrub forest along the river. Outside the park, wild ungulates comprised only about a quarter of leopard kills. Leopards hunting or living outside the park switched to killing domestic stock in the same size classes as they took inside the park.

I became aware of the tremendous adaptability of leopard predatory behavior when I examined the food habits of leopards living in Meru Betiri National Park, a rainforest area in Java that is home to very few ungulates. There, leopards

shall see, this size seems ideal for the exploitation of a wide range of prey sizes and prey types.

Are there behavioral adaptations that contribute to the leopard's wide geographic distribution and ability to live in man's shadow? Leopards live in a diverse range of habitats, seeming equally at home in semidesert and rainforest. They penetrate into deserts along watercourses although apparently, in the Kalahari, they are independent of water supplies but drink regularly when water is available. They inhabit the great rainforest areas of Africa, but do not live in the tracts of mangrove forest, the Sundarbans, found at the mouth of the Ganges. (In historic times they did inhabit the northern fringe.) Also they do not live on the rainforest-clad islands of were eating mostly primates. I also examined the food habits of leopards from a number of areas in Africa and Asia, where reliable data have become available. If there is one or more abundant ungulate species in the 20 to 50 kilogram (45 to 110 pound) size range present in a habitat, the leopard focuses its hunting on those animals. Leopards do not seem to spend much time hunting primates in those habitats, even though they may be quite abundant, and they do not spend much time pursuing smaller prey animals. Where ungulate prey of this size class is present but not at a high density, leopards do prey on primates, and primates may make up as much as 30 percent of their diet. In habitats where the 20 to 50 kilograms (45 to 110 pound) size class of ungulates is essentially absent, leopards switch and eat a high proportion of primates where these are available. In the Kalahari, leopards killed ungulates in this size class and also killed smaller prey as encountered, for example, genets, springhare, bat-eared foxes, black-backed jackals, aardwolfs, porcupines, and aardvarks. Some leopards specialize in exploiting a single resource at a time, as many owners of dogs have learned. This is not a limiting feature in leopard predatory tactics; it is a manifestation of their ability to switch to, and focus on, a readily available prey resource.

HOME RANGES

The home ranges of adult female leopards, which Mel Sunquist and I established using radiotelemetry at the edge of the Royal Chitwan National Park in Nepal, ranged from 6 to 13 square kilometers (2.25 to 5 square miles) in an area of very high ungulate biomass. John Eisenberg estimated home ranges to be about this size for leopards that lived in Wilpattu National Park in Sri Lanka. These home ranges were focused around water holes where prey were concentrated. In the Huai Kha Khaeng Wildlife Sanctuary in Thailand, Alan Rabinowitz found leopards had home ranges of 11 to 37 square kilometers (4.25 to 14.25 square miles). The home-range size for leopards in Serengeti National Park in East Africa has been estimated by a number of investigators and varies from 16 to 60 square kilometers (6.25 to 23.25 square miles). In Tsavo National Park, Kenya Patrick Hamilton found that leopards' ranges varied from 11 to 121 square kilometers (4.25 to 46.75 square miles). At the extreme, a radio-tagged adult male and adult female, in the Stellenbosch Mountains in South Africa, had home ranges of 388 and 487 square kilometers (150 and 188 square miles) respectively, and the ranges of two males in the Kalahari were about 400 square kilometers (almost 155 square miles) in size.

Thus, the largest leopard home ranges exceed the smallest by a factor of 80. For vertebrates in general, the size of an animal's home range depends on metabolic needs, and carnivores such

Gérard Lacz/NHPA

as leopards, which have a large portion of flesh in their diet, have particularly large home ranges. The variation in leopard home ranges in different habitats can be attributed to food availability. Within a carnivore species, differences of six to as much as 20 fold in home-range size are not unusual, but the 80-fold difference in home-range size found in leopards is remarkable.

The way the home ranges of breeding adults are arranged in relation to each other also shows considerable flexibility. Observations we made in Chitwan indicated that the home ranges of females were essentially exclusive, with little overlap between them. Males were apparently territorial as well, and a male territory enclosed the territories of a number of females. In Wilpattu National Park in Sri Lanka, areas around some of the water holes were occupied exclusively by a single adult male and a single adult female. In a dry tropical forest in Thailand, Alan Rabinowitz found partial but not extensive overlap between the home ranges of males and between females. The land tenure pattern that seems to be emerging for leopards is one of considerable flexibility, the exact attributes of which depend on the abundance and distribution of food resources.

The dispersal system in leopards appears to be flexible, and young animals do not always leave their natal areas when they become independent. There are a number of examples of larger male leopards remaining in the ranges of their mother for some time, but these were not followed until they entered the breeding population. On the other hand, Mel Sunquist tracked young male leopards in Nepal leaving their natal area at only 15 to 16 months of age. The dispersal patterns of leopards remain unknown, but if young females and/or males have a tendency to leave their natal areas to breed, it could result in increased vulnerability as leopard habitats become increasingly fragmented.

▼ Leopards carefully stalk their prey using stealth and the advantage of cover to closely approach a gazelle or sambar. Once near, leopards rush explosively, grab the animal by its throat, and suffocate it. When the prey dies, it is dragged into a tree or thick cover where the leopard begins to feed.

Mark Deeble and Victoria Stone

Stephen J. Krasemann/DRK Photo

REARING YOUNG

The time just after birth, and the whole suite of behaviors associated with rearing, are critical in the life of a cat. My colleagues and I were able to follow the movements of a female leopard during the first six weeks after she gave birth. She moved her two cubs three times within a 25 hectare (62 acre) area of tall grass during this period. During the third week, the female stayed with the cubs for 33 hours, was gone for 36 hours, then returned and stayed for 29 hours. This pattern was repeated at six weeks of age. All told during these early weeks, she spent about half her time with or in the close vicinity of her young, and when she departed it was usually for more than 24 hours. When the cubs were seven weeks old, a fire swept through the tall grass area where the cubs were

hidden. The mother was away, but the cubs were able to escape the fire on their own. When the female returned she immediately found them and moved them again. We came to think of this rearing site not so much as a den, but a cub-rearing area, the features of which complemented the leopard's behavior in absorbing and/or deflecting harm to the cubs. During this six-week period she used a home range of about 8 square kilometers (just over 3 square miles). She could cross it easily in two hours or less. Spending such long periods away from her young was evidently dictated not only by the time needed to hunt and kill her prey, but by the fact that once she made a kill she had to stay with the dead animal to protect it from scavengers and consume it before it decomposed (a quick process in hot, humid climates).

▲ A leopard leaves its mother at the age of 16 months to two years. Some young leopards will disperse to areas that are a great distance from their mother's territory. Others live independently but remain in or near their mother's territory for extended periods of time. Dispersal is fraught with danger for leopards. Not only do they risk starvation because they are not yet expert hunters, they are also at risk of being killed by competitors and, of course, man.

HOW TO TELL A LEOPARD BY ITS SPOTS

SRIYANIE MIHTHAPALA

Rudyard Kipling, in his classic *Just So* stories, wove a tale of "How The Leopard Got His Spots" and in it wrote that if one examined any leopard carefully "there are always five spots." Rudyard Kipling was wrong — there *aren't* always five spots. A leopard has spots on its face, chest and feet, rosettes on its body and flanks, and rings on its tail. The spots on its face form patterns which vary among individual leopards, just as facial features differ among humans.

The number of spots on the muzzle and their relative positions are different on different leopards, and also different on either side of an individual leopard's face. Spots on the forehead form discernible shapes such as circles, ovals or squares; there are lines, or spots in a line, immediately below the eyes, while on the chest, spots sometimes form a necklace.

About two decades ago, Colin Pennycuick and Judith Rudnai described a method of identifying individual lions by using whisker spots. Because their method was quantitative, we were able to modify it for identifying individual leopards. In those specific areas where spot patterns varied, we described characters and gave different values for alternative states. For example, on the muzzle there were several spots above and along the whiskers. We used the first row of spots that had whiskers (row D) as a reference line for character descriptions of rows A, B, C and E. We described character number 2 as the number of spots in row A, and defined value number 1 as two or fewer spots, while value number 2 was three or fewer spots. We were able to use spacing as well as alignment of spots as characters with alternative values. Lines, spotted lines or a combination of both under the eyes, and the presence or absence of a "necklace," were also used. Thus, we were able to define each animal by a combination of values — a spot pattern identification code, much the same as computer barcodes on the back of books.

Once this code was defined, we had to answer two questions: were some characters more variable than others, that is, were some characters more useful than others for identification, and how reliable was the code, that is, was each combination of values unique?

We answered the first question by calculating how often each character value occurred and then we added up the frequencies of all values in a combination. This told us how probable it was that a given spot pattern code would occur. Once we had this probability, we were able to use a mathematical formula to calculate how much information was conveyed by each spot pattern. With that information, we could then figure out which characters were most variable and hence which were most useful for identification. We found that characters such as the number of spots in rows D, C and B contributed more information than others.

We answered the second question of reliability of identification by figuring out how probable it was for no animals or one individual to have identical identification codes. If the sum of these probabilities was larger than 0.95, then we would be 95 percent certain of reliable identification. If the sum of these probabilities was larger than 0.99, then we would be 99 percent certain.

We used this method of identification in a sample of 21 leopards from Sri Lanka, and found that it was effective for distinguishing 19 leopards with 95 percent reliability, and 15 percent with 99 percent reliability.

▶ At first glance, identifying a leopard by its spots seems impossible. But careful analysis of face, forehead, and throat spot patterns produces reliable individual recognition.

Row A
Row B
Row C
Row D
Row E

Joe McDonald/Animals Animals

Stanley Breeden

COMPETITORS

The life of any predator, even a predator the size of a leopard, can be confounded by the presence of competitors, and tigers and lions are potentially deadly obstacles for leopards. There is a long-held saying that in many habitats "...where tigers are numerous, leopards are few." In lowland rainforest wildlife reserves in Java, leopards were indeed very rare when tigers occurred there. With the extirpation of tigers from those areas, leopard numbers increased. George Schaller noted that, in the Serengeti, habitats used by leopards were strongly influenced by the presence of lions.

I was able to compare the behavior of a female leopard and a female tiger using essentially the same area in Chitwan. The two cats hunted the same ungulate species but the tiger usually took large prey which was 45 to 90 kilograms (100 to 200 pounds) in size. The tiger's kills included adult axis deer, sambar, and wild swine, as well as adult domestic water buffalo. The two cats were active both day and night but not always at the same time. As the temperatures climbed before the monsoon, the leopard was more active during the day and evening, and the tiger's activity gravitated to the early morning. When the grass was thick and lush after the monsoon, both cats used the forest

and grassland in much the same way. After the February fires, the tiger restricted herself mainly to the forest where the large species of prey were concentrated. The leopard, meanwhile, frequented the burned-over area where she could find the small hog deer. The tiger often walked along roads but the leopard did so only for short distances; they both used different trails and crossings. Thick vegetation was obviously an important factor tempering relations between the leopard and the tiger. So, in general, without this thick vegetation leopards and tigers would encounter each other more frequently in Chitwan National Park, and the tigers with their greater size advantage would drive the leopards from an otherwise suitable habitat for, like African lions, tigers will pursue leopards and kill them if they have the opportunity.

This interspecific social dominance has been a strong selective force in leopard evolution. The tiger or lion had first choice of food and space, and if the leopard had challenged that priority it would have been unlikely to win. To survive, the leopard has adapted its ways to live in areas that are unsuitable for the tiger, and evolved habits that reduce the possibility of overlap with the tiger's use of resources. Curiously, the leopard's

▲ These leopards in Dudhwa National Park, India, are courting with their usual abandon in a most unusual habitat. Most leopard matings occur in cover on land.

▼ When mating, the male leopard grasps the skin on the back of his mate's neck. He maintains this grip for several seconds until mating is completed. The female then turns and swats the male away with a forepaw.

Anthony Bannister/NHPA

113

HOW MANY LEOPARDS ARE THERE IN AFRICA?

ROBIN MEADOWS

Trade in leopard skins rose dramatically in the 1960s and early 1970s, reaching an estimated high of 60,000 skins sold per year. This prompted the Convention of International Trade in Endangered Species (CITES) in 1975 to list leopards as endangered. However, to the people living in African villages, where leopards killed livestock and even children and the elderly, these great cats seemed only too abundant. To re-evaluate the status of leopards in Africa, CITES commissioned two biologists to estimate the size of the population.

In their controversial 1987 study, Rowan Martin of the Zimbabwe Department of National Parks and Wildlife Management and Belgian biologist Tom de Meulenaer stated that there were about 700,000 leopards in Africa — enough to warrant moving them from the endangered list to the threatened list, which would have eased protective measures such as the international ban on buying leopard skins. Other leopard experts consulted by CITES overwhelmingly rejected the study and so, despite Martin and de Meulenaer's recommendation, African leopards still enjoy the strictest protective measures.

Because counting leopards in a large area is not feasible, Martin and de Meulenaer developed a computer model to estimate the number of leopards in Africa. Besides accounting for birth rates, death rates, and other factors that affect population size, their model made three notable assumptions: first, if an area had a suitable leopard habitat then the cats were living there; second, if leopards lived in an area, the population would be as big as the area could support; and third, the number of leopards an area could support depended on the amount of rainfall the area received. (Previous research has shown that compared to dry areas, those with lots of rain have bigger populations of carnivorous animals, such as leopards, presumably because wet areas have more plants and thus can support bigger populations of the herbivorous animals that carnivores eat.) Martin and de Meulenaer assigned a rainfall value to each vegetation type in the 38 African countries inhabited by leopards, and then used existing vegetation maps of Africa to estimate the amount of rainfall — and therefore the number of leopards — in each country.

To check their model's estimate of 700,000 leopards in Africa, they compared previous population estimates for individual countries to those made by their model. The results were virtually identical in the case of Kenya, which was the only country with an estimate based on extensive field work: the field study predicted that there were about 11,000 leopards in Kenya, and the model predicted that there were about 10,000.

While some of the experts who reviewed the results of the Martin–de Meulenaer study agreed that leopards may have been plentiful in some areas of Africa, the consensus of the reviewers was that the model was invalid because its assumptions were false. Reviewers refuted the assumption that all areas of suitable habitat would contain leopards by pointing out, for example, that leopards no longer survive in several of the areas deemed suitable by the model because they have been hunted by man to protect livestock. Reviewers also disagreed with the assumption that the number of leopards in an area depended on the amount of rainfall, saying, for instance, that the forests with the most rain have extremely small populations of herbivores and thus could not be expected to support large populations of carnivores. In addition to questioning the model's assumptions, reviewers who had estimated leopard populations in specific areas believed that the model's estimates were far too high — for example, whereas the model predicted that there were over 23,000 leopards in South Africa, one of the reviewers predicted that fewer than 3,000 lived there.

Due to these flaws, the reviewers concluded that the Martin–de Meulenaer model's estimate of leopard numbers in Africa was unreliable, and as such was an insufficient basis for CITES to move African leopards from the endangered list to the threatened list. Unless it is proven that the African leopard population is robust enough, these great cats should not be hunted for fur or sport.

deference to the lion and the tiger has produced traits that give it the best chance of surviving human impact. As the social subordinate, the leopard has developed adaptability and, with it, the ability to alter its behavior as conditions change. In the face of growing human pressures it has proved more resilient than the tiger or lion.

For nearly a decade Mel Sunquist, Charles McDougal, and I monitored and radio-tracked leopards living at the edge of the Royal Chitwan National Park in Nepal. We were startled to find that the leopard population at the edge of the park was not replacing itself. Here, it took an average of 46 months for a female leopard to produce another female, whereas the females on our study site survived or remained an average of 37 months — that is, not long enough to replace themselves. This finding altered our view about leopards; it suddenly was apparent that they were not immune to the forces that were threatening Asia's other big cats. What was wrong?

Leopards do not shy away from carrion (dead and rotting flesh), and if they are disturbed will frequently return to their kills. Thus, the leopard can easily be poisoned. People can, and do, lace killed prey with pesticides, and lay cable snares along a leopard's approach route into villages, and livestock-grazing or holding areas. The leopard hangs tough in the face of change, but the very traits that serve the leopard so well also make them especially vulnerable to certain methods that humans employ to get rid of them.

► Like most big cats, leopards spend about two-thirds of their time resting and surveying their environment. Leopards lie up in thick cover but also frequently rest on limbs and crotches of trees. Leopards come to the ground to hunt, however, and only rarely find prey in trees.

JAGUARS

LOUISE H. EMMONS

Of all the great cats, jaguars (*Panthera onca*) have remained one of the most elusive. The private lives of lions, tigers, leopards, and cheetahs have been watched by millions on television, and the affluent can pay for a safari to see them, but no amount of money can guarantee the sight of an undisturbed wild jaguar. All that researchers have been able to learn of jaguar behavior has been by indirect means: following the disembodied movements of the radio signal from a collared cat, collecting its droppings, or reconstructing events from kills or tracks on a beach. Jaguar study is one of the most challenging areas of field work, but also one of the most long and arduous. Months of effort are needed to learn a few precious facts, often without ever seeing the animals.

Similar to leopards in color and average weight, jaguars differ from them in build: they have shorter, thicker legs, and larger feet; shorter backs, and larger heads, with stouter canine teeth. The largest jaguars are much heavier than leopards, but sometimes smaller in linear size. The aura of a jaguar is of great power, not speed or graceful beauty; a heavyweight wrestler rather than a runner.

▼ Giant jaguars (*Panthera onca*), once roamed throughout North America, and rivalled the ancient European cave lion in size. Even at its present smaller size, the jaguar is the third largest felid (after tigers and lions) and its jaw muscles and teeth are so well-developed that it is considered the most powerful of all the big cats. Today jaguars live only in Mexico, Central America, and South America as far as northern Argentina.

Comstock

HABITATS

Jaguars are animals of forested or densely vegetated habitats; they can venture into open grasslands to find prey, but retreat to the brush or forest for most of the day. Historically, their range covered many habitat types including the wooded canyons of the Sonoran Desert and the riverine forests in the southwestern United States, the vast rainforests of South and Central America, the flooded grassland/forest mosaics of the Venezuelan Llanos and Brazilian Pantanal, the thorny thickets of the Chaco of Bolivia and Brazil and the Cerrado of eastern Brazil, and the Pampas of Uruguay. Jaguars do not seem to adjust well to cold, and they stay in the lowlands below 1,000 meters (3,300 feet), although they have been recorded above 2,000 meters (6,500 feet), and historically lived between the latitudes of about 35° north and south.

The speciality of jaguars among the big cats is their strong association with wet and waterside habitats, from which they take prey. They regularly travel along river margins, haunt the borders of lakes, and swim great distances across large rivers. They choose waterside spots to rest, and are most easily seen and commonly photographed as they lie on logs over the water in the morning sun. Radio-tracking in the forest/grassland mosaic of the Brazilian Pantanal showed that jaguars spent about 70 percent of their time in forest and less than 30 percent in grassland, and in any of these locations were located a mean distance of only 0.5 kilometer (0.3 mile) from water. The greater Rio Amazon and Paraguay Basins are extremely flat, and during the six months of the rainy season, vast areas of both forest and bordering grasslands are covered with sheets of water intersected with

Loren McIntyre

◄ Jaguars are most often found in forests or habitats with dense vegetation. They may venture into grasslands at night to make a kill but retreat to cover during the day. Being good climbers, jaguars often rest in trees but they are believed to hunt almost entirely on the ground.

natural levees. Jaguars seem to thrive in these seasonally flooded regions.

The use of wet and waterside habitats by jaguars may help them to avoid competition for prey with pumas, which are present throughout their entire geographic range. During a sampling period in a rainforest study area in Manu National Park, Peru, jaguars left tracks inside the forest on dry land on 35 days and puma on 32 days; puma used exposed river and lake margins on only five days, while jaguar traveled these on 39 days. This difference between the species is likely to be the direct result of hunting for particular kinds of prey.

LAND TENURE
The way in which individuals of a species occupy a habitat is a product of their social organization. Our knowledge of jaguar behavior comes from following radio-collared individuals. But, this knowledge is still rudimentary because jaguars are difficult both to capture for collaring and to follow once collared, and only a few members of a population have ever been radio-tagged at once, or for more than a fraction of their lives (one to two years).

All of the four radiotelemetry studies of jaguars have shown that females have home ranges that overlap those of a small number of other females — perhaps two overlapping on any one part of an area. The young use their mother's home range until they become independent. Home ranges of females are from 10 to 70 square kilometers (4 to 27 square miles). Males have home ranges that overlap those of neighboring males to a lesser extent, and perhaps in some cases not at all. Male home ranges are superimposed on those of females and are two to three times larger, 28 to 168 square kilometers (10 to 65 square miles), so that each male home range contains within it those of several females. Jaguar densities in fairly undisturbed populations have been estimated to be from one per 15 square kilometers (5.75 square miles) in Belize, to one per 64 square kilometers (25 square miles) in the Brazilian Pantanal.

Any spot of terrain may thus be used by a number of resident jaguars, but they seem to avoid each other so that only one at a time is hunting in a given area. When two males are close to each other, they sometimes counter-call with bouts of roaring (a pulsed series of single, deep grunts, each like a single rasp of a bow across the strings of a bass fiddle), suggesting territorial defense. Females also roar. A cat will enter a part of its home range, circulate within it for three to ten days, then abandon that area for several weeks before returning for another visit. In Manu National Park in Peru, an adult, resident female used a particular portion of her range 13 percent of the time, and returned there once or twice each month. A male used the same area less often and more irregularly.

Mutual avoidance while hunting may be common to several species of cats, and in Manu, jaguars and pumas seem to stay out of each other's way, as do jaguars among themselves. Any cat looking for prey would be less likely to find it in an area just visited by another cat hunting the same prey.

A TASTE FOR TURTLES

The strength and enormously powerful bite of a rainforest jaguar is most often needed, not for subduing a tapir (the only mammal much larger than itself that it will ever meet), but for piercing the armor of reptiles. In the untouched rainforest of Peru, one-third of the prey individuals identified from scats were turtles, tortoises, and caiman. Jaguars kill both land tortoises (*Geochelone denticulata, G. carbonaria*) and river turtles (*Podocnemis unifilis*) by brute force, breaking the top of the carapace (the thick, hard shell) with their teeth. Species of each genus are opened in a different way. The high crowned, wrinkled dome of tortoises provides "tooth-holds" for the jaguar's canines, which can penetrate the comparatively thin top of the shell through to the bone below. The smooth, flat carapace of river turtles offers no hold for teeth and, unlike the tortoise's shell, is apparently thicker on the top than at the edge. Jaguars open them by breaking the carapace edges, and making holes on both sides rather than enlarging a single hole to include the top. Giant river turtles (*P. expansa*) are so large that jaguars are said to scoop out the bodies from between the carapaces with a paw. Caiman are apparently killed with a crushing bite to the neck, and opened, along the sides of the body, where there are no bony armor plates. No other great cats have been reported to focus on armored reptiles as prey, and this diet may be the reason broken canines are often seen on jaguar skulls.

A taste for turtles and caiman (also fish and capybaras) may be the main impulse that brings jaguars to the waterside, and this food habit may have a long history: Pleistocene (2 million to 10,000 years ago) fossil turtles found in deposits with jaguar bones reveal cat-like toothmarks. However, the future of this relationship looks dim. In Amazonia, all large chelonians (turtles and tortoises) are intensely pursued by man for food. Giant river turtles survive in only a few, dwindling, fragmented populations, and the other species are increasingly rare or virtually gone wherever man occurs.

▲ The remains of the land tortoise (above) and the river turtle (below) show just how the jaguar tackles the carapace of these difficult prey.

Fiona Sunquist

HUNTING BEHAVIOR

Jaguars hunt both day and night, usually with a peak of activity in the early part of the night and rest periods in the middle of the day. Their chief activity seems to reflect that of their major prey: in the Brazilian Pantanal they feed mainly on diurnal species, and are most active by day, and in Belize, where their primary prey is all nocturnal, they are most active by night. In rainforest areas in Belize, male jaguars were active close to 60 percent of the time, which is a great deal, and implies that considerable effort is required to find prey.

There are few eyewitness accounts of jaguars attacking or killing prey, and the slim knowledge of their hunting tactics is all derived by reconstructing signs at kill sites or from following tracks. Jaguars primarily seem to hunt by simply walking until they surprise a prey animal and then making a short charge to capture it. In Manu National Park, a jaguar was seen walking along a lake margin and suddenly rushing at a limpkin (a bird), which it missed. In the same locality, track sequences on beaches showed jaguars walking

steadily along, then apparently sighting prey, breaking straight from a walk into a full charge for distances of 7 to 30 meters (23 to 98 feet), that is, only a few enormous strides. Anecdotes suggest that jaguars also lie in wait on top of high logs over trails and then pounce on prey that passes below, but possibly the jaguars were simply resting on a log when prey chanced by. Jaguars eat several forest canopy species such as spider monkeys, but it is not clear how they obtain them. Cats certainly capture monkeys that forage near the ground by day, but it is highly unlikely that they succeed in catching active monkeys in trees, nor is there direct evidence that jaguars hunt arboreally by day. Do they find the rare spider monkey that has fallen to its death? Or can they locate the sleeping sites of arboreal animals and climb to capture them at night? We don't know.

When a jaguar has captured a large mammal, it kills it by a powerful bite to the head, neck, or throat, often puncturing the skull near the ears with the canines, or dislocating or crushing the neck vertebrae. Jaguars are the only big cats to

▲ Jaguars thrive in well-watered habitats. Radio-tracking studies show that they rarely venture more than 0.5 kilometer (0.3 mile) from water. Jaguars seem especially suited to exploiting habitats in the Amazon Basin that are partially submerged in water for some months of the year.

▲ (Top) By using stream banks and other waterside habitats, jaguars may avoid competition with pumas for prey. The distribution of jaguars and pumas overlaps through much of the jaguar's range, but jaguars frequently kill prey that are water dependant such as capybara, river tortoises, and caimans.

▲ (Bottom) Jaguars kill caiman with a crushing bite to the neck. They open the caiman's body along the sides as they are not protected by heavy armor plates. No other big cat regularly hunts and kills reptiles for food.

regularly kill prey by piercing the skull. After making a large kill, a jaguar drags it into the shelter of a thicket to feed on it.

PREY

In densely forested habitats such as rainforest, most terrestrial animals are solitary or live in pairs, and only a few, such as peccaries, form herds. Individuals or small groups tend to be thinly dispersed in large home ranges throughout the forest. Large fruiting trees may briefly attract many local animals, but such trees are rare and isolated. Vegetation in rainforest blocks the view, so that only animals within a very short distance can be seen. These factors combine to make it hard for either a hunting jaguar or a hunting human to predict the whereabouts of animals in the forest.

For this reason, jaguars in the forest seem to eat almost any vertebrate that they can catch. In a sample of only 40 prey individuals identified from jaguar scats in Manu National Park, there were 20 mammals, including 11 species: two opossums,

one anteater, one monkey, one deer, one olingo (a small carnivore), one peccary, one squirrel, and three large rodent species. The remaining 20 prey included birds, fish, turtles, a lizard, and caiman. This striking diversity of prey shows that the jaguars did not pass up even tiny morsels, such as a snail or a small skink. Clearly, the jaguars acted as if they could not count on finding large or favored prey species. Parallel studies of prey populations on the study area showed that jaguars took mammal prey species in about the same ratios as those species occurred in the area. There was one exception: jaguars ate collared peccaries more often than expected from their numbers, showing that jaguars were able to specifically seek these out to a small extent.

The opportunism of jaguar hunting tactics in rainforest is highlighted by comparative studies in different regions. In a large sample from Cockscomb Basin in Belize, over half of all prey taken were armadillos, and the next most common prey (9 percent) were deer and pacas.

Fifteen other species were eaten in lesser numbers. Once again, these numbers closely reflected the ratios of the prey species in the study area. At La Selva, Costa Rica, jaguars eat large numbers of sloths.

In habitats with much grassland, especially those with limited supplies of water, the distribution of prey becomes much more predictable than it is in forest. Large mammals in such habitats often live in herds and/or at high densities and need water, and the open habitat makes them detectable from a distance. In open habitats, big cats, including jaguars, can learn to predict the whereabouts of particular prey species, so that their array of prey becomes a smaller set of preferred species rather than a random smorgasbord (although they still take a wide array of items). In the Pantanal of Brazil, a grassland/ forest mosaic, jaguar prey chiefly on capybara and peccaries, which they apparently find so easily that they often abandon kills with large portions remaining uneaten. In rainforest, evidence from

scats shows that this seems not to be the case, as large animals such as peccaries are entirely consumed, including the feet and hooves.

The little available data strongly indicate that jaguars in rainforest areas are on average much smaller than those in grassland habitats, perhaps weighing only half as much. One can speculate that this is because in grassland areas jaguars are able to find large prey more easily and often, and well-fed youngsters can develop to a larger size. Being small in size may be an advantage to rainforest individuals, as they would need smaller amounts of food and fewer of their smaller prey. Nonetheless, even in rainforest habitats, rare individual males of both puma and jaguar reach extremely large sizes. Perhaps these giants had outstanding mothers that fed them exceptionally well, and maybe there were no siblings to share their food, or perhaps they learned exceptional hunting strategies. Genetic factors could also play a role in producing the rare and often legendary giant males that appear at intervals in all habitats.

▲ Jaguars live and hunt alone. The home range of a female may overlap with those of one or two other females. Male home ranges include the home ranges of a number of females and these may be exclusive or they may overlap those of other males. Female home ranges vary in size from 10 to 70 square kilometers (4 to 27 square miles), and those of males are two to three times larger.

► Jaguars are opportunistic hunters, usually taking prey in about the proportion of its occurrence in the area. In one study area, more than half of the jaguars' diet was pangolins; in another area, capybara and peccaries were important. Other prey include opossums, rodents, deer, anteaters, and primates.

Claudia Wright/Partridge Productions/Oxford Scientific Films

► Jaguars give birth to between one and four young after a gestation period of about 100 days. Young jaguars stay with their mother for about two years before they disperse. Little is known about this period in the lives of wild jaguars as only recently have jaguars been studied by radio-tracking and most have been followed for only short periods of time.

Andi Cole

JAGUARS AND MAN

There is currently no method to accurately estimate jaguar populations over large regions. Thus far, the only reliable data have come from studies where every animal in an area is identified and its home range measured, a process that takes several years for a tiny population. All such studies have been done in regions with high prey and jaguar numbers. It is unlikely that the results can be extrapolated to most of the rest of the geographic range of the jaguar, where prey and probably predator are at lower densities. We urgently need a better method to count rainforest cats.

During the 1960s, prior to the Convention of International Trade in Endangered Species (CITES), jaguars were hunted extensively for their skins. Hunters penetrated deep into the most remote regions of Amazonia, supported by organized trade networks that reached even the smallest indigenous villages. In 1965, 1,113 jaguar skins were legally exported from the Peruvian Amazon town of Iquitos alone. If jaguar densities in the region are assumed to have been about 1 per 30 square kilometers (12 square miles), this single year's export, from one town, represents the entire jaguar population of 33,000 square kilometers (12,740 square miles). Considering that much of the trade did not pass through legal channels, and there were other points of export, it is obvious that the effects of this level of hunting would have been catastrophic within a few more years.

The CITES agreements were dramatically effective in curbing the skin trade. Although poaching is still rife in many areas, the number of fur-bearing animals taken seems to be a fraction of the former tally. A strong index of the recovery of these animals is that the single species most threatened by the skin trade, the giant otter, which was brought to the edge of extinction, has returned to at least some of the rivers where it has not been seen for decades.

Reduction of the skin trade has relieved jaguars from persecution in the far, uninhabited corners of their geographic range, but

Alan and Sandy Carey

unfortunately, jaguars and man have thus far proven incompatible in the same habitats. As human populations have spread, jaguar populations have shrunk. Within the main geographic refuge of jaguars, the rainforests, most of the human populations occupying the same area obtain their meat by subsistence hunting. All prey species of the jaguar are also eaten by man and have become increasingly scarce near inhabited regions. In addition, hunters almost always shoot any jaguar they encounter by chance. Populations of jaguars seem reduced, though not extinguished, in most inhabited regions of Amazonian forest.

The most threatened populations of jaguars are those in areas that have been developed for cattle ranching. Individual jaguars learn to prey on livestock such as cattle and horses, causing direct conflict with ranchers. With the exception of a handful of enlightened ranch owners who protect wildlife, stockmen generally aggressively exterminate all jaguars whether or not they are

cattle-killers. In addition, ranch hands hunting for meat in remaining forests often decimate the game species on which jaguars depend, thus making it more likely that jaguars will prey on cattle. The habit of shooting at every jaguar seen can further aggravate the situation as wounded cats may be especially prone to seeking out easily found prey such as livestock. Finally, their own behavior seems to be a liability: jaguars are not as shy and secretive as pumas, and as a result, seem to walk into human view and get shot more often.

The geographic range of the jaguar is surrounded by lands undergoing rapid development for cattle pasture and agriculture. Consequently, once large populations in the north, south and east are now extinct or dramatically reduced. There are only an estimated 1,000 remaining jaguars in all of Mesoamerica (Central America and Mexico); half of them in Mexico and half in all the other countries combined. The great rainforests of Amazonia are the last refuge for jaguars and most of their prey.

▲ Jaguar numbers continue to fall as a result of continuing habitat encroachment. Throughout their range, more and more land is being converted for pasture and agriculture. Ranchers and farmers do not tolerate jaguars, but pursue and kill them. Unlike the shy and retiring puma, jaguars are bold and do not avoid people; they are thus easily shot.

SNOW LEOPARDS

RODNEY JACKSON

For centuries, the snow leopard (*Panthera uncia*) of Central Asia has been a creature surrounded by mystery and folklore. For example, it is common belief among Central Asia's highland villagers that snow leopards do not eat the meat of their victims, but live only by sucking their blood. (This belief is probably explained by the small punctures made by the cat's canines when they suffocate their kill, and by the instances when a villager disturbs the cat at its kill before it has had a chance to begin eating.) There is also the story of Milarepa, Tibet's great Buddhist poet-saint, who lived from 1052 to 1135. A mountain snowstorm stranded Milarepa for six months in the Great Cave of Conquering Demons, where he had gone to live in solitude and pursue his devotions. When the snow finally melted, six of his followers went to find his body, but found that he had been transformed into a snow leopard.

In reality, the snow leopard, is rarely sighted, even by enterprising mountain peoples, it seems to be endowed with an almost uncanny ability to blend into the rocky vastness it inhabits. It is often placed in a genus by itself, its structure revealing adaptations for life among rugged mountains — large forepaws, short forelimbs, well-developed chest muscles, and a 1 meter (3 foot) long tail.

Snow leopards are sparsely and discontinuously distributed through the mountains of Central Asia — "the roof of the world" — with a population of unknown size. The species ranges from the Hindu Kush mountains of Afghanistan into Pakistan; along the Karakorum Range and Pamir Range to the Tien Shan, Altay, and Syan ranges along the border between the People's Republic of China, the USSR, and the Mongolian People's Republic; southward through Qinghai, Gansu, and Sichuan provinces of China into Tibet and the Himalayan countries of Bhutan, Nepal, and India — a potential range of more than 2.5 million square kilometers (almost 1 million square miles).

Inhabitants of alpine and subalpine zones, snow leopards are usually found above 3,000 meters (9,800 feet) although they have been reported as low as 600 meters (2,000 feet) in the USSR. During summer months they range as high as 5,500 meters (18,000 feet). Snow leopards are most closely associated with arid and semi-arid steppe habitats, and some parts of their range, such as the massifs of the Gobi Desert of Mongolia, Tibet's vast Chang Tang, and the hostile northern rim of Ladakh, are virtually devoid of vegetation. In Pakistan and India, snow leopards are said to migrate down into oak, fir, or rhododendron forest for the winter, and in parts of the USSR they are said to remain in conifer forest all year round.

Himalayan tribesmen and Tibetans have a saying: where bharal (or blue sheep) occur, so one will find snow leopards. To this might be added the Asiatic ibex, an important prey in the extreme

Michael Dick/Animals Animals

west of the cat's range, where there are few or no bharal. But the bharal, described by biologist George Schaller as an "aberrant goat with sheep-like affinities," shares with the cat its entire range, which covers the enormous Tibetan plateau and fringing Himalayan and Kunlun mountains. Predator and prey, both superb rock climbers, live above the tree line, in sparsely vegetated fields and alpine pastures in steep terrain well-dissected by ravines or gullies and interspersed with cliffs or broken bands of rock. Since life among cliffs tends to discourage predators like the wolf, it is not surprising that snow leopards are the main predator of bharal — after man, that is.

Although snow leopards depend heavily upon bharal and ibex, in reality they are an opportunistic predator, taking anything from a yak weighing more than 200 kilograms (440 pounds) to a diminutive musk deer of about 10 kilograms (22 pounds), or from the resplendently colored Impeyan pheasant to the social marmot. Small prey may be very important in some parts of their range. For example, in Qinghai Province, China, Schaller found that 45 percent of their summer diet consisted of marmots. For the rest of the year, when the marmots are hibernating, the snow leopards must subsist more heavily upon bharal, or if these are at low density, on livestock.

Secretive habits, low numbers, a sparse distribution, and difficult field conditions have long hindered attempts at studying the snow leopard. When I first visited its habitat in Nepal's remote Kanjiroba mountain range in 1976, very few accounts of its behavior or natural history

▼ The solitary-living snow leopard (*Panthera uncia*) ranges widely over the high mountains of central Asia. Superbly adapted to the rigors of its cold, high-altitude habitats, this secretive cat is seldom seen, even by local people.

CONSERVATION OF A FLAGSHIP SPECIES

Throughout the vast area that snow leopards inhabit, they exist precariously, threatened by hunters seeking them either for their magnificent pelt, or because they have been stealing livestock (prey upon which they must increasingly depend as humans erode their natural prey base). The International Union for Conservation of Nature and Natural Resources (IUCN) lists them as endangered. The number remaining in the wild is not known, although some biologists put the population as high as 5,000. Even if there are that many, they would occur in small pockets, thinly spread over a very large area, and most likely isolated from each other. Conservation biologists question whether such isolated sub-populations could retain genetic viability for long. As the countries with known or potential snow leopard habitat (Afghanistan, Bhutan, China, India, Mongolia, Nepal, Pakistan, and the USSR) expand their efforts toward high altitude ecological protection, so they increase the base of information upon which to assess such protection and management questions.

In parts of China, Pakistan, and India, where snow leopards were formerly frequently sighted, they are now very rare. While the illegal fur trade has certainly been a major factor, the scarcity of prey must be a significant element in the decline of their numbers. For example, in the Tian Shan mountains of Xinjiang, China, biologist George Schaller counted only six ibex in a 250 square kilometer (95 square mile) area formerly known for its large ibex population. Not far away, local people reported that 11 snow leopards had been killed by two men several years previously, presumably because they were considered a threat to the area's livestock industry. Unfortunately, this pattern is being repeated in many parts of Central Asia.

Although snow leopards are protected in most countries, enforcement is hampered by difficult terrain, inconsistent policies on the part of governments, and a thriving fur trade catering to an ever-increasing tourist market. Conservationists, however, can hardly blame poverty-stricken tribesmen for killing a rare snow leopard in hope of making a quick 50 or perhaps 200 dollars — a year's income to some. Rather, the blame must lie with the middlemen and furriers who collect raw pelts or make the fur coats to satisfy the black markets of Europe, North America, and Asia, as well as the person who sports the end product. A full-length coat may require up to 16 snow leopard skins and sell for upwards of US$60,000.

While the establishment of national parks or reserves is vital to the protection of snow leopards and their prey, conservation must embrace broader strategies in order to preserve genetically viable populations. Living standards of people sharing the same habitat must be improved, and ways found whereby people can benefit in tangible ways from the presence of wildlife.

The snow leopard stands as a flagship species at the apex of the food chain: by protecting snow leopards, so we provide sufficient habitat for myriad other plants and animals. Just as the snow leopard is a striking symbol of the world's loftiest highlands, so it could become an unwitting environmental ambassador — an animal envoy for ecological balance and international cooperation in the race to overcome political and social barriers toward a global conservation ethic.

▲▶ (Top) A skinned snow leopard carcass. (Center) Bhote villagers with a snow leopard skin they were willing to sell for about US$10. (Bottom) Villagers use sharpened bamboo spears tipped with poison to kill snow leopards and their prey. Until recently large regions in the snow leopard's range were virtually uninhabited by people. With expanding human populations, however, local people and their livestock have invaded many areas, decimating natural prey populations and leaving the snow leopard with little choice but to prey on domestic animals. People respond by killing snow leopards. The sale of skins also adds to these peoples' annual incomes.

Terry Whittaker/Frank Lane Picture Agency

◀ A female snow leopard nuzzles a 10 month old cub while another cub looks on. By this age, cubs are probably traveling with their mother while she hunts. A mother's home range may be as large as 39 square kilometers (15 square miles). Snow leopards prefer to hunt blue sheep, or bharal, and ibex, but will also take marmots and musk deer.

existed. With several Nepalese associates and fellow biologist Gary Ahlborn, I led the first successful attempt at in-depth study of this elusive cat, in Nepal's Langu Gorge.

As little can be learned about a species' behavior or ecology without marking individual animals, we fitted radio-collars to three males and two females and tracked their subsequent movements. While the tagged cats exhibited many traits typical of other solitary felids, there were some important differences. Like tigers, they tended to move to a new place each day, unless on a kill, which could occupy them for up to a week. However, straight-line distances between consecutive-day locations averaged 1 kilometer (just over half a mile), which is less than half that traveled by tigers, jaguars, or pumas — all felids that live in far less rugged or precipitous terrain than the snow leopard. In all species the actual distance covered was much greater than the straight-line distance, due to circuitous, zig-zag travel patterns. Furthermore, in Langu Gorge elevational differences of over 4,000 meters (13,000 feet) exist within distances of a mere 7 kilometers (4.5 miles). Occasionally, a snow leopard would move from one end of its range to the other within a 12 or 24 hour period, covering linear distances of about 7 kilometers (4.5 miles). Snow leopards exhibit a distinct preference for traveling along major ridgelines, river bluffs or cliffs, and other well-defined landscape "edges." They prefer to rest in places with good vistas such as rocky promontories and cliff ledges.

We found the snow leopards in Langu Gorge to be crepuscular, that is, most active around dawn until about 10 a.m., and then again in the late afternoon and evening. They would spend much of the night bedded on or near a cliff. In Ladakh and elsewhere in Central Asia, they tend to be more nocturnal, a pattern most pronounced where they are hunted for their pelt or because of livestock thefts.

HOME RANGES

Home-range sizes varied widely between individual cats, ranging from 12 to 39 square kilometers (4.5 to 15 square miles) and averaging about 21 square kilometers (8 square miles). Assuming the Langu cats are representative of their species, snow leopard home ranges are similar to those of common leopards occupying Africa's bush country, but larger than leopards inhabiting Asia's prey-rich lowland wildlife reserves. Pumas in North America tend to have much larger home ranges, but they are bigger felids.

Although the Nepalese tagged cats did not occupy separate summer or winter ranges, seasonal movements of snow leopard and ibex have been reported from regions of Central Asia experiencing lengthy snowfall periods. These areas include, the Pamirs, Tien Shan, and the Karakorum Range. Some seasonal movement may also occur in certain areas of China and Tibet where the availability of prey such as wild ungulates, livestock, and marmot fluctuate markedly.

The cats did not appear to patrol the boundaries of their home ranges, but they visited most parts of it at intervals of several days to two or more weeks, mostly traveling alone. Although reports exist of snow leopards traveling and even hunting in pairs or larger groups, few observers have been explicit about the animals' sizes, and

Terry Whittaker/Frank Lane Picture Agency

traveled routes and repeatedly scent marked them. Prominent topographic features, such as large rock outcrops or ridgeline promontories, were more likely to be marked and revisited.

It is possible that this marking system enables individual snow leopards residing in a common area to share its resources with minimal strife, and to avoid contact that could otherwise result in serious injury or death, especially among males. Also, remaining well spaced may improve their chances of capturing wary prey.

An adult snow leopard is thought to require about 20 to 30 bharal annually, and the Langu Gorge is an ideal habitat for both predator and prey. Steep cliffs and other landscape edges abound, and near a major stream and river confluence is an extensive grassland that is a highly productive bharal habitat. Post-mating densities of bharal on these slopes exceed 15 to 20 sheep per square kilometer (40 to 52 per square mile) compared to 2.6 per square kilometer (6.7 per square mile) in a population inhabiting more typical Himalayan terrain but under relatively heavy harvesting pressures from humans, and 8.8 to 10 per square kilometer (23 to 26 per square mile) in a protected wintering population near our study area.

Our radio-tracking data revealed that snow leopards kill large prey about once every 10 to 15 days, a figure which compares favorably with kill rates in pumas. Langu snow leopards used their kills efficiently, consuming everything except for skeletal parts, the hide, and most of the viscera. They remained on kills for as long as a week, but averaging three to four days. Judging by how well the snow leopards guarded their kills, loss to vultures or other scavengers appeared negligible; neither were many animals interrupted or chased away from their meals by humans, as happens in other areas.

Snow leopard density was estimated at 5 to 10 animals (excluding cubs) per 100 square kilometers (13 to 26 per 100 square miles). Compared with estimates from elsewhere, the Langu Gorge population is extremely dense. For example, snow leopard numbers are widely estimated, from the incidence of marking, at about 0.7 per 100 square kilometers (1.8 per 100 square miles) in Ladakh, and a mere 0.35 to 0.53 (0.9 to 1.4 per 100 square miles) in the Taxkorgan Reserve of Xinjiang, China. In order to maintain a dense population, snow leopards would have to make efficient use of an unequally distributed food resource. Different patterns of establishing home ranges, land tenure, and social marking may occur in less favorable habitats where there are fewer snow leopards and where man and wildlife coexist precariously. If we are to protect this magnificent endangered cat, we need to learn more about its ecology and how best to achieve sustained utilization of its fragile mountain habitat.

▲ Although snow leopards have a stocky appearance, due to a thick coat, they are actually slightly smaller than leopards — but equally good predators. Snow leopards frequently take prey larger than themselves but, unlike other big cats, which occasionally kill people, snow leopards are not known to do so.

▶ Many expeditions, organized by the world's large museums, went in search of the elusive snow leopard after its discovery by westerners in 1761. It is only in the last 20 years, though, that wildlife biologists have been successful in studying the snow leopard's behavior and ecology in the wild. It remains the least known of the big cats.

such sightings are most likely of a female and her nearly independent offspring, or of recently independent siblings briefly traveling together. On average, the Langu radio-collared cats remained 2 to 3 kilometers (1.2 to 1.9 miles) apart.

The ranges of the five snow leopards overlapped almost entirely, although duplicate use of any particular area was separated by time. In the usual pattern of solitary felids, females occupy exclusive ranges which are shared by their offspring until they disperse, become transients, and then find or establish ranges of their own. The offspring usually disperse soon after becoming independent of their mother. However, several adult males may, if food supplies are adequate and if some mechanism exists to facilitate mutual avoidance, share a common area.

Snow leopards have a social marking system of scrapes (scuffs made as the animal rakes the ground with its hind paws), rock-scenting, and deposition of other signs which presumably identifies the particular snow leopard, its sex, relative age, and reproductive status. In Langu Gorge the intensity of marking peaked during the mating season, from January through March. Both sexes visited particular rocks along regularly

PUMAS

JOHN SEIDENSTICKER

The early Dutch traders in New York, so the story goes, were puzzled by the fact that the lion skins they obtained were those of females only. When questioned about this and asked why they never obtained skins with long manes, Indian hunters assured the traders that, indeed, there were such animals, but they lived in the most inaccessible mountainous places. It would be foolhardy to attempt to capture them, they said. Bewilderment over the relationship between the puma (*Felis concolor*) and the other big cats has a long history. In the past two decades we have learned that there really isn't much about pumas that is lion-like, other than color, and even the color varies from gray to reddish.

Stephen J. Krasemann/Bruce Coleman Ltd.

▲Pumas (*Felis concolor*) are solitary-living animals; a mother and her two to four young are the largest social groups. Young stay with their mother until they are 18 to 24 months of age, then leave to live and hunt alone. Pumas are widely-spaced in nature not because they are anti-social but because they must cover large areas to find enough prey to sustain themselves.

Confusion about this big cat begins with its common name: American lion, mountain lion, cougar, puma, panther, painter, catamount (cat on a mountain). When my colleagues and I studied the behavior and ecology of this cat in the Salmon River Mountains in Idaho, USA, we referred to it as "cougar." Cougar Creek Tom was a particular favorite. I don't know why we did it, but when we wrote our scientific reports we referred to it as American or mountain lion. Puma is a Native American word (Inca) from South America, which I have come to believe is an appropriate and distinctive name that avoids the misunderstanding of panther or lion and their African and Asian namesakes. But I sense that no one name will be accepted because of the size of the puma's geographic range and the regionalism of people who claim this cat as their own.

Extending over 110 degrees latitude — from the Straits of Magellan to the Canadian Yukon — the puma has the most extensive range of any terrestrial mammal in the western hemisphere. A solitary hunter, the puma is a cat of the rainforest, of coniferous forest, of chaparral, breaks, canyons and broken country, of mountains and the strips of stream-side trees, and brush that stretches out into the valleys and plains from the mountains, and, during the past century, of the great deciduous forests of eastern North America. Pumas can live and hunt in what appears to us as open country. A puma uses the grain of the land, the topography, grass, sage or other low bushes to shield its presence, stalk, and kill, and to conceal its prey from scavengers. Pumas are like a light breeze: when one is present, you know it; you can feel it, but you don't see it.

THE PUMA'S PLACE AMONG THE LARGE CATS

I had the great privilege of spending two years in the Salmon River Mountains of Idaho snow-tracking and radio-tracking pumas. Shortly thereafter, I spent several years in southern Asia probing the lives of leopards, tigers, and, briefly, lions. Making comparisons among the *Panthera*

Alan & Sandy Carey

cats is relatively straightforward. There are the obvious differences in size and social structure, and the manifestations of these differences — what John Eisenberg has called "variation on a common theme." I found that putting the puma into this comparative picture was not a natural fit, but the reasons for this were not immediately obvious.

It has been only since the mid-1960s, with George Schaller's pioneering work, that the *Panthera* cats have been objects of ecological and behavioral inquiry. Research on the puma also dates from about the same time, with the groundbreaking studies carried out by Maurice Hornocker and Wilbur Wiles. Before this, it was the hunting literature that shaped perceptions

about these cats, and this did, in fact, present very different portraits of the eastern hemisphere *Panthera* and the western hemisphere puma. The hunting literature on tigers and leopards was about the thrill of the hunt and about these cats as killers of deer, of livestock, and of humans. To be sure, the puma kills cattle and horses, and they are specialists at hunting and killing deer and elk, but examples of man-killing by this shy cat are very rare. *Panthera* cats, on the other hand, do kill humans under some circumstances. Pumas never figured prominently as objects of hatred in the pioneering, antipredator attitudes in North America, as did the wolf, for example. Ridding the country of the last "outlaw" wolves became the

▼ Pumas have the largest geographical distribution of any western hemisphere terrestrial mammal. Historically they ranged from northern Canada to Patagonia, from the Atlantic to the Pacific. They occupy diverse habitats from rugged snow-covered mountain slopes to steamy lowland tropical forest.

Comstock

Tom McHugh/Photo Researchers Inc.

▲ Despite their size and strength, pumas are shy and retiring. Unlike the big cats of Asia and Africa, which can become man-killers and even turn to people as a major source of food, pumas avoid people. Only a few cases of pumas attacking people have been documented.

subject of pulp magazines, as did the hunting of "man-eating" tigers, leopards, and lions. There were no "outlaw" pumas. Driving pumas into trees with aggressive, barking hunting dogs was discovered to be an extremely effective means of capture very early on. In contrast to pumas, leopards will actually eat dogs when they have an opportunity to catch them.

In more than half of its geographic range the puma is today the largest cat, but this is a relatively recent development. The circumspect demeanor of the puma may be a survival tactic that has its genesis in the evolution of the puma as a smaller player and social subordinate in the Pleistocene (2 million–10,000 years ago) assemblage of western hemisphere big cats and other very big carnivores. The ancestry of the puma remains largely unknown. Stephen O'Brien and his colleagues,

using the tools of molecular genetics, have discovered that the puma is in the Pantherine group rather than closely allied with the small living species of cats of Europe, Africa and Asia, or South America. There is a possible connection with the now-extinct cheetah-like cats that roamed North America until the end of the Pleistocene, about 10,000 years ago. Certainly the demeanor of the puma is more cheetah- than leopard-like. Tigers, leopards, and lions communicate with long-distance calls — roars — that leave no doubt about their presence in a landscape. Pumas do not announce their presence with long-distance calls, although the calls of a female puma in estrus can actually be quite loud. Like other cats, pumas use a covert marking system of scrapes and scent marks in places that are obvious to other pumas but not to other species.

STRUCTURE AND FUNCTION

Pumas living in rainforest, near the equator and mostly within the range of the jaguar, can be half the size of pumas that live in the northern and southern parts of their range. In Idaho, adult females weighed 40 to 45 kilograms (88 to 99 pounds) and adult males were 50 percent larger, 65 to 75 kilograms (145 to 165 pounds). Giant males that approached 90 kilograms (200 pounds) have been reported by reliable observers, but these must be very rare individuals. A comparative study of body proportion in the larger cats demonstrated that the puma has the greatest difference in the length of the anterior and posterior limbs. The relatively longer hind limbs of the puma are an adaptation for jumping.

The puma's ability to adapt to environmental change is apparent when its natural history is examined in areas with seasonal variation as well as great variation in habitat and topography. This characterizes the environment of the Salmon River Mountains in central Idaho. In winter, accumulated snow forces deer and elk to concentrate in the lower canyons. From September through May, pumas kill and feed primarily on mule deer and elk, which, except for fawns and adult female mule deer, are far larger than themselves. Pumas drag kills to protected sites and cover them with whatever is available be it snow, leaves, or pine needles. They remain in the vicinity of the kill for up to 19 days, venturing out of the area for short trips only, until the kill is completely consumed. A kill not closely guarded would be quickly eaten by one or a number of hovering scavengers such as golden eagles, ravens, and coyotes.

▲ Among the cats, pumas display a proportionately greater difference in the length of the forelimbs compared to the hind limbs. Hind limbs that are much longer than forelimbs are an adaptation for jumping, which enable the puma to move with relative ease through steep canyons and ravines.

C.C. Lockwood/Animals Animals

Alan & Sandy Carey

▲ Pumas are as adept as tigers at capturing preferred large prey like deer, but they are also as good as any of the small cats at capturing lesser prey. Raccoons, beavers, ground squirrels, mice, birds, even grasshoppers are eaten when big game is scarce.

What I found absolutely astounding is that pumas, both males and females, killed adult male elk. A bull elk is seven times the size of a female puma. In a study comparing the ratio of prey size amongst the cats (using modal [most frequently taken] prey weight divided by adult female cat weight) the puma, with a ratio 2.4 to 1, was far above all the other cats: the ratio of prey size of the puma is twice that of the snow leopard (1.4 to 1); and modal prey size for a female leopard and lion is about one to one.

In the southwestern United States — where deer do not move to winter ranges — deer is a staple in the diet of pumas throughout the year. During summer in the Salmon River Mountains,

when deer and elk are widely dispersed over the high ridges and rolling forested high country, pumas do leave the lower canyons, but they concentrate their hunting in areas rich in the colonial-living Columbia ground squirrel, which weighs 500 grams (1 pound); only occasionally do they kill deer and elk. In Amazonian Peru, Louise Emmons found that pumas preyed on small rodents, opossums, bats, and lizards. The majority of their prey were agoutis and pacas ranging from 1 to 10 kilograms (2.2 to 22 pounds) in weight. In the Torres del Pine National Park in Chile, an area of rolling, steppe-like hills and scattered woodlands, pumas most frequently killed guanacos and the introduced European hare. So,

depending on availability, pumas can and do take prey animals varying greatly in size.

Pumas are active day and night in the Salmon River Mountains, but they tend to be more active in the day during summer than during winter (their principal summer prey, Columbia ground squirrels, are diurnal). Pumas are active while snow is falling and during widely differing conditions in cloud cover and temperature. Light rain seems to matter little, but they are less active during periods of long heavy rain. I found that deer and elk kills had been made in the evening, at night, and mid-morning.

In winter, between kills, radio-tagged pumas traveled on average each day between 2 and 3 linear kilometers (1.2 to 1.9 miles) — the actual distance traveled was much farther — and they rarely spent more than one day in the same location. Males, especially transient males, moved significantly farther each day than females, and in summer averaged 5.5 kilometers (3.5 miles) a day. Snow-tracking pumas revealed that they seldom traveled along frozen waterways and trails, as did coyotes wintering in the same areas. Pumas zig-zagged back and forth through thickets, moved around large openings, under rock overhangs, up and down little ravines, and back and forth across small creeks. The impression I gained in tracking them was that using this procedure they were constantly moving through the country in a way

▲ During their first three months of life, puma cubs are left behind, in thick cover or in a cave, while their mother hunts. Later, their mother takes them with her to feed on kills and to explore and learn about their environment.

that optimized encounters with prey and provided them with the best possible positions in terms of cover from which to launch attacks.

When unknown pumas are tracked in the snow, their travels at first seem random and without bounds. This perception was emphasized in much of the early writing on pumas. My mentors, Maurice Hornocker and Wilbur Wiles, by recapturing marked pumas with hounds (in the lower Big Creek drainage, a major tributary of the Middle Fork of the Salmon River), demonstrated that the number of resident breeding adults in the area remained stable over a number of years and that the animals confined their movement to specific areas where they were captured year after year. In addition to the resident breeding adults, there was a component of younger adults in the population that moved through this area but did not remain. This idea of land tenure was confirmed through the radio-tracking methodology I used when I joined the project.

HOME AREAS

Radiotelemetry allowed us, for the first time, to accurately measure the size of puma home areas and the extent of puma movement. Winter and spring home areas of resident males varied from 41 to 220 square kilometers (16 to 85 square miles), and those of resident females varied from 31 to 105 square kilometers (12 to 40 square miles). Summer areas were adjacent to the winter and

spring home areas but extended into higher elevations; the summer area for one male was 292 square kilometers (113 square miles), and the summer area for females varied from 114 to 207 square kilometers (44 to 80 square miles). The total home area over a year was 453 square kilometers (175 square miles) for one male, and between 173 and 373 square kilometers (67 and 144 square miles) for four females. We found that the home areas of resident males were largely distinct from those of other males. The degree of overlap between the home areas of females varied from nearly total overlap for three females to partial separation for three others females.

Variation in the size of home areas of both males and females demonstrated that the amount of terrain a breeding puma used was not a simple function of body weight and metabolism or some psychological limit. We discovered that the land over which a puma roams is variable in terms of cover, topography, number of ungulates and carrying capacity, and vulnerability of prey. The size of a puma's winter area does not directly correlate with the density of deer and elk. For a stalking predator like the puma to succeed in killing a large and potentially dangerous ungulate, it must approach undetected to within a critical distance. This depends on a number of suitable environmental conditions, and not surprisingly prey are killed more often in some parts of the home area than in others. This variation in

▶ The puma has become rare wherever people dominate the landscape. In the United States, where the current puma range is about half the size of its historical range, pumas live almost exclusively in the mountains of the west, having been all but extirpated in the eastern United States during the nineteenth century. An exception is the remnant population of Florida panthers.

PUMAS IN CALIFORNIA

ROBIN MEADOWS

The question of hunting pumas (mountain lions) for sport in California has been hotly contested for decades. From the early 1900s to the early 1960s, the puma was hunted for bounty to protect livestock, but in 1963 it was designated a non-game animal because people were concerned that it might become extinct in California. Over the next two decades, the hunting status of the puma oscillated between game and non-game before returning to game status in 1986. However, since then, California pumas have still not been hunted for sport, in part because would-be hunters have been thwarted by lawsuits brought against them by anti-hunting groups. Standing at opposite poles of this controversial issue are the Mountain Lion Preservation Foundation (MLPF) and the California Department of Fish and Game (DFG), which is the department responsible for managing the state's wildlife.

The DFG recommends regulated hunting of pumas. According to their estimates, the California puma population has more than doubled since the early 1970s, reaching at least 5,100 in 1988, and pumas now occupy about half the land in the state. While acknowledging that habitat loss may threaten the

puma in parts of southern California, the DFG says that the statewide population is robust enough to sustain regulated hunting. One DFG proposal is that hunters be allowed to shoot some of the pumas that would be shot anyway, including those that are killing livestock or wild prey species that are threatened with extinction, such as bighorn sheep.

On the other hand, the MLPF opposes hunting pumas in California for any reason, saying that too little is known about their status. They argue that the DFG's population estimate is too high and that the number of livestock killed by pumas is too small to warrant hunting them. The MLPF says that only 5 percent of California's domestic sheep were killed by pumas while 11 percent were killed by domestic dogs. The MLPF further claims that pumas are severely threatened by the continuing loss of habitat, and that development has divided them into isolated groups, some of which may be too small to reproduce successfully.

The question of "to hunt or not to hunt" the puma was decided by California voters in 1990, when an initiative was passed banning the hunting of the puma for sport.

environmental structure results in differences in the suitability of home areas, the amount of terrain a resident puma uses, and the degree of overlap of female areas.

Site attachment for breeding adults as I have just described is not a requisite for survival, but rather a phenomenon that comes into play during the reproductive phase of the puma's life cycle. For a female with young, the best strategy for exploiting the food resources necessary for rearing kittens is to gain familiarity with, and attachment to, the best available site. Males, on the other hand, gain reproductive advantage by maintaining areas not inhabited by other breeding males. The more home areas with potentially breeding females they include the better, as long as they do not overextend. There appeared to be little or no overt aggression amongst the pumas we observed, although other investigators have observed puma males fighting. Land tenure in pumas is based on prior rights; puma home areas are altered in response to the death or movement of other residents, and young adults establish home areas only as vacancies become available.

The expected life span of adult pumas is long, and the resulting slow rate of population turnover means that vacant areas where young pumas might settle and successfully rear young are widely scattered. Vacancies can be found only through a non-restricted pattern of dispersal movement, that is, one that allows pumas to readily colonize new areas of habitat, such as those created by extensive fires (which create conditions suitable for the development of excellent ungulate habitat where it was previously nonexistent or marginal).

This pattern of dispersal adds yet one more dimension to the great flexibility and adaptability to environmental change that we see in pumas, and has led to a remarkable recovery in numbers and distribution through many areas in the western United States. Because pumas kill deer and elk, and sometimes kill cattle and horses, they were relentlessly hunted in the United States until at the end of World War II sizable puma populations remained only in the remote regions of the western mountains and in southern Florida. Eventually, in the mid-1960s, attitudes about the use of wildlands and the role of big predators in wilderness systems began to change. This led the states in which pumas remained to limit or place moratoriums on killing them, and poisoning was greatly curtailed. The puma responded to this protection in the west, but there was no such recovery in the eastern United States, even though there was a remarkable recovery in suitable habitat, and a great increase in the white-tailed deer population. With the exception of southern Florida there was simply no surviving remnant population from which a recovery was possible; and, it has to be said, even the future of the Florida puma is tenuous.

Stephen J. Krasemann/DRK Photo

CHEETAHS

TIM CARO

Cheetah is a word derived from the Hindu "chita" meaning spotted one. Cheetahs (*Acinonyx jubatus*) have several unique morphological features not found in other living felids: a slight build, long thin legs, and a small, delicate skull. Their light brown coat is covered with large and small solid, round, black spots that are scattered over the body. Some individuals, called "king" cheetahs, from Central Africa have a blotched coat as a result of possessing an identical pair of recessive alleles for coat pattern. *A. jubatus* is the last surviving species of at least four cheetah species that lived in both North America and the Old World during the Pleistocene (2 million–10,000 years ago). Seven subspecies are currently recognized from subtle differences in their coats, although analyses of the blood proteins suggests that the differences between some subspecies are trivial. *A. jubatus* once had a wide distribution throughout Africa and southwest Asia, but its range is now confined to savanna and Sudano-Sahel vegetation zones south of the Sahara. A relic population of perhaps 200 animals still survives in Iran and possibly northwest Afghanistan.

Cheetahs are notable not only for their beauty and unusual build, but also for their hunting technique which involves a concealed approach towards prey, followed by a sudden rapid dash and very fast chase of less than 300 meters (330 yards). They are much more active during the day than other cats, relying on visual means to locate their prey. As a result of these attributes, cheetahs were used for the sport of coursing in Asia prior to the Assyrian dynasty, in Libya during the reign of the Pharaohs, and by Mogul emperors in India between the thirteenth and sixteenth centuries. Despite prolonged attention from the nobility, the behavior and ecology of cheetahs has been documented only very recently.

► Female cheetahs live alone except when rearing cubs. Males live alone or in permanent groups of two to four, called coalitions. Males in coalitions are often siblings and share kills such as this springbok. In general, coalitions kill larger prey than lone males or females.

▼ In historical times, cheetahs (*Acinonyx jubatus*) ranged throughout the dry areas of Africa, the Arabian Peninsula, Asia Minor, and as far east as India. Today, substantial numbers of cheetahs survive only in Namibia and Kenya. In Asia, only fragmented populations remain.

SOCIAL STRUCTURE

Compared with other felids, cheetahs have a unique and highly flexible social structure. In East Africa, females live alone unless they have cubs accompanying them, a characteristic shared with females of other solitary species. Males, however, either live alone (approximately 40 percent of individuals) or in permanent groups of two (40 percent), three (20 percent), or occasionally four. These groups, termed coalitions, last throughout the lifetime of the males, a period of up to eight years in the wild. Coalitions are normally made up only of sibling males from the same litter, but approximately 30 percent also include additional, unrelated males. In southern Africa, persistent reports suggest that cheetahs live in larger groups containing more than one adult female, and also in groups containing adults of both sexes, but these accounts have yet to be confirmed.

In the Serengeti National Park in northern Tanzania, cheetah density is high, reaching 1 per 10 square kilometers (2.5 per 10 square miles). Female cheetahs have huge (800 square kilometer/ 310 square mile) annual home ranges because their movements closely follow the migratory routes of Thomson's gazelles, which make up 90 percent of the female cheetah's diet in this area. A female remains in one locality within her range for several weeks until hunting becomes poor, then she moves a few kilometers to an area with more prey. Annual ranges are too large to be defended effectively against other females and there is extensive range overlap; nevertheless, females do show avoidance behavior.

Clem Haagner/Ardea London

FOUND IN GROUPS

Years	Coalitions of males
Months	Mother with cubs
	Adolescent siblings
Months	
or days	Adolescents or lost
	cubs parasitising
	unrelated adults
Days	Males and females
	in consort

FOUND ALONE

Years	Single males
Months	Pregnant females
	Lactating females
	with cubs in den
	Single adolescents

▲ The social structure of free-living cheetahs is flexible, as the above table shows. For different periods of time and for various reasons, different social patterns are exhibited.

In contrast to females, some males (approximately 30 percent) scent mark and actively defend their territories against other males, but these ranges are much smaller (40 square kilometers/15.5 square miles) than those of their female counterparts. Other non-territorial males wander over large areas of the Park as do females. The siting of territories is fixed in that boundaries do not alter after a change of ownership. Each territory contains a certain amount of cover either in the form of vegetation growing in riverbeds or tall rocky outcrops on the savanna landscape. Large expanses of short grass plains between territories appear unsuitable for territory occupation. At any one time there is a maximum of 10 territories occupied on the Serengeti Plains and woodland border, and competition for these limited sites is severe, with males dying in contests over ownership. In fights, a male will first use its weight to pin down its opponent, and then attempt to suffocate it with a bite to the neck, while its coalition partners deliver repeated bites to the haunch and genitals. This fighting technique means that coalitions of males are better able to acquire territories and hold them than single males; single males become residents only if territories are voluntarily vacated or if there

are few coalitions to compete against. Competition for territories results in high mortality among males, skewing the adult sex ratio by as much as 1:2 in favor of females. Although the costs of territory acquisition and defense are great, the reproductive benefits are high because female cheetahs temporarily gather in territories during their annual migration, capitalizing both on cover and a high concentration of gazelles. As yet, it is unknown whether females choose to mate with certain males or give birth in particular territories.

REPRODUCTION AND DEVELOPMENT

Mating has been observed very rarely in the wild and is a brief affair lasting less than a minute; nevertheless, males often remain with females for as long as two days, either in anticipation of estrus or to guard the female after mating with her. When a male coalition locates a female there can be mild aggression between the males, but these confrontations are slight compared with fights between coalitions. In the single observation of a pair of males mating in the wild, both males copulated, suggesting paternity among some littermates may be mixed.

After a 90 to 95 day gestation period, as many as six, but usually fewer, cubs are born in a lair

CHEETAH SPEED

RICHARD A. KILTIE

If an Olympic competition could be arranged among the world's mammals species, cheetahs would likely win the gold medals in the 200 and 400 meter sprints (without steroid supplementation!). Obtaining precise, reliable measurements of the maximum speed of cheetahs has been difficult, but it is generally conceded to be about 110 km/h (68 mph). In comparison, some antelope have maximum speeds approaching 100 km/h (62 mph), canids about 70 km/h (44 mph) and humans about 40 km/h (25 mph). What gives cheetahs their celebrated swiftness?

A stride is one cycle of sequential footfalls, that is, two steps for a biped and four steps for a quadruped. The speed of an animal equals its stride frequency times its stride length. Anything that causes an animal to have a longer or quicker stride will increase its speed. Felids in general have anatomical adaptations that promote relatively long strides. These include a

digitigrade stance (only the "toes" touching the ground), lateral placement and heightened mobility of the scapula (the shoulder blade), and heightened flexibility of the spine. For increasing stride frequency the main adaptation consists of a reduction of the distal mass of the limbs, which serves to heighten the rate at which the limbs can be oscillated.

Cheetahs differ from other cat species primarily by taking these features a little bit further. In comparison to other large felids, cheetahs have proportionately somewhat longer limbs, longer scapulae, longer lumbar portions of the vertebral column (between the ribs and the pelvis, allowing greater spinal flexion), more consistently vertical orientation of the foot bones and leg bones, and larger muscles for flexing and extending the spine.

Considered one at a time, none of the cheetah's differences from other cat species is very large, but the net effect of them all is to make cheetahs champion sprinters.

situated among boulders, in tall vegetation, or a marsh. Cheetah cub mortality is very high during the first two months of life, but surviving cubs are brought out of the den at six to eight weeks and from then on accompany their mother. The cubs have a peculiar natal coat which is light gray and woolly on the cub's back and black on its belly. Many functions have been ascribed to this coat, but its main function is probably to camouflage cubs against carnivores, such as lions and spotted hyenas, and against raptors, such as martial eagles and crowned hawk eagles. The natal coat is entirely lost by four months, exactly the time cubs are strong and agile enough to outrun these predators. If a mother loses her litter during this time, she comes back into estrus within days.

Cheetah cubs are extremely playful from the time they first emerge from the den until eight months of age. They stalk, chase, and wrestle with each other, particularly during the first two hours of the day; some mothers take part in bouts of chasing and fleeing as well. Cubs begin to hunt many different species in their environment when they reach three months of age. Small birds such as francolins are the focus of most hunts by groups of young cubs, although they never catch them. At five months, cubs start to chase small carnivores, mostly jackals, but by the time they are eight months old, the cubs are mostly stalking inappropriately large prey, such as adult giraffes or elands. Cubs are actually responsible for less than 10 percent of the kills eaten by the family.

▲ This sequence of movements illustrates the rotary gallop of a sprinting cheetah. The hind limbs land first on alternate sides, and this is followed by a phase of floating, when no feet touch the ground. The forelimbs then land on alternate sides, and this is followed by a period of crossed flight, when all feet are gathered under the body.

▼ After an incredible burst of speed the cheetah will overtake this fleeing Thomson's gazelle. A slap to the gazelle's leg will trip and knock it down, and to kill, the cheetah will bite down on the animal's throat until it suffocates. Cheetahs must consume their prey quickly because lions, wild dogs, and hyenas readily steal their kills.

Mitsuaki Iwago

When cubs first leave the den and accompany their mother, she captures and kills prey for them as would any adult female. When the cubs are three months old the mother brings live prey, such as newborn Thomson's gazelles and hares, back to the cubs and releases it in front of them. The cubs canter after the fleeing prey and attempt to slap it to the ground; on the few occasions it escapes, the mother retrieves it for them. This way cubs soon learn to kill for themselves. Nevertheless, when they do separate from their mothers, at between 14 and 18 months, they are still very poor at capturing prey. Littermates remain together for up to six months after leaving their mother, but after that time the females leave their siblings. The male siblings stay together for life. The daughters range over an area that partially overlaps their mother's home range, but the sons establish territories that are 20 kilometers (12 miles) or more outside their natal range. Sexual maturity in females occurs at 20 to 24 months; in males it occurs at two and a half to three years of age.

Jonathan Scott/Planet Earth Pictures

▲ Separated from its mother and herd, a confused baby Thomson's gazelle is easy prey for a young cheetah in Kenya's Masai Mara Game Reserve. Inefficient hunters, young cheetahs frequently start their chase too early, allowing more experienced prey animals to escape.

▶ Three young cheetahs follow their mother on a late afternoon expedition on the East African plains. Cheetahs rest and sleep at night, generally hunting in the late morning and early evening when competition from nocturnal and crepuscular predators is less keen.

Cubs that are not yet fully grown but who have lost their family through ill fortune will attempt to associate with unrelated cheetah families or even male groups for as long as they can, sharing meat caught by the adult females or by the males. Single adolescents or adolescent groups have also been observed to latch on to an unrelated family for several weeks. Despite suffering aggression from the mother, parasitic cubs and adolescents seem to steal sufficient meat to survive and, for very incompetent hunters, this may be their only means of survival.

Arthus-Bertrand/Ardea London

CHEETAH CUB MORTALITY

KAREN LAURENSON

Cheetahs, like other felids, must conceal their newborn cubs in a lair or den for several weeks as the cubs are born blind and unable to walk. For these first six to eight weeks, cheetah cubs are reliant on their mother's milk, and they grow and develop quickly. After leaving the lair, the cubs follow their mother when she hunts and eat meat from her kills, finally leaving for an independent life at 14 to 18 months of age.

The first months of life are particularly critical for cheetah cubs. In the Serengeti National Park in Tanzania about 90 percent of all cubs born will die before reaching three months of age. Causes of mortality while the cubs are in the lair include predation, abandonment by the mother, grassfires, disease, exposure, and possibly infanticide by cheetah males. Of these, predation imposes the heaviest toll, accounting for more than 50 percent of deaths. Lions, spotted hyenas, jackals, and birds of prey will kill cubs if they find them. Cubs have no defense except to hiss and spit. If prey is scarce, mothers may be absent from the lair for up to 48 hours while hunting. Furthermore, if she is unable to kill sufficient prey to meet the extra demands of lactation, she may be forced to abandon her litter. This may be a relatively frequent occurrence in areas where cheetahs rely on migratory prey because prey can move beyond the mother's commuting distance from the den.

Cubs that do survive to two months are still extremely vulnerable. While in the lair the cubs are at least partly concealed from predators, but once they begin to follow their mother they are all too visible. They are unable to run fast enough to escape attacks, and they may not even recognize predators as being dangerous. Their normal response to an attack is to scatter, so it is unlikely that a predator would run after and kill the whole litter at one time. Nevertheless, by three months of age three out of five cubs, on average, that left the lair will have died.

Cheetah mothers do change their behavior to minimize the vulnerability of their cubs to predators. Where possible, they choose a lair that offers good protection and one that is away from other predators. They will move the cubs a short distance to a new lair about every five days, probably to prevent the build-up of odors that undoubtedly occurs. When returning to the lair, they are extremely vigilant and may sometimes wait until after dark to join their cubs, thereby not drawing attention to the location of their den. In comparison to females that are on their own, mothers with small cubs are very alert to danger. Mothers may aggressively attack a predator by rushing at it, slapping it, and chasing it off, even if it is posing no immediate threat. However, being small and lacking powerful jaws, a female cheetah is still relatively defenseless against a group of lions or hyenas or a single, determined, large carnivore. In some cases, therefore, she endeavors to lead the cubs away.

Throughout their range in Africa, cheetahs exist at low densities compared to other major predators. With cub mortality so high, cheetah populations seem to be limited primarily by the number of young that can be raised to maturity. As predation is the most important cause of cub mortality,

Mark Deeble and Victoria Stone

▲ These three baby cheetahs were killed in their den by a female lion while their mother was away hunting. To avoid predation during the early months of their lives, cheetahs rely on their mother's protection as well as concealment in dens and heavy vegetation. Larger carnivores, however, are not intimidated by the mother and may drive her away and kill the young. The mother's ability to protect her young is further reduced because she may have to be away from her cubs for up to 48 hours at a time to kill enough prey for herself and the cubs. In the Serengeti National Park in Tanzania, about 90 percent of all cubs born die before reaching three months of age.

cheetahs may be able to raise larger litters where other predators have been eliminated or exist at low densities, for example, on livestock ranches or pastoral areas. In Namibia, a large population of cheetahs was once tolerated on ranches, and the average litter size was reported to be four, as compared to approximately two in East African parks. Thus, protected areas, while ensuring a plentiful supply of prey, may actually keep cheetah numbers below carrying capacity because of the protection also given to large predators. In evolutionary terms, the large litter size of cheetahs (up to eight recorded in captivity) compared to other felid species may be a strategy for maximizing reproductive success in those few situations where litters do survive the numerous causes of mortality.

John Downer/Planet Earth Pictures

HUNTING AND FEEDING

In Serengeti, cheetahs do not become proficient hunters until they are at least three years old. Independent adolescent and young females are less successful at catching prey than adults mainly because they fail to crouch down when gazelles are scanning their surroundings for danger and so are often seen by their quarry. Also, they tend to start their unconcealed rush towards prey too early, allowing prey to get a head start on them. Finally, younger cheetahs abandon chases prematurely, apparently not daring to knock prey over even though they are gaining on it.

Cheetahs normally take medium-sized ungulate prey in the 20 to 50 kilogram (44 to 110 pound) range. In Kafue National Park in Zambia, they kill mostly puku; in Namibia they take springbok; and in the Transvaal and Kruger National Parks they take impala. In East African parks, Thomson's gazelles, impala, and Grant's gazelles are chosen. These are only general descriptions because on the Serengeti Plains prey preferences are strongly dependent on the size and ages of the cheetah hunting party. Among

males, coalition members stay together while hunting, and normally choose to hunt wildebeests weighing 80 kilograms (176 pounds) or more; single males usually hunt adult Thomson's gazelles in the 20 kilogram (44 pound) range, even though they are capable of pulling down wildebeests on their own. Coalitions have no greater hunting success than single males but when they do kill, the prey that they capture is large enough to provide each coalition member with more meat, even after dividing it three ways (for example), than a lone male gains from a single kill.

Like adult male coalitions, groups of adolescent littermates seem to prefer capturing large prey, such as adult and subadult Thomson's gazelles, whereas adolescents that are on their own hunt small newborn gazelles and hares. When littermates hunt together one adolescent often takes over the chase and knocks the prey down even if its sibling is unable to. However, cheetah littermates do not stay together because they have greater hunting success, rather, it is because groups suffer less harassment from spotted hyenas and rival male cheetahs.

▲ Cheetahs prefer flat, open habitats, where their view of the surrounding area is unobstructed. Cheetahs are more diurnal in their activity patterns than other cats, and so may rely more on their visual sense to detect prey. Cheetahs often use high vantage points like broken tree limbs and rock outcroppings to survey the surroundings both for prey and potential predators.

THE GENETIC PERIL OF THE CHEETAH

STEPHEN J. O'BRIEN

The cheetah is descended from a handful of survivors of a global extinction that occurred at the end of the last Ice Age, more than 10,000 years ago. Before then, the cheetah roamed throughout North America, Europe, Asia and Africa. After the global catastrophe, which eliminated the mammoths, the mastodons, the giant ground sloths, and sabertooth cats, the cheetah survived only in certain regions of Africa and Central Asia. The cheetah is still paying a steep price for its survival of those prehistoric events.

Our knowledge of the cheetah's legacy grew out of the frustrations of private breeders and zoological curators unable to breed cheetahs in captivity. A physiological explanation for the cheetah's reproductive difficulties emerged when scientists examined cheetah spermatozoa and found a low sperm count and a high degree of developmental abnormalities in the sperm. These reproductive defects were congenital abnormalities resulting from the expression of damaging genes that appear when close relatives interbreed. When the techniques of molecular biology were applied to the cheetah, a startling genetic situation was found: the cheetah turned out to be remarkably homogeneous.

Individuals of any species have approximately 100,000 genes, and most species of animals have molecular genetic diversity in 30 to 50 percent of them. The cheetahs were found to have 10 to 100 times less variation in their intrinsic genetic material than is normally found in other cat species, or indeed, in mouse or man. Cheetahs are so similar to each other in genetic terms that they do not recognize individual differences between surgically exchanged tissue grafts. Such genetic uniformity had never been discovered in a free-ranging population before. The only time that comparable genetic uniformity was achieved was in deliberately inbred laboratory mice or livestock.

The genetic findings told us that the cheetah must have had a unique history, one that involved extensive interbreeding among close relatives despite instinctive tendencies in mammals to avoid incest. We now think that the cheetah was headed for extinction at the end of the Pleistocene, about 10,000 years ago, but that by some stroke of luck the species survived — perhaps it was only a single pregnant female that survived the holocaust. We were not there, so it is impossible to be precise about the exact scenario, yet the consequences in the cheetah today are apparent and troubling. The species as a whole is suffering from the effects of what we call inbreeding depression. When breeding between related individuals occurs there is an increase in the expression of mutant genes that have accumulated over time, but they are not normally damaging because their effect is offset by a second normal gene. (We inherit two genes for every trait, one from each parent.) Inbreeding causes an increase in the incidence of two unhealthy genes in the same individual.

A second peril that threatens the cheetah's survival is not so obvious, but may be more insidious. A species that sheds indigenous genetic diversity homogenizes the genes that encode the components of the immune system. This causes the entire species to be susceptible to infectious disease agents, viruses or pathogens, which periodically evolve into a form that can overcome the disease defenses of a single individual. Unfortunately this danger has recently been realized in a series of outbreaks of a nearly benign virus, feline infectious peritonitis virus, which decimated a number of captive cheetah colonies. The virus has a mortality rate of 1 to 5 percent in genetically diverse domestic cats; the same virus killed 50 to 60 percent of the cheetahs in recent outbreaks.

Does the remarkable genetic hangover of the cheetah spell doom for the species? The answer is not necessarily, because there are some encouraging signs. First, the cheetah is a survivor; it has survived and even increased to tens of thousands since its ancestors passed through the ancient population bottleneck. The lion's share of the damage of a population contraction occurs in the first few generations, so the cheetah's survival is actually a success story as much as a scary one. Second, there are at least two subspecies of cheetahs in Africa and their hybridization might actually improve the cheetah's chances. Third, there are other threatened species that have survived similar bottlenecks (for example, the northern elephant seal) and gone on to increase their numbers dramatically after the implementation of legislative protection. The cheetah's future may be in our hands, and the irony of the story may be that while technological advances are eliminating the habitat of this treasured but endangered species, they may also play a key role in orchestrating the survival of the cheetah.

▼ This king cheetah from Transvaal, South Africa, represents the results of a captive breeding program, which focuses on rare or unusual color forms rather than on maintaining the genetic integrity of the species. The king cheetah displays a rare coat pattern type, and it was once thought to be a separate species. Modern captive breeding programs strive to ensure that all of the genetic diversity of a species survives. This is particularly important for cheetahs because they have one of the lowest levels of genetic diversity found in any group of wild mammals.

Gerald Cubitt

Steve Bentsen

CONSERVATION

In the early 1970s, a survey showed that the world population of cheetahs totalled approximately 14,000 animals only, down from an estimated 28,000 recorded 15 years earlier. Individuals were still distributed widely across 25 African countries but existed at low densities; only in Kenya, Botswana and Namibia did numbers exceed 2,000 animals. Even in protected areas, densities were low compared with lions and spotted hyenas, probably as a result of the very high rates of cub mortality and adult deaths (resulting from intrasexual combat).

Cheetahs are classified as endangered, being listed in Appendix 1 (which includes species that are most threatened) to the Convention of International Trade in Endangered Species (CITES). The main threat to their survival across Africa is thought to be habitat encroachment, caused by the spread of agriculture into areas formerly used by pastoralists for grazing cattle. On a regional basis, uncontrolled and sophisticated hunting from vehicles of dama and dorcas gazelles has almost certainly contributed to the decline of cheetahs in the Sahel. In Namibia, cheetahs are shot legally as vermin, and hunting of cheetahs has just started again in Zimbabwe. In southern Africa and in the Horn of Africa, a limited skin trade exists. In all probability, the only long-term prospects for survival are in areas with effective protection, but even here cheetahs are threatened by high densities of predators. An investigation into the status of cheetahs in Africa and new ways of protecting them is currently under way.

In captivity, cheetahs have a poor breeding record. Only one litter of three cubs was reputedly raised in the stable of 3,000 cheetahs belonging to Akbar, the Mogul emperor. The next litter was born in the 1950s, and although breeding performance is far better now, fewer than 25 percent of adults breed more than once. Currently the Species Survival Plan under the auspices of the American Association of Zoological Parks and Aquariums (AAZPA) has a research team investigating behavioral, physiological, and other aspects of captive breeding in order to solve the problem. Even though a self-sustaining captive population would halt the continued export of free-living cheetahs to zoos, there are no firm plans to reintroduce cheetahs from captivity into the wild and, at present, captive breeding represents little more than a holding action.

▲ Coalitions of male cheetahs defend territories that include areas suitable for breeding females to den and protect their young cubs. This is costly for males, as good territories are in short supply. Many males are killed in fierce territorial fights with other coalitions. As a result, adult females may outnumber adult males by a ratio of two to one.

▼ Young cheetahs lose their distinctive natal coats at about four months of age, which is when they are agile enough to outrun most potential predators. This is also the time when mother and cubs are ready to leave the den areas for good and begin to lead nomadic lives following migrating herds of gazelle.

Jonathan Scott/Planet Earth Pictures

BOBCATS AND LYNXES

S. DOUGLAS MILLER

It was actually just a blur shooting across the path in front of me, but I knew instantly that I had finally seen my first wild bobcat. Or had I really seen anything? The mind does play tricks, and it happened so quickly and unexpectedly as I was walking along that South Alabama riverbed almost 20 years ago. However, apparitions don't leave tracks, and the spoor confirmed my sighting. During the next six years of research on this species, I was privileged to observe many bobcats throughout the southeastern United States but what I still remember most is that first "meeting."

▲ The Eurasian lynx (*Lynx lynx*) ranges through Europe as well as temperate and boreal Asia. It is one of five species within the *Lynx* genus; the others include the bobcat (*L. rufus*) of Mexico and the United States, the North American lynx (*L. canadensis*) of the northern United States, Canada, and Alaska, the Spanish lynx (*L. pardinus*), found only on the Iberian Peninsula, and the caracal (*L. caracal*), whose range encompasses the dry areas of Africa, the Middle East, Asia Minor, and India.

Historically the North American lynx (*Lynx canadensis*) was widely distributed in northern North America, throughout all of Canada except Prince Edward Island, reaching south into the northern tier of the United States; the bobcat (*L. rufus*) was present in all 48 adjoining states and northern Mexico; the Eurasian lynx (*L. lynx*) was most broadly distributed throughout the boreal forests of Europe and the Soviet Union with scattered populations in Palestine, India, China, and Pakistan; and the Spanish lynx (*L. pardinus*) was distributed throughout the Iberian Peninsula. Today, only the bobcat retains most of its original distribution, though populations in some states are very low and are given complete protection. Over the past 100 years, changing land uses, coupled with heavy hunting, have contributed to the significant reduction in the range of the Eurasian lynx. The Spanish lynx is also much reduced in numbers and occurs primarily in the south of Spain and in parts of Portugal. After years of decline due to habitat loss, the North American lynx is making a comeback in the upper areas of the United States.

Within the genus *Lynx*, the bobcat exhibits the greatest success in adapting to varying habitat conditions. Viable populations are found in areas as diverse as Georgia's coastal marshes, the Arizona desert, the Maine woods, and the Colorado Rocky Mountains. Both North American and Eurasian lynxes are most often found in association with large unbroken expanses of northern evergreen forests. The Spanish lynx appears to be midway between the others in its habitat preference.

What makes a *Lynx* a *Lynx*? Members of this group appear similar in several features. They are all medium-sized cats, with a gray or tawny coat and varying degrees of black spots, dorsal stripes, and barring on the legs. Although coloration varies greatly among lynxes and bobcats, bobcats tend to range in color from a rusty red to a yellowish brown to gray; the North American lynx is most commonly gray or light brown with faint spotting; the Eurasian lynx is gray to yellowish gray; and the Spanish lynx is the most heavily spotted. They all have a prominent facial ruff and their ears are tipped with tufts of black hair. This latter feature is

particularly pronounced in the Eurasian lynx, which also has heavily furred paws, an apparent adaptation for surviving and hunting in snow country. All have a relatively short tail, which, in the North American, Eurasian, and Spanish lynxes, is tipped completely in black, and in the bobcat is tipped black on the dorsal surface and white on the ventral surface. The ventral surface, or belly, of these cats is usually heavily spotted, and it is this single trait that has accelerated the demand for lynx and bobcat pelts since the 1975 ban on international trade in the pelts of other spotted cats, including ocelots, leopards, and cheetahs.

The annual harvest of bobcats and North American and Eurasian lynxes is regulated and there is no legal harvest of the Spanish lynx, which is considered an endangered species.

Among bobcats and lynxes, tail lengths vary from 11 to 24 centimeters (4.5 to 9.5 inches), total body lengths (including tail) from 65 to 130 centimeters (25.5 to 51.25 inches), height at the shoulder from 45 to 75 centimeters (17.75 to 29.5 inches), and weight of adults from 4 to 38 kilograms (9 to 84 pounds). However, the typical average weight is 8 to 14 kilograms (17.5 to 31 pounds). The females are generally smaller than

▼ The Eurasian lynx (*Lynx lynx*), pictured below, and the North American lynx (*L. canadensis*) possess large paws with thick fur padding. These paws function like snowshoes to improve locomotion on ice and snow — an important adaptation for these cats which inhabit coniferous forest habitats that are covered in ice and snow for much of the year. Relatively large body size and long soft fur are other adaptations of these cats for life in cold climates.

Michael S. Quinton

the males in all of the *Lynx* species. With few exceptions, the upper end of the above measurements represent the Eurasian lynxes of the Soviet Union, followed by the North American lynx, the Spanish lynx, and then the smallest, the bobcat. The relatively high shoulder height and thick fur of bobcats and lynxes makes them appear much larger than they actually are.

FEEDING HABITS

Prior to 1950, most of the research on bobcats and lynxes tended to be either taxonomic or anecdotal accounts of distribution and general behavior. It was not until the late 1940s and 1950s that the

▲ ▶ A bobcat (*Lynx rufus*) stalks a muskrat then, using its forepaws, flips and grabs the rodent before delivering a killing bite to the neck. While bobcats and lynxes kill a wide variety of prey — from birds to adult white-tailed deer and caribou calves — the mainstay of their diets is rabbit and hare. Population numbers of bobcats and northern-dwelling lynxes vary in accordance with prey abundance, which can fluctuate greatly from year to year.

Michael S. Quinton

▶ (Opposite page) The Spanish lynx (*Lynx pardinus*) is distinguished from the Eurasian lynx (*L. lynx*) by its small size and well-defined spotting. The Spanish lynx inhabits open forests and thickets, and its range once overlapped with that of the Eurasian lynx. Today, this endangered species exists only in a few remote areas of the Iberian Peninsula, primarily in the southwest.

Michael S. Quinton

feeding habits of bobcats and lynxes were examined. Bobcats and lynxes are opportunistic and will take advantage of any potential food situation, which results in maximizing energy-gain versus energy-expended. This, of course, is not a conscious decision but rather a result of eons of natural selection. A list of the food items found in a year-long study of any of the lynxes or the bobcat, could easily top 45 items, and have a representative from every class in the animal kingdom. However, when one looks at the data by frequency of occurrence, it becomes quite obvious that bobcats and lynxes specialize in the capture of animals about the size of the lagomorphs (rabbits or hares). Rodents (rats, squirrels, and mice) are usually second in observed frequency. There is much documentation that suggests that the North American lynx in Canada is so dependent upon snowshoe and other hares that their numbers fluctuate in a regular 10-year cycle following the boom and bust of hare populations. A phenomenon called "switching" has been observed in some North American lynxes, where during periods of hare scarcity they are able to switch to an alternative prey without experiencing a major population decline.

There are also seasonal differences in the food habits of bobcats and lynxes. Large prey, including a number of cervids (members of the deer family), occur in their diets more frequently in the winter and early summer than at any other time. The winter is a time when deer are stressed and the lynxes are able to take advantage of heavy snow conditions to kill them. Bobcats and lynxes kill deer and other large animals by biting through their trachea (windpipe) and holding on until the animal suffocates. The occurrence of deer in the diet of bobcats and lynxes in late spring is also likely because of the increased availability of newborn and young animals. The Eurasian lynx, particularly the larger individuals in Scandinavia and the Soviet Union, are reported to kill deer and other large prey more frequently than other members of the *Lynx* genus. The Spanish lynx preys heavily on rabbits and waterfowl.

Bobcats and lynxes are solitary except during the mating season; they are also secretive, and generally thought to be nocturnal. However, recent studies have documented that there are two peaks of increased activity during a typical 24-hour period. These are at dusk and dawn, with several resting times during the night, indicating that the lynxes are crepuscular rather than nocturnal. Their method of hunting is fairly typical for the cat family; lacking great speed, they rely on their well-developed senses of vision and hearing to locate prey. Once a potential meal is detected, a bobcat or lynx makes a slow deliberate stalk, keeping its body as concealed as possible. When within striking distance (about 10 meters/33 feet), it makes a bounding rush toward its prey. If it misses

Ferrero-Labat/Jacana

SKIN TRADE

For one to understand the current status of bobcats and lynxes, it is necessary to review not only their biology but also the equally significant role that politics and international trade have had on these species. Lacking the fabled ferocity of lions and tigers, these medium-sized members of the cat family are seldom the leading characters of fairy tales or myths. But this is not to say that they haven't been credited with the demise of every missing fowl, lamb, piglet, or small game animal since time immemorial! Their purported villainy, deserved or not, resulted in a bounty being placed upon them in North America and throughout much of Europe. Bounties may have had some impact upon local populations, and the efforts to eliminate predators in general contributed to significant reductions in historical ranges. The latter is particularly true for the Eurasian and Spanish lynxes. Little was known about bobcats and lynxes, but there seemed to be little concern that any of them were in any particular danger of extinction throughout the first half of this century.

This anonymity ended rather abruptly in 1975 when the Convention of International Trade in Endangered Species (CITES) placed the ocelot, the tiger, and the cheetah on its Appendix I list. CITES was established in 1974 because of the concern that international trade was contributing to the decline of certain plant and animal species. Nearly 100 countries are now party to the terms of CITES, which basically categorizes plants and animals into one of three Appendices (I, II, or III) depending upon their trade-related vulnerability to extinction. An Appendix I listing provides the most protection, by banning all commercial trade in those species or the products made from those species. With the exception of a rare Mexican subspecies of the bobcat (*Lynx rufus escuinape*), the remaining species and subspecies of the *Lynx* genus were placed by default onto the Appendix II list, the members of which could be traded internationally if "closely" monitored. When the legal trade in pelts of the large spotted cats stopped in 1975, fur buyers and furriers rushed to find a suitable substitute. The spotted "belly" fur of the bobcat and lynx became the substitute, and harvest levels from the United States and Canada rose dramatically, reaching over 84,000 in 1984.

Regulated international trade in these cats continues today amid a growing controversy surrounding the wearing of furs. Though the market for bobcat and lynx furs has leveled off, it is still significantly higher than before 1975. In a one to two year period after that decision, prices for bobcat pelts rose from US$10-$15 to an average of $125, with $250 not being unusual for an exceptional one. The rise in value of a lynx pelt was even more dramatic, often exceeding $600. An estimated 60,000 to 80,000 bobcats and 18,000 to 20,000 North American lynxes were entering the international market as late as 1987. The Eurasian lynx, which is harvested in the Soviet Union and Scandinavia, contributed 6,000 to 7,000 skins to this market. The data that have been collected in the past 15 years, along with the annual harvest and monitoring surveys, suggest that in North America most populations of bobcat and lynx are stable or increasing. In Europe major populations of lynx are present in Scandinavia and the Soviet Union, while there are smaller populations in eastern Europe. There have been several attempts to reintroduce the lynx into Austria, Germany, and Switzerland, but these have achieved only partial success because of opposition from farmers, who fear predation on livestock, and hunters who fear competition for roe and red deer. The Spanish lynx remains in fairly low numbers, being most common in central Spain and the Coto Donana in the south of Spain.

▼ Coats made of cat fur are becoming increasing unpopular in the West.

Zefa-BAUER

on the initial pounce, as is frequently the case —
the success rate is about one in six — it rarely
pursues the prey very far.

REPRODUCTION

Reproductive behavior is similar among all
members of the *Lynx* genus. They come together
briefly for mating between December and April,
with the earliest breeding occurring at the lower
latitudes of their distribution. A male may breed
with a number of different females but females
typically mate with only one male. Following
mating, the male and female part company and the
female is solely responsible for raising the one to
six (but usually two to four) kittens born after a
63 to 70 day gestation period. Den-site selection
varies but is typically in a cave, under a rock ledge,
in a hollow log, or under the upturned roots of a
fallen tree. Kittens are born with their eyes sealed,
and they open after nine or ten days. Lactation lasts
for three to four months, though kittens begin to
eat some meat during their second month, and
they stay with the female until the beginning of

Marty Cordano/DRK Photo

▲ Bobcats (*Lynx rufus*) are blind and
helpless at birth, but they mature quickly.
By about nine months of age, they are
independent of their mother, and able to
catch small prey. Females can breed in
the spring following their birth, and
thereafter produce one litter per year.

◄ A bobcat (*Lynx rufus*) resting on a
bird's nest in Arizona. While bobcats
and lynxes readily climb trees to escape
predators like pumas, wolves, and dogs,
they spend most of their time on the
ground. These animals are also strong
swimmers and have been known to cross
wide rivers.

the next breeding season. Female kittens are capable of breeding in their first year, while males do not become sexually mature until their second year. Young males typically disperse and travel long distances in search of a suitable unoccupied territory, whereas females often settle near, or partially within, the range of their mother. Whether or not first-year females breed is dependent upon the availability of prey and the overall population density of lynxes or bobcats in the area. If prey is limited, or the cat population is

► A bobcat (*Lynx rufus*) in north-western Montana. Montana and northern Idaho are among the last strongholds of this species in the conterminous United States. They once ranged as far south as Colorado in the west and as far as Pennsylvania and Illinois in the east.

▲ North American lynxes (*Lynx canadensis*) are generally solitary. Females raise young without male assistance and they live in exclusive home ranges. Large male home ranges sometimes overlap those of other males and usually overlap several female home ranges. When prey populations collapse, however, lynxes may abandon their home ranges to seek areas where pockets of prey remain.

high, then breeding is unlikely, although the likelihood of dispersal to a new area is greater. Lynxes and bobcats can live for 15 years or more in the wild, retaining their reproductive capabilities for that time.

HOME RANGES

By analyzing radiotelemetry data, biologists have found that the home-range requirement of bobcats and lynxes vary seasonally, and depend on both the availability of prey and the presence of other cats of the same species. They also vary depending upon the sex and age of the individual. Home ranges vary from 6.5 to 240 square kilometers (2.5 to 92.5 square miles) for the North American lynx; from 12 to 100 square kilometers

(4.5 to 39 square miles) for the Spanish lynx; 15 to 120 square kilometers (5.75 to 46.5 square miles) for the Eurasian lynx and 0.9 to 42 square kilometers (0.4 to 16.2 square miles) for the bobcat. Generally male home ranges are larger than female home ranges; and while female ranges seldom overlap, male ranges often encompass two or more female ranges. In fact adjacent adult male ranges may overlap separate ends of one female's range. Adult ranges are larger than juvenile ranges, and juveniles are tolerated within the range of an adult until they become sexually mature. In the northern latitudes and in areas of low prey density, the home ranges are typically larger.

The question of whether or not lynxes and bobcats will defend their home range from

members of the same species has not been fully answered. Different studies have revealed varying degrees of "territoriality." Generally though, bobcats and lynxes maintain exclusive home ranges. In addition to this apparent spatial separation, these cats maintain a temporal or time separation by avoiding being near adjacent or marginally overlapping areas at the same time, except of course during mating. Home range or territorial boundaries are probably conveyed through scent marking, which helps the cats avoid injury caused by direct conflict—a serious situation for a solitary predator. When a territory becomes vacant through the death of an occupant, other cats move in very quickly, often within a couple of days, to claim all or part of the area. This suggests

that the maintenance and adjustment of home ranges is a dynamic process.

Bobcats and lynxes are predators that have demonstrated their resilience and adaptability by surviving a wide range of threats and by living in many varied habitats. Although their harvest for international trade will likely continue, it is at least regulated. The far more serious and impending threat to bobcats and lynxes is the continuing fragmentation and loss of habitat as a result of the growth of our population, and our ever-increasing demands on the natural environment. To maintain viable populations of these species, land managers must develop a better understanding of, and respect for, the habitat requirements of these fascinating cats.

OCELOTS AND SERVALS

FIONA C. SUNQUIST AND MEL SUNQUIST

The ocelot (*Felis pardalis*) and serval (*Felis serval*) are medium-sized cats with different evolutionary histories. They live on separate continents in very different habitats: ocelots live in forests whereas servals generally hunt in more open woodlands and grasslands. However, both cats make their living catching essentially the same type of food — small rodents.

STRUCTURE AND FUNCTION

Scientists generally agree that the archetypal felid was a forest-dwelling cat. It was certainly an agile climber and leaper, which probably lived by catching rodents and other small prey in dense cover. Today, the ocelot and the majority of the world's small- and medium-sized cats make their living in a similar way. Camouflaged by their dappled coats, they live primarily by hunting rodents in forests and woodland.

▲ Until ocelots (*Felis pardalis*) were protected by the International Convention of Trade in Endangered Species in 1975, their beautiful spotted coats were much in demand by furriers. Ocelots remain rare throughout their range from southern Texas through Central America, and as far as Argentina in South America.

▶ Elegant with their long legs and large ears, servals (*Felis serval*) are almost fox-like in appearance. They inhabit well-watered grasslands, are primarily rodent hunters, and they do well even in close proximity to people.

Potential rodent prey is not, however, confined to forests. In Africa and other parts of the world, rodents can be far more abundant in open grasslands than they are in tropical forests. For instance, in the Serengeti the Nile rat has been known to reach biomass densities as high as 470 kilograms per square kilometer (2,680 pounds per square mile), this being roughly five times greater than rodent density in the tropical rainforest of Cocha Cashu in Peru. Though savanna rodents are usually eaten by birds and foxes, some cat species such as the serval have evolved behaviors and physical characteristics that allow them to take advantage of this abundant food resource.

A cursory glance reveals that ocelots and servals are superficially quite similar. Both are medium-sized spotted cats that weigh about 10 to 12 kilograms (22 to 26 pounds). But a closer look reveals some striking differences. Whereas the ocelot has typical felid proportions, the serval looks a bit like the cat world's version of a giraffe.

Stalking through the grasslands on their stilt-like legs, servals seem strangely uncatlike in shape. Rather than the compact crouching body plan of the ocelot and most other cats, the serval seems designed to attain maximum height. A small slim face dominated by a pair of large ears sits atop a very long neck. Relatively, the serval also has the longest legs of any member of the cat family, and its front legs are considerably longer than its hind legs. Long legs usually mean speed, but the serval is not a particularly fast runner. This is because, strictly speaking, it is not the serval's legs that are long but its feet! Elongated metatarsal bones in the

Bruce Davidson/Animals Animals

▲ Although sometimes hunted for their spotted fur, servals seem to be holding their own in their range in sub-Saharan Africa. Servals were once found in the Atlas Mountains of North Africa, but have not been seen there for many years.

▶ Ocelots either walk slowly or sit and wait while hunting. Whether living in semi-desert (above) or dense forest (below), stalking ocelots take advantage of all available cover and the camouflage of their coat to conceal their approach. When close to prey, ocelots pounce, then bite and shake the animal until it is dead. They take a variety of small prey, primarily rodents.

they occupy a fairly narrow set of microhabitats, and are highly dependent on dense cover. Because they can climb well and are often found resting in trees, ocelots were previously thought to spend most of their time in trees. Radiotelemetry studies have proved differently. Ocelots, in fact, do almost all their hunting on the ground and only occasionally choose trees as rest sites during the daytime. Ocelots are strong swimmers and are able to cross rivers and move between patches of high ground in seasonally flooded habitats. They are active mainly at night but can sometimes be found hunting during the day, especially during cloudy or rainy weather.

Servals live only on the continent of Africa, in well-watered grasslands, scrub, woodlands, or reed beds. They can climb but only do so occasionally — when pursuing a particularly tempting meal or when they are being hunted by dogs. Usually they hunt and rest on the ground.

HUNTING
A hunting serval walks slowly through the high grass, scanning the area for sounds. This cat uses its huge dish-like ears to focus in on the rustlings made by rodents as they move unseen through vegetation. A hunting serval is so tuned in to sounds that it may stop and sit for 10 minutes or more, eyes closed, just listening. The specialized "sound hunting" technique of the serval is so sensitive that a strong wind can interfere with its ability to pinpoint prey. Unless they are extremely hungry, these cats rarely bother to hunt in windy weather; instead they rest and wait, postponing the hunt until the wind dies down.

As soon as it hears something move in the grass, the serval swivels its head and pinpoints the exact position of the sound. Then, after a short careful approach, it pounces like a fox, springing high with all four feet off the ground. If the first attempt misses, the serval will follow its prey with a swift succession of stiff-legged jumps — chin tucked into its chest, tail up, bouncing high into the air as if on a trampoline.

Servals also use the high bouncing pounce to flush animals from cover. They gallop through the grass in a zig-zag pattern, leaping high into the air; anything that moves is caught immediately. Other cat species use a combination of sight and hearing to catch their prey, but keen eyesight is not much help when dense grass and vegetation make small prey essentially invisible. The serval relies instead on its huge ears to pinpoint the noises made by potential prey. In order to get an accurate fix on the sound, the serval needs an elevated vantage point, hence the long legs.

Besides providing a vantage point for the serval to "hear into" tall grass, this cat's long legs also pack a powerful punch. The serval uses its front feet to deliver a series of formidable blows that can kill or stun prey. When hunting a larger

palms and soles of the serval's feet add inches to its height. An adult serval can stand more than 60 centimeters (24 inches) high at the shoulder, and may be 20 or more centimeters (8 or more inches) taller than an otherwise similar-sized ocelot.

Compared to the highly specialized serval, the ocelot has the typical cat-like shape. A heavily spotted coat is the ocelot's most variable characteristic, and its short close fur can range from cream to tawny yellow or gray, with solid or open-centered dark spots that sometimes form chains or stripes.

Ocelots are found in South and Central America, and in a small portion of North America. However, within this broad geographical range, animal that might fight back, the serval springs up into the air, strikes hard with all four feet, bites, and then leaps away. Servals can kill quite large snakes by bashing them with a series of swift hammer-like blows.

Cats are not known for their digging abilities but servals can, and often do, dig for their meals. Huge ears make their hearing so acute that they can actually locate prey underground, and they frequently use their long toes, which are tipped with strong curved claws, to hook rodents and fledgling birds out of tunnels. Servals have also learned a highly refined "dig and wait" technique that they use specifically to catch African mole rats, which are generally difficult to catch as they live exclusively underground in long tunnels: a serval locates a mole rat tunnel, scratches a hole in it, then sits and waits with one paw upraised (ready to capitalize on the fact that mole rats hasten to repair any damage to their tunnel system); at the first sign of movement, the serval slams its paw down, hooks the mole rat and flings it away; the serval then follows with a lightning pounce before the stunned victim can recover.

The serval also uses the "hook and jab" technique for catching fish, and captive servals have been observed to hook fish out of a basin of water with several fast jabs of a foreleg and a deft scoop of the wrist. Like ocelots, servals seem to have an affinity for water. They often hunt in foot-deep water, in marshes and shallow pools, where they stalk wading birds and catch frogs. One scientist working in Tanzania watched a young serval catch and eat at least 28 frogs of different sizes in a three-hour period.

Whether it is feeding on frogs or mice, the serval's big ears, uncatlike shape and specialized hunting technique translate into more meals per pounce than the average cat, which is lucky if it gets one meal for every 10 hunting attempts. Nearly one in every two of the serval's pounces results in a kill, making it one of the most successful of all feline hunters.

Like the serval, ocelots use two basic strategies to catch prey — they either walk slowly or sit and wait. The slow "hunting-walk" technique of the ocelot involves moving very slowly, watching and listening for prey. When the cat sees or hears something it stops, then, taking advantage of all the available cover and its camouflaged coat, it carefully stalks the prey until it is within range. A quick pounce, bite, and shake, and the ocelot has its meal. Using this technique, ocelots probably kill whatever catchable prey they encounter. Using the "sit-and-wait" hunting method, an ocelot typically travels to a location where it sits and waits for 30 minutes to one hour or more. It then quickly moves to another area where it sits and waits again. When moving between these "sit-and-wait" stops, ocelots travel two or three times faster than they do when using the slow hunting-walk technique.

Alan & Sandy Carey

Ron Austing

Roguenant/Jacana

▲ Female ocelots may give birth to as many as three kittens but the usual litter size is just one. They rear their kittens on territories that range in size from 2 to 10 square kilometers (about 1 to 4 square miles). When rearing a kitten, a female may spend 17 of every 24 hours hunting in her territory to find enough prey to support it and herself.

female ocelots typically vary from 2 to 10 square kilometers (about 1 to 4 square miles) while those of males are 5 to 18 square kilometers (about 2 to 7 square miles). Both species maintain their ranges in similar ways: they urine spray, make scrapes by raking the ground with their hind feet, and leave their feces in prominent places. Males and females hunt alone but they are not asocial. While traveling about their ranges, neighbors encounter each other along boundaries and come to know each other by sight and smell. Associations lasting for a day or two are known for both ocelots and servals; some of these associations are for mating purposes, but others are for unknown reasons.

After a gestation period of 79 to 82 days, ocelots may give birth to as many as three kittens; however, the more usual number of young in a litter is one. Servals have a shorter gestation period, about 74 days, and litters can consist of as many as five kittens, but more usually two or three.

Female ocelots and servals show similar behavior patterns when they have young, and both species raise their young alone, without help from the male. Immediately after her kittens are born, a mother spends most of her time at the den, leaving only to drink or hunt nearby. Later, when the young become more mobile, she has to increase her hunting efforts to feed the extra mouths. This is clearly a difficult time for females of both species, and many young die at this stage. A study carried out in the Ngorongoro Crater showed that female servals with young had to spend twice as much time hunting as those without young. For servals, and probably other cats too, prey capture rates remain the same per distance traveled whether females have young or not, and this means that females with kittens have to travel farther to catch more food. By doubling the normal daily distance traveled, female servals probably double their food intake.

Ocelots may have a more difficult time finding and catching food than servals. One radio-collared female ocelot in Peru was monitored after she gave birth. When her kittens were one month old, the female doubled her normal activity and spent as much as 17 of every 24 hours hunting. Despite her efforts, the young died. Even when female ocelots are not nursing young, they spend almost half of every 24 hours hunting. The long gestation period of the ocelot and the subsequent small litter size and slow maturation of young, may be adaptations for living under conditions where food is hard to find and where a cat needs to spend much of its day hunting in order to meet its normal daily energy requirements.

Over their range, both ocelots and servals live at relatively high densities. In Peru and Venezuela, ocelot densities have been calculated to be between 40 and 80 adults per 100 square kilometers (between 100 and 200 adults per 100 square miles). Data on serval density are more

Despite the fact that servals and ocelots may individually weigh as much as 13.5 kilograms (30 pounds), both these cats sustain themselves on surprisingly small prey. Most of the ocelot's diet consists of rodents and small mammals weighing less than 1 kilogram (2.2 pounds) that is, less than 10 percent of its own body weight. The majority of the serval's prey is even smaller, over 90 percent consisting of prey weighing less than 200 grams (7 ounces), which is less than 2 percent of an average female's body weight.

SOCIAL SYSTEMS

Both ocelots and servals appear to have similar social systems — neighboring females occupy small, essentially non-overlapping ranges, and males hold larger ranges that overlap with the ranges of one or more females. Range sizes of

Frédéric/Jacana

scanty, but sightings in the Ngorongoro Crater suggest that these cats may live at densities of approximately 40 per 100 square kilometers (approximately 100 per 100 square miles).

In their own way, both ocelots and servals are highly specialized rodent catchers, and as such, both cats benefit humans by killing rats and mice. On the other hand, both species are also known to make raids on domestic poultry, and many ocelots and servals are shot every year for these chicken-killing habits.

If success in the biological world is measured by an animal's ability to survive and breed, then the serval's ability to survive in more open habitats probably makes it a more successful cat than the ocelot. The serval has been able to exploit high rodent populations in open grasslands and woodlands by virtue of its morphological and behavioral specializations. These specializations are very similar to those found in the canid family, a group that also preys extensively on small rodents in open habitats. With its large ears, small slim face, and long legs, the serval resembles a fox or a maned wolf rather than a cat. The hunting behavior of the serval is also canid-like. The high bouncing pounce, the scanning of an area for sounds, and digging, are all hunting behaviors

shared more with the dog family than with other members of the cat family.

Although radio-tracking studies of ocelots have shown that this cat sometimes hunts in more open areas at night, it remains a species that is strongly tied to dense cover. In all the areas inhabited by them — from the thick brushy chapparal vegetation of Texas to the tropical rainforests of Peru — ocelots do not seem to be able to survive where forest or thick brush has been eradicated. Unfortunately, both the deforestation of much of South and Central America, and the demand for the ocelot's beautiful spotted coat, have combined to endanger this cat. The ocelot was placed on the endangered species list of the International Union for the Conservation of Nature and Natural Resources (IUCN) in 1989.

Servals also are sometimes persecuted for their spotted skins, but they seem to be able to survive alongside human activity better than many other spotted cats. Servals thrive on the rats and mice that go hand in hand with agricultural activity, and they are quite common in rural areas in many parts of Africa. As long as they are not hunted, these graceful long-legged cats can survive in man-altered habitats and co-exist with humans. This will be the ultimate measure of their success.

▲ Serval young grow extremely rapidly, reaching the size of their mother within about seven months. Like ocelots, female servals raise their young alone on a relatively large territory. Females rearing young spend twice as much time hunting as females without young.

161

WILD CATS AND FERAL CATS

WARNER C. PASSANISI, DAVID W. MACDONALD AND GILLIAN KERBY

The "domestication" of the wild cat probably began in Egypt approximately 4,000 years ago. However, despite its close association with humans since that time, much of the domestic cat's behavior and ecology has, until recently, remained shrouded in folklore and mystery. During the past few years, research into the lives of free-ranging domestic cats, combined with studies of the European and African wild cats, has cast new light on the biology of the most familiar member of the cat family.

▲ A wild cat devours a partridge in this mosaic, which is housed in the Naples Museum. Distributed throughout Europe, Africa, and parts of Asia, the wild cat (*Felis silvestris*) was the progenitor of the domestic cat. Domestic and wild cats are believed to be of the same species, and interbreeding was probably common in the past.

The domestic cat derived from either the European wild cat or the African wild cat. On grounds of both biology and protocol, taxonomists differ on exactly how to classify these similar cats, but current practice is to group all three cats into one species, *Felis silvestris*. The stocky European wild cat (*Felis s. silvestris*), the racily-built African wild cat (*Felis s. libyca*), and the domestic cat (*Felis s. catus*) are thus all subspecies. Irrespective of the proprieties of zoological nomenclature, the close relationship between wild cats and domestic cats is emphasized by the difficulties a team of Scottish zoologists encountered in trying to tell them apart on the basis of skull morphology. Using the skulls of contemporary skeletons they found no measure that reliably separated true European wild cats from domestic cats. However, using museum skulls from the last century, differences were more apparent, and hybridization between the subspecies was probably less common then than it is today.

BEHAVIOR AND ECOLOGY
Apart from the difficulties in distinguishing wild and domestic cats anatomically, it is interesting to look at how different they are behaviorally and ecologically. Has domestication unnaturally stretched the behavioral flexibility of the domestic cat, or would the wild ancestor behave in the same way if confronted by the same ecological circumstances? A recent radio-tracking study of African wild cats in Saudi Arabia indicated that they were organized rather like European wild cats, in that they were solitary-living. When observed around human refuse wild cats remained solitary, whereas feral domestic cats formed colonies. Perhaps the domestic cat's capacity to form large aggregations may have been fostered by domestication over the past few thousand years.

This brings into question whether the domestic cat's social organization is a valid topic for study, or if colony formation is simply a product of domestication. Although the domestic cat has had a lengthy association with man, and undoubtedly has been subject to intense artificial selection for certain traits, we believe that this does not invalidate the search for an adaptive basis for

its contemporary behavior. Free-ranging domestic cats exhibit no behavior that has not been documented in other felids, and there is little to suggest that man has sought to alter their social behavior in any way that is otherwise directly counteradaptive and likely to confuse the interpretation of their behavior now. Humans have made accessible certain resources, such as highly clumped and predictable food sources, to which cats like many other carnivores have adapted, and which they can utilize efficiently.

The domestic cat has long been a favorite subject for many aspects of scientific, laboratory-based research. It is the primary experimental model for many human genetic and physiological abnormalities, including nutritional, metabolic, oncologic, immunological, parasitic and reproductive disorders, and has become the focus for much research into the conservation and management of endangered felids. Much of what we presently know about the domestic cat's behavior has also resulted from detailed research

▼ A South African wild cat. Across their wide distribution, wild cats live in diverse habitats from deciduous and coniferous forests to scrubby brush and even croplands. Variations in body size, coat color, and spotting and striping characterize wild cats as being from different parts of their range.

Des & Jen Bartlett/Survival Anglia

▲ A wild cat in Namibia's Etosha National Park. Capable of taking prey the size of young dik-dik and duikers, wild cats are known to feed mainly on small mammals such as rodents and hares. They also prey on birds up to the size of guinea fowl.

► While very little is known about the social behavior of wild cats, they are believed to be solitary and territorial — the typical felid pattern. Primarily nocturnal, wild cats are seldom seen, even when they live in close proximity to human settlements.

Gunter Ziesler/Bruce Coleman Ltd.

on captive animals in artificial laboratory conditions. Only recently have researchers begun to investigate the behavior and ecology of domestic cats in more natural environments, and to question whether the aggregations or colonies of domestic cats are real societies.

The domestic cat is one of the most adaptable of all mammals: it lives in habitats ranging from subantarctic islands to busy industrial cities, and cat densities vary from less than 1 to more than 2,000 per square kilometer (less than 3 to more than 5,000 per square mile). The domestic cat also varies widely in its dependance upon man; the

degree of association with people ranges from nil on uninhabited islands to almost continual contact in crowded metropolises. The remarkable flexibility in the ecological circumstances of different populations makes the domestic cat a promising subject for the study of intraspecific variation (variation between members of the same species) in spatial and social organization.

It seems highly likely that a major factor contributing to the variation in the social system of the domestic cat is the distribution, richness and predictability of important resources such as food, shelter, and nest sites. Although cats can show many different levels of social organization, in general domestic cat populations can be divided into cats that are solitary and cats that are part of a group. Solitary cats are most likely to occur where resources are widely dispersed and relatively unpredictable, while groups will be favored where resources are highly predictable, rich and patchy.

Even though some cats live solitary lives this does not mean that complex relationships between members of the same species do not occur. Relationships need not be based on immediate, short-distance modes of communication, such as visual cues, but can also involve olfactory and vocal cues. For instance, male and female solitary domestic cats and European wild cats, appear to use scent marks to delineate territories.

Home ranges of solitary animals vary from those found on subantarctic Dassen Island, where the average home ranges are less than 20 hectares (50 acres) for females and more than 40 hectares (100 acres) for males (the density of cats is approximately 30 per square kilometer/78 per square mile), to the home ranges of cats found on the subtropical grassland in Victoria, Australia, where an average female range is more than 170 hectares (420 acres) and more than 620 hectares (1,530 acres) for males (with a density of approximately 1 to 2 cats per square kilometer/2.6 to 5.2 cats per square mile). Group-living cats tend to range over smaller areas than those of their solitary counterparts. In the small fishing village of Ainoshima, Japan, which has a density of more than 2,000 cats per square kilometer (more than 5,000 cats per square mile), the average home range of group-living females and males is 0.5 and 0.7 hectares (1.25 and 1.75 acres), respectively. On the agricultural lands of Illinois, USA, where cat density is approximately 6 per square kilometer (15.5 per square mile), female and male ranges are approximately 112 and 228 hectares (277 and 563 acres), respectively. Since 1978, our own research has concentrated on the social organization and behavioral ecology of free-ranging, group-living cats based on farms in southern England. We have observed four populations in particular, ranging in size from 4 to 70 members, each of which is at least partially provisioned by humans, but with little other direct interference. Radio-tracking combined with careful observation of individuals has revealed that whereas females in these circumstances tend to operate within a 5 to 20 hectare (12.5 to 50 acre) area centered around farm outbuildings, males can travel more than 80 hectares (200 acres), and may sometimes visit females of other farms.

Every colony that we studied seemed to be based on a core group of related females; structured matrilines (kinships through the female line) with largely overlapping ranges, living around the resource center of the site. On the other hand, the larger ranges of adult males generally encompassed those of several females, and some overlapped those of other males. Away from the farmyard, cats tended to travel alone and seemingly without obvious reference to each other's activities. However, when within the farmyard their behavior was far from socially random. Cats chose to sit together, and each individual favored the company of some over others. These associations were not merely whimsical "friendships," but ones largely governed by the age, sex, status and blood ties of the individuals involved.

This close scrutiny of the private lives of farm cats revealed the complexity of their social relationships. We observed that large colonies embraced several groups of cats whose members frequently interacted within the group, and to a much lesser extent outside their immediate social circle. The overall pattern within a colony of cats was of well integrated, amicable groups. This was in marked contrast to the unanimous hostility with which members of a particular group treated outsiders. Although females warded off most would be female immigrants, males tended to be aggressive towards other males.

It has become evident that asymmetries in the flow of certain interactions between certain individuals may be important indicators (and, perhaps, reinforcers) of the social relationships between individuals in the population. In some colonies, and between some cats, this asymmetry is particularly marked for certain rubbing behaviors, notably facial rubbing. A female will often approach a male by rubbing her lips, cheek, and forehead against his face, but he rarely rubs on her. (Such rubbing behavior may also involve the subtle transfer of scent marks.) Similar asymmetries may differentiate relationships between adult females. Kittens also deploy their favors in a way that is far from random. Loosely speaking, within a family group those in receipt of rubs correspond to dominants in a linear pecking order. However, we prefer, rather than the step-ladder analogy of classical dominance, to think of farm cat society as a wheel, with certain types of interaction (especially rubbing behavior) flowing from socially (and sometimes spatially) peripheral

John Downer/Planet Earth Pictures

individuals to socially central ones at the hub — a centripetally-structured society.

REPRODUCTION AND REARING YOUNG

Free-ranging domestic cats exhibit a promiscuous mating system, with no long term bonds between adult males and females. The remarkable variation in cat social and spatial organization is mirrored in the flexibility of mating and reproductive tactics between members of the same species. There is no paternal care of kittens, thus male investment in offspring is restricted to successful fertilization of receptive females. Adult males tend to follow one

▲ Feral domestic cats take advantage of human refuse and of the rodents — mice and rats — that congregate around garbage. Such a concentrated food resource may form the center of activity for a group of feral cats. As a result, these cats appear to be more social than their wild counterparts.

Karen Tweedy Holmes/Animals Animals

◄ Groups of feral domestic cats are based on a core of related females who occupy overlapping ranges. The center of these ranges is usually a food resource, often a farm. Male ranges include those of several female groups and sometimes overlap with those of other males.

► About a third larger and more sturdily built than the domestic cat, the wild cat of Europe has a reputation for ferocity when cornered. Man is the wild cat's biggest predator, but wild cats are also preyed on by lynx and other larger cats.

Arthus-Bertrand/Jacana

► Wild cats from Africa are the likely ancestors of domestic cats, which are believed to have been tamed in Egypt about 4,000 years ago. Today, African villagers still adopt wild cat kittens and keep them as pets.

Gerald Cubitt

► (Opposite page) Wild cats bear only one litter of two to three kittens a year. Young mature quickly, and begin to hunt with their mother by about 12 weeks of age. At about five months of age they are independent, and by the end of their first year, are fully mature adults.

Throughout the breeding season, male–male competition is often intense and wounding is common, however, when males are in the presence of an estrous female, such competition is subtle, with little actual physical aggression.

In large colonies, estrous females are often surrounded by up to seven adult males in consort, and they may be inseminated by as many as ten different males during a single estrus. There are some indications of active female choice of mating partner. For instance, estrous females seem to advertise their receptive status by frequently rubbing and spraying on prominent objects, and by spending more time than usual traveling relatively long distances away from their core area; it appears that such females may be actively enticing particular males to follow them.

Virtually all adult females of the large cat populations in southern England are fertile, and, depending on the level of nutrition, a single female can produce a maximum of three litters of one to nine kittens between January and late October. Females exhibit two different forms of mothering behavior: either they are solitary mothers and raise their litters alone, or they are communal breeders with at least two, and up to four, mothers raising a combined litter. A high degree of birth synchronization may facilitate communal care of offspring, although there have been cases of pooled litters as much as seven weeks apart in age. Communal breeding appears to be favored when the mothers are closely related; we are presently analyzing genetic evidence to test this assertion. Further research into the communal care of kittens is underway to ascertain the costs, such as

of two alternative mating tactics: either "staying" with a single female throughout the receptive phase of her estrous cycle (one to four days), copulating with her frequently (up to nine intromissions or a maximum of 27 minutes per hour) but usually not enjoying exclusive access to the female during that time; or "roaming" over a large area in search of receptive females with whom to copulate, but leaving any one female after a few hours.

An individual male may adopt both tactics either within or between breeding seasons. The males who "stay" appear to secure fewer matings than those enjoyed by males who "roam." But, as has been shown by several studies of wild vertebrates, male copulation success does not necessarily signify actual reproductive success. At least some litters have more than one father, and work is in progress to ascertain what factors determine which males father most kittens.

attraction of predators including infanticidal males and females, increased aggression, mixing up of litters and the enhanced spread of infectious diseases, and the benefits, such as increased thermoregulation and defense of young, shared suckling responsibility, grooming by unrelated mothers, "maternal" learning and the possible transfer of antibodies to kittens via milk.

Infanticide by males (and females) has been observed several times in populations of group-living domestic cats. Female domestic cats with dependent offspring tend to strongly rebuke adult males if they approach their kittens. The total time during which kittens are attended by a nursing (and perhaps guarding) female is significantly greater for communal litters, where females share the nursing duties, than for single litters. As is true of communal cub rearing in lions, communal rearing of kittens appears to be an adaptation against infanticide. The majority of observed infanticidal episodes in domestic cats have involved the killing of kittens from single litters.

Male coalitions have not been documented in domestic cat populations, so why then, if female domestic cats form large socially bonded groups do males not form coalitions to monopolize them as lions do? Many of the differences between the two species can be explained by the size and distribution of their food resources. Lions hunt together to ambush and overpower large prey as well as to defend large carcasses, cooperation for which farm cats have no need. Also, perhaps the distribution of lion prey causes female lions to be so spread out that males could not effectively defend several prides. Furthermore, male lions (but not cats) require almost continual association with females, as they rely on them for hunting.

The argument often advanced to explain why male lions do not fight over access to their females, but rather take turns to mate, is that they are so dependent on each other for defense of the pride that rifts caused by mating rivalry would be overwhelmingly disadvantageous. In addition, they are often brothers, and so have a vested interest in each other's reproductive success. Amongst male domestic cats, on the other hand, there is no known cooperation of a similar order, nor any evidence of long term brotherly alliances.

In our larger colonies, adult male cats rarely fought over females during courtship, but in the small colony a single male seemed able to drive away all other intruding males. Perhaps, in a colony that otherwise accommodates several adult males, it is simply impossible for any one male to monopolize the matings. That is not to say that they don't find other ways of competing. It may be that the order of insemination is crucial (perhaps being the first, or last, to mate ensures a better chance of successful fertilization) and competition may occur between sperm as they race to fertilize the eggs. But why don't they fight over females?

Jany Sauvanet/NHPA

In principle, for it to be worthwhile for an individual to escalate a contest to bloodshed it must have evidence that the rewards will outweigh any costs incurred. In a large colony of cats, at least three factors may minimize the benefit of fighting to a male cat. First, in colonies attended by several adult males, who may be closely related, their fighting prowess may be closely matched (feeble contestants may have been thrashed before they got close to a receptive female), and to emerge as overall victor any one male would have to beat not one but several rivals. Being the first to enter the fray could also mean the first to become exhausted! Second, with several adult females all likely to come into estrus at roughly the same time, and being widely spread out, the difficulties of monopolizing them would be great. Thirdly, and exacerbating the first two problems, cats' claws are such fearsome weapons that it is hard to imagine even the victor emerging unscathed from any serious combat. Finally, if our observations of infanticide are a general phenomenon, and if, as would be expected, kitten-killers spare their own offspring, then kittens of uncertain paternity might have a selective advantage. All these factors make it unlikely that the costs of fighting outweigh the reward measured in additional surviving kittens sired. However, until genetic studies reveal the paternity of kittens, we can only speculate on the reproductive success of the farmyard lions.

To return to the similarities and differences between feral and domestic cats and their wild ancestors, we stress that it is very difficult to study wild felids. Feral domestic cats are often used to living alongside man and are therefore amenable to study and observation; most other felids live in wild terrain, and are hard to locate and almost impossible to observe directly. The use of radiotelemetry has revealed some information about their spatial organization but very little is known about their social behavior.

We know that more than one subspecies of *Felis silvestris* may occur in the same types of habitat, and we have some evidence that their behavioral repertoires are broadly similar. Evidence from field studies also suggests that in similar habitats, their diet and ranging behavior are similar. In common with many other species cat, we find a negative correlation between population density and home range size (the higher the density, the smaller the home range size) which is likely to be linked to the availability of food: ranges increase with decreasing food availability. Where the food supply is stable and evenly distributed, exclusive ranges are found, but where food occurs in large clumps that are unevenly distributed throughout the habitat, we find overlapping ranges. The farm cats described in this chapter are at this extreme of the spectrum with very many individuals sharing the same core feeding area.

Angelo Gandolfi

The spacing pattern of males is also dependent on the distribution of females during the breeding season. Males seek to maintain access to both food and mates and tend to adopt exclusive ranges where there are high numbers of females evenly distributed through the area, but favor a roaming strategy when females are at low densities. In colonies of feral cats where densities are high overall, there may be areas of low and high female density within a very small area resulting in overlapping male ranges.

As with other felids, there is a clearly defined breeding season and males do not share in parental care. In some cat species there is evidence

of reproductive loyalty between male and female in successive years, but this has not been observed as a general phenomenon in free-ranging domestic cats as we have no information on other subspecies of *Felis silvestris*. Very little is known about breeding behavior and kitten development of either *Felis s. libyca* or *Felis s. silvestris*.

Most close relatives of the domestic cat live in habitats where food is scarce for at least part of the year. They occupy large, exclusive ranges and adopt a solitary existence for most of the year. Studies of the European wild cat and domestic cat, in an area where food is seasonally rare, have shown that both subspecies adopted this strategy.

However, there may be differences between the behavior of the subspecies in areas where food is abundant and stable, which may in part reflect the influence of domestication. Preliminary evidence from our Saudi Arabian study indicates that African wild cats persisted in a solitary existence when feral cats in the same area formed groups at high densities around the clumped food supply provided by a rubbish tip. The process of domestication may have facilitated the predisposition to group living found among *Felis s. catus*. Until there have been more studies of the behavior and ecology of wild subspecies of *Felis silvestris* this conclusion will remain speculative.

▲ Like other felids, solitary wild cats probably use olfactory signals to communicate without actual encounters. When they do meet face to face, however, cats employ vocal, and visual signals to express their mood and intentions.

LITTLE-KNOWN CATS

JILL D. MELLEN

► Ranging from southern Texas to northern Argentina, the jaguarundi (*Felis yagouaroundi*) hunts mainly on the ground during the day. Its diet includes small- to medium-sized mammals such as mice and rabbits, as well as birds, arthropods, and fruit. Despite its unusual appearance — it lacks spots and resembles a weasel or marten — its behavior is definitely feline.

▼ Native to Central Asian deserts, steppes, and barren rocky mountainsides, the Pallas' cat (*Felis manul*) climbs sheer cliff and rock faces with ease. Weighing only about 3 kilograms (6.5 pounds), the Pallas' cat appears larger than it really is because of its dense, fluffy fur, an adaptation to habitats with cold, snowy winters.

O f the 37 species of cats found throughout the world, we are most familiar with the larger cats: lion, tiger, leopard, snow leopard, jaguar, cheetah, and clouded leopard. These species have been studied to a greater or lesser degree both in the field and in captivity. With the exception of the cheetah and the clouded leopard, the larger cats breed readily in captivity. The remaining members of the cat family, however, have not fared as well. At best, the small cats breed inconsistently in zoos. A systematic examination of the physical, social, and genetic environments of small cats in a captive setting seemed necessary to determine which of these factors most closely correlated with successful reproduction. To this end, I collected more than 650 hours of behavioral data on a total of 65 male and 69 female individuals representing 20 species of small cats at eight zoological institutions.

The study provided me with the unique opportunity of getting a first-hand view of the behavior of many small cats (accomplished through careful measurements of their behavior and captive environments). I quickly came to realize that the zookeepers taking care of these cats had a much greater insight into the behavior and "personalities" of them than I ever would. All of the keepers with whom I had the pleasure to work contributed greatly to my knowledge.

Jill D. Mellen

CHARACTERIZATION OF SMALL CATS IN CAPTIVITY

The behavior of wild felids has been described as "generally one of inactivity punctuated by forays in search of food." In captivity, the behavior of small cats may be described as generally one of inactivity punctuated by brief bouts of scent marking and even briefer bouts of social interaction — only 1 to 2 percent of their time is spent in this way.

The most extraordinary aspect of studying so many species of small cats was my discovery that from species to species the social and scent-marking behaviors of each were remarkably similar. At one zoo I watched the courtship behavior of the tiniest cat, the rusty-spotted cat (*Felis rubiginosa*), over a three-day period. I was amazed to see a pattern of courtship that virtually mirrored that of every other species of cat I had studied, including the courtship of the largest of the cats, the Siberian tiger. At another zoo I watched a male jaguarundi (*F. yagouaroundi*) "patrol" his large, naturalistic enclosure. In German, the common name for jaguarundi is "weasel cat" — a very apt name, because this South American cat much more closely resembles a weasel than a felid. It has very short legs, a rounded head with small rounded ears, and proportionately a very long, thick tail. What I found truly fascinating was that although this cat didn't look very cat-like to me, he "sharpened" his claws on a log, just like every other felid; he scraped with his hind feet when he urinated and defecated; and he cheek and neck rubbed, then rolled on his back when approaching an estrous female — all patterns I had seen in many other species. The only omission I detected was that whereas the other species of cats sprayed urine on vertical objects such as bushes, I never saw jaguarundis doing this. I think the legs of a jaguarundi are just too short and its tail too long.

The species of cat I enjoyed watching the most was the beautiful Pallas' cat (*Felis manul*) of the Himalayan steppes. The ability of the Pallas' cat to negotiate rocky crevices is a marvel — with their short stout legs, these cats appear to flow up or down an almost vertical rock face. Their ears are positioned at the sides of the head, presumably an adaptation to their hunting style of peering over boulders while stalking their prey. Pallas' cats have a noteworthy "personality." Their facial expression gives the impression that they are irritated with everything in their surroundings. Zookeepers who have cared for them in captivity agree with this characterization. One keeper dangled a lure at the end of a string in an attempt to play with the several different species of small cats in her charge. All but the Pallas' cats seemed to enjoy stalking, chasing, and catching the lure. The Pallas' cats, instead, stared at the keeper, giving her the unique Pallas' cat threat pose of "sneering" (quivering the lips over the canine teeth), all the while the lure was in the exhibit.

Sadly, there is no longer a viable population of Pallas' cats in North American zoos. Although several zoos had limited success in the 1970s with breeding these wonderful cats, that captive population has now died out. Most were the descendants of one pair brought in from the wild in the early 1970s. Unfortunately, the fate of the Pallas' cat population in captivity was the rule, not the exception. The captive populations of most species of small cats in both North America and Europe are headed towards extinction.

Another small cat I studied, the sand cat (*F. margarita*), originally ranged throughout the Sahara of Africa and into the Arabian Peninsula. The pads of its feet are covered with long hair to protect it from the hot sand. Its contact call is a short, bark-like vocalization. Sand cats respond to close human contact, such as a keeper entering their enclosure, by crouching down and seeming to ignore them. It is as though they are hoping that the human intruder will go away soon. The docile personality of sand cats has contributed to their demise. In the 1960s, sand cats were collected for the pet trade, although their survival rate as pets was very low. Further, wild specimens sunning themselves on rocks were often shot for "sport." The subspecies most often found in zoos is *F. m. scheffeli* from Pakistan, and this subspecies may well be extinct in the wild. The Pakistani sand cat is represented in zoos by less than a dozen individuals, all of which are descendants of one wild-caught pair. All of the sand cats held in European zoos have died out. This same trend appears to be occurring in North American zoos.

Keith and Liz Laidler/Ardea London

► The smallest of the felids, the rusty-spotted cat (*Felis rubiginosa*) weighs only about 1 kilogram (2.2 pounds). Little is known about this species in its natural habitat in Sri Lanka and southern India, but the climbing abilities it displays in zoos suggest that it hunts in trees.

Ron Austing

► The zoo population of sand cats (*Felis margarita*) is small and highly inbred, therefore, this cat in captivity is likely to become extinct. Wild sand cats may be faring little better. They are believed to be extinct in Pakistan, and their status in the rest of their range, from the Sahara to the Arabian Peninsula, is unknown.

Stouffer Enterprises/Animals Animals

► Solitary and nocturnal, the small but fierce black-footed cat (*Felis nigripes*) inhabits arid parts of southern Africa. It uses rocks and stones for cover while stalking prey such as mice and gerbils. It spends the day hiding in termite holes and abandoned burrows to avoid predation by larger carnivores.

Ron Austing

► Servals (*Felis serval*) are solitary, except for mothers and young. The young leave their mother's exclusive territory when they are about one year of age. Servals are among the few small cats that breed relatively often in zoos, suggesting an adaptability to human presence that may contribute to their survival in the wild.

► (Far right) Averaging some 15 kilograms (33 pounds) in weight, caracals (*Lynx caracal*) are able to take prey as large as impala and reedbuck. More typical fare includes birds, rodents, hyraxes, dik-dik, and antelope fawns. Caracals hunt at night, and like most cats, are solitary.

Phyllis Greenberg/Comstock

The black-footed cat (*Felis nigripes*) of southern Africa is similar to the sand cat in appearance, size, and habitat use. (The black-footed cat does indeed have black feet, and the backs of its hind legs are also black.) However, the personalities of the two species are as different as night and day. While the sand cat is extremely docile in its interactions with humans, the black-footed cat is best described as "tenacious," "fierce," and "humorless." While these terms seem almost comical when describing a 2.25 kilogram (5 pound) cat, every keeper who has worked with this species has respect for this cat.

I watched one black-footed cat stalk a free-ranging jungle fowl which was foraging near the cat's enclosure. She flattened herself against the ground with her large ears out to the side (in a position I termed "airplane ear posture"), and in a serpentine manner, appeared to flow from one rock to the next, creeping closer to the "prey." I'm sure this is an adaptation to hunting in an open habitat. The jungle fowl never seemed aware of the cat, and she continued to stare intently at the bird, teeth-chattering and tail flicking, until it moved out of her sight.

It is regularly reported that black-footed cats attack small sheep four times their weight. They are said to fasten onto the neck of the sheep and hang there until the jugular vein is pierced. This may be the source of the Bushmen story that tells of black-footed cats that attach themselves to the neck of giraffe. Most of the black-footed cat zoo population is inbred, which means that many of the cats share common ancestors because they were bred with closely related individuals. Although the captive population is somewhat larger than that of Pallas' or sand cats, this population is not what demographers would call a healthy one.

Another of the *Felis* species found in Africa is the serval (*F. serval*). It is one of the most common species of small cats maintained in zoos and, relatively speaking, it breeds quite readily in captivity. In my study of small cats I observed five different pairs of servals. During aggressive encounters, servals have a unique, ritualistic method of fighting: usually, while both are seated and facing one another, one cat places its front paw on the chest of the other individual, and the second cat responds by repeatedly "bobbing" its head up and down, sometimes biting at the raised paw of the first cat. Paul Leyhausen, a German ethologist who has studied small cats extensively in captivity, termed this raised-paw behavior a "paw prod." Sometimes this interaction escalated to an actual cat fight with hissing, spitting, striking with paws, and even biting, but most often the paw prod was followed by a protracted "stare-off" which finally ended when both cats moved away. Ironically, while servals typically breed very well in captivity, of the five pairs I observed in the course

▶ About the size of a domestic cat, the South American Geoffroy's cat (*Felis geoffroyi*) lives in scrubby woodlands and bush. It hunts alone on the ground for small birds and rodents. Beyond this, little is known of its natural history, but thousands are trapped and killed each year for their beautiful black-spotted fur.

Frank W. Lane/Frank Lane Picture Agency

▶ Closely related to the margay and ocelot, the oncilla (*Felis tigrina*) is a tropical forest dwelling cat. Little is known about its habits. Even the extent of its distribution in South America is a mystery.

E. & P. Bauer/ZEFA

▶ Within its large range, which includes parts of northern Africa, Europe and Asia, the jungle cat (*Felis chaus*) varies in size from 4 to 8 kilograms (8.75-17.5 pounds) in tropical India and Thailand to 16 kilograms (35.25 pounds) in temperate Central Asia. Jungle cats inhabit diverse habitats from dense forest to wet reed beds.

Gerald Cubitt/Bruce Coleman Ltd.

of my study, only one pair produced offspring. Female servals show very overt estrous behavior. Their rate of urine marking increases sharply during estrus (from a rate of once or twice per hour when not in estrus to more than 30 times per hour when in estrus). Every female in my study sprayed urine directly into the face of the male on more than one occasion. Despite the definite change in behavior in the female during estrus, and the dramatic increase in interest shown by the male toward the female, I never directly observed one successful copulation. Approaches by the males were vehemently rebuffed by each female in my study. It's still a mystery to me that the captive serval population seems to be thriving.

Yet another African cat is the caracal (*Lynx caracal*). This medium-sized cat is similar in size to the serval but is found in the much more arid regions of southern and Central Africa as well as the Middle East. This species is referred to as caracal "lynx" because of the long ear tufts similar to those of the Eurasian, Spanish and North American lynxes, and bobcats. The caracal's ear tufts, however, are much longer and more pronounced than those on any other species of cat. One theory holds that the tufts at the ends of the cat's ears allows them to hear better, serving as "antennas." Presumably, if the tufts were cut off, the cat would not hear as well. While this is an interesting theory, the tufts probably have little to do with aiding the hearing of this cat. Caracals do appear to use the tufts to accentuate facial expressions. They "ear flick" at one another as a mild threat. Caracals, like servals, are fairly common in zoos and like servals, seem to reproduce readily in captivity.

In addition to the weasel-like jaguarundi, I had the opportunity to study several other species of small cats native to South America. The rarest captive representative is the delicate-looking pampas cat (*Felis colocolo*). The size and shape of the pampas cat is similar to that of a domestic cat, except that the pampas cat has a fine-boned, long-legged appearance. This cat also has a long "mane" of hair around its neck. The tip of its nose looks like a spot of pink putty was pressed there. The coat color and pattern varies widely on pampas cats, ranging from reddish to gray to reddish-gray with black spots; some melanistic cats have been found. The pampas cat is thought to be mainly a nocturnal, terrestrial predator, which presumably preys upon small mammals, such as guinea pigs, and birds. One piece of the puzzle with regard to their diet was provided by a scientist studying Magellanic penguins in Argentina. She came across a satiated-looking pampas cat dozing in the middle of a penguin nest.

The captive population of pampas cats is similar to that of Pallas' and sand cats. There are fewer than a dozen individuals held in North American and European zoos and most are

Warren Garst/Tom Stack & Associates

descendants of one wild-caught pair. As with the Pallas' and sand cats, this population, as it stands right now, is not self-sustaining and will eventually become extinct. The tiniest of the felids, the rusty-spotted cat (*Felis rubiginosa*) from Sri Lanka and southern India, consists mainly of closely related individuals at two zoological institutions.

Some captive populations of small cats exist in substantial numbers, but are of unknown origin or subspecies. These include the wonderful fishing cat (*F. viverrina*) of Asia that readily dives, head first, into water in pursuit of fish. Other Asian species, the jungle cat (*F. chaus*) and the leopard cat (*F. bengalensis*) were once popular in zoos, but again due to benign neglect, their numbers in captivity are dwindling. The margay (*F. wiedii*) of South America is still fairly common in zoos. This truly arboreal cat is able to descend trees head first by wrapping its hind legs around a tree trunk in a manner similar to tree squirrels. Most margays arrived in zoos from the private sector. As with virtually all exotic animals, these cats make poor pets and disgruntled owners invariably donate their animals to local zoos. Thus, the current captive population of margays is composed of many human-raised (and often socially inept) cats of unknown origin — a combination that is not conducive to successful captive breeding programs. The Geoffroy's cat (*F. geoffroyi*) of

central South America represents yet another small spotted cat from the neotropics. While the captive population is well over two dozen individuals, most are related to one very prolific pair. The tiny oncilla (*F. tigrina*) is found only in the private sector outside of its native South America and the rare flat-headed cat (*F. planiceps*) of Asia, is represented in captivity by a lone geriatric animal.

Other species of small cats are all but unknown to us. The marbled cat (*F. marmorata*) of Asia looks like a miniature clouded leopard with slightly shaggier fur and a long tail. Only a half dozen specimens are held in captivity; four are not in breeding situations. The beautiful African golden cat (*F. aurata*) is represented by three older specimens held in one zoo in England. Its "cousin," the Asian golden cat (*F. temmincki*), is represented by less than a dozen specimens in North America, Europe and Australia, with only four or five females in breeding situations, most being related to a single female. The Bornean bay cat (*F. badia*) is known from only four museum skins; no live specimens have ever been held in zoos. Although museum specimens of Andean mountain cats (*F. jacobita*) have existed for over 100 years, it wasn't until 1980 that two Argentine scientists were able to observe and follow a single individual for about two hours. Their description of this silver-gray cat drinking from a stream,

▲ The margay (*Felis wiedii*) frequently encounters other South and Central American tree-dwellers like this tamandua, a small anteater. Margay frequently hunt in trees for rodents, birds, reptiles, and insects.

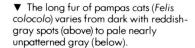
▼ The long fur of pampas cats (*Felis colocolo*) varies from dark with reddish-gray spots (above) to pale nearly unpatterned gray (below).

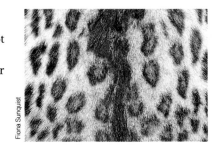
Fiona Sunquist

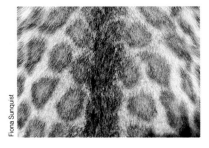
Fiona Sunquist

► Arboreal forest dwellers of South and Southeast Asia, marbled cats (*Felis marmorata*) are like small clouded leopards. Rarely seen in the wild, little is known of their natural history or conservation status, and only about six marbled cats exist in zoo collections.

Rod Williams/Bruce Coleman Ltd

► (Opposite) the Asian golden cat (*Felis temmincki*) typifies the status of small cats in zoos. Few captive Asian golden cat individuals exist, few females are in breeding situations, and they are highly inbred. Small cats are poor breeders in captivity, and soon they are likely to be lost from zoo collections. Most small cats are also threatened in the wild.

► A rare glimpse of the Andean mountain cat (*Felis jacobita*) – only one other has been observed by scientists in more than a century. Even more enigmatic is the Bornean bay cat (*F. badia*), which is known only from a single museum specimen dating from 1874 and a few other skins.

G. Ziesler/APL/Orion

► Confined to small areas of Chile and Argentina, the kodkod (*Felis guigna*) is rare and perhaps threatened with extinction due to habitat destruction. Like other rare and elusive mammals, the kodkod may slip away before we learn anything about its biology and behavior.

Eduardo J. Ramilo/Focus

► Clouded leopards (*Neofelis nebulosa*) have been described as having a big cat's head on a small cat's body. Clouded leopards hunt on the ground and in trees, killing large prey like deer, monkeys, and pigs as well as smaller animals like birds and porcupines.

Ron Austing/Photo Researchers Inc.

strolling along a path, and then napping for a few minutes, represents the sum total of our knowledge of this rare cat. Another South American cat, the kodkod (*Felis guigna*), may exist in South American zoos and possibly in the private sector in the United States, but little else is known. Several Chinese desert cats (*F. bieti*) were once in Chinese zoos, but currently a lone female housed at the Beijing Zoo is perhaps the only captive representative.

The last of the enigmatic cats virtually unstudied in the wild is neither a large cat nor a small one, but rather one that shares characteristics of both groups. In essence, the clouded leopard (*Neofelis nebulosa*) has the skull and dentition of a large cat, but the body of a small one. Its most striking feature is its extremely long canine teeth (proportionally longer than those of any other felid species), and it has been likened to the extinct saber-toothed cats. This cat looks somewhat like a larger version of a marbled cat, with a long, low-slung body and an even longer tail. Its wide paws allow it to run along the underside of branches and grasp monkeys, squirrels, and birds in the tree tops. The Malaysian word for clouded leopard, in fact, means "branch-tiger" or "tree tiger," but they may also spend considerable time on the ground. The behavior of clouded leopards also resembles that of both large and small cats and yet matches neither. Like a small cat species, it purrs, but cannot roar; its method of eating food and its body postures, however, are closer to those of the large species of cats.

Clouded leopards are extremely difficult to breed (only 20 percent of the captive population has reproduced), due mainly to the notoriously high incidence of males killing females. A retrospective analysis of these incidences suggests that females are often killed by males when they are coming into estrus, and in association with feeding. In order to reduce the number of fatal encounters, clouded leopards are now paired with an appropriate mate when both are very young (often less than six months of age). These youngsters form a strong pair bond and remain together for life. These early, "life-time" pairings pose significant problems for the successful management of the captive population. What does one do with the older, unpaired animals? What happens to a clouded leopard whose mate has died? The answers to these questions appear to lie in some of the newly developed artificial means of propagation. While natural breeding is always preferred, the clouded leopard represents one of the best examples of the necessity for artificial breeding. To that end, the development of successful artificial insemination and embryo transfer techniques may be the only hope for maintaining a healthy captive population of these cats. Unfortunately, these methods have not, to date, been perfected.

OVERALL FINDINGS

What did I discover about the behavior of small cats and captive environments, and why do small cats breed so inconsistently in zoos? First, I found that the scent-marking and social behavior of small cats were remarkably similar in all of the species I studied. The most distinct species-specific aspect was each species' vocalizations. While all hissed and spat and yowled during aggressive encounters, the contact calls they used were quite different from species to species. It is important to note here, however, that in the wild these small cats utilize a wide range of habitats: some are arboreal, some terrestrial, some semi-aquatic; they inhabit open scrub, desert, or tropical rainforest; and they prey on chickens, pikas, fish, birds, small monkeys, or burrowing rodents. These aspects are what each cat is really all about, and they were aspects I could only imagine in my study of captive animals. So, while what I saw emphasized the similarities among small cat species, it should be remembered that each species occupies a unique niche in its native habitat.

I found that through systematic behavior observations, I could detect estrus in females. (This is in contrast to more invasive, more expensive, and yet to be perfected methods such as biochemical analyses of blood, urine, feces or saliva.) The most pronounced change in behavior took place not in the female, but in the male. As a female came into estrus but was not yet receptive to mounts by the male, the male's rate of scent marking dramatically increased as did his interest in the female. He spent most of his time either scent marking, following the female, or intently watching her every move. Until the female was truly in estrus (that is, when she allowed the male to mount her), she responded to the male's behavior by avoidance or overt aggression.

Through systematic observations I was also able to predict success and compatibility between potential males. The pattern described above, of a female coming into estrus and the male's response to it, is typical of a reproductively successful pair. Successful males avidly pursued females, following, approaching, sniffing them, responding to aggressive swipes by staying just out of reach, rolling on their backs, and neck-rubbing. Reproductively unsuccessful cats were characterized by either extreme aggression or actively and avidly "ignoring" their partners. While this ploy may be adaptive in defusing an aggressive situation, it appears to be counterproductive when a female cat is in estrus.

While pouring over zoo records I also discovered a wealth of information about these little-studied cats that had not previously been documented, including gestation rates, the duration of estrus, average litter sizes, sex ratio of kittens, whether particular species produced litters seasonally, and age at sexual maturity.

Stouffer Enterprises/Animals Animals

Source: ISIS and Alan Shoemaker

CENSUS OF SMALL CATS IN CAPTIVITY

Common Name	Scientific Name	Number of Specimens
serval	F. serval	169
bobcat	Lynx rufus	156
Eurasian lynx	L. lynx	110
caracal	L. caracal	92
ocelot	Felis pardalis	76
margay	F. wiedii	58
Geoffroy's cat	F. geoffroyi	35
fishing cat	F. viverrina	33
jaguarundi	F. yagouaroundi	32
black-footed cat	F. nigripes	31
jungle cat	F. chaus	28
leopard cat	F. bengalensis	27
Asian golden cat	F. temmincki	22
Pallas' cat	F. manul	12
rusty-spotted cat	F. rubiginosa	12
pampas cat	F. colocolo	10
Pakistan sand cat	F. margarita scheffeli	9
European wild cat	F. silvestris silvestris	8
African wild cat	F. s. libyca	6
marbled cat	F. marmorata	4
jaguarundi (endangered subspecies only)	F. yagouaroundi	2
flat-headed cat	F. planiceps	1
Mexican bobcat	Lynx rufus escuinapae	1

▲ The fishing cat (*Felis viverrina*) of South and Southeast Asia lives up to its name: crouching on a stream-edge rock or a sandbank (above top) a fishing cat stalks its aquatic prey then seizes the fish with its paws (above right). Fishing cats can also catch fish with their mouth (above) and have been reported to dive deeply for prey. Largely confined to wetland habitats, fishing cats feed on aquatic animals, such as snails, but also take small mammals, birds, and snakes.

What correlations were apparent between the captive milieu and reproductive success? Could I determine the optimal captive environment for small cats? Surprisingly, I found that size of enclosure and number of den sites available were not critical to reproductive success. It would appear that most zoos provide enclosures large enough for these cats, and virtually all provide at least one den box in which the females can give birth. Neither age difference between mates nor type of diet proved to be significant factors in successful reproduction.

Three factors did correlate with successful reproduction in captivity. The number of medical treatments a cat received and the number of cats housed together negatively correlated with reproductive success. In other words, cats with chronic health problems and cats that were

housed in groups larger than a single male with a single female were likely to be reproductively unsuccessful. These two factors seemed intuitively obvious to me — a chronically ill animal is not likely to reproduce, and given the solitary nature of cats, attempts to maintain groups larger than a single male and female would not seem like a good idea. The third significant factor was a surprise. I found that the more time a keeper spent interacting with the cats under his or her care, the more likely those cats were to reproduce. Again, given the solitary nature of these cats, I would not have predicted this outcome. However, in retrospect, this result makes perfect sense. Keepers are an inevitable part of any zoo animal's life. It seems that unless small cats feel "comfortable" with their human caretakers, they are not as likely to be successful breeders. I also found substantial

indirect evidence that nursery-reared cats were much less likely to reproduce than maternally-reared animals.

The most alarming result of the study was the preliminary genetic and demographic analysis I did on the size and relatedness of small cat populations in captivity. Species represented by fewer than 30 individuals, unless immediately and aggressively managed, will eventually cease to exist in captivity. Some populations, such as the rusty-spotted, Pallas', sand, black-footed, pampas, Asian golden, Geoffroy's, and Scottish wild cats, are already highly inbred as well as small. I suspect that the ultimate reason for reproductive failure in many of these small cat species is due to inbreeding depression.

The potential for bringing more individuals into the captive breeding population is confounded by the fact that most of these cats are, in fact, endangered species. Legally (and morally) this means that animals brought in from the wild cannot be exported from the country of origin.

What can be done to save these wonderful little cats? Any plan to do so must certainly be a concerted effort among countries of origin, zoos worldwide, and international conservation organizations. The International Union for Conservation of Nature (IUCN) produces taxonomic analyses for animals in danger of extinction. This organization is currently developing a global conservation plan for felids, and this plan promises to be an important starting point for a cooperative effort between the active conservation of cats in their native habitat and the captive breeding plans for zoos.

IRIOMOTE CAT

FIONA C. SUNQUIST

In 1965, Yukio Togawa, a Japanese writer and naturalist, heard rumors of a new kind of cat that could be found on the remote and mountainous island of Iriomote. When Mr. Togawa arrived on the island, he found that the house-cat-sized animal was well known to the native people. In fact, they occasionally caught it in snares set for wild boar, and considered its meat to be a great delicacy. Mr. Togawa brought two skins and three skulls of the mysterious cat back to mainland Japan and took them to the National Science Museum in Tokyo to be studied by taxonomists. Two years later, in 1967, the Iriomote cat (*Felis iriomotensis*) was declared a new species, and became one of only a handful of new mammal species to be discovered in the last 30 years.

Officially part of Japan, Iriomote Island is actually geographically closer to Taiwan — it is some 2,100 kilometers (1,300 miles) south of Tokyo and only 200 kilometers (125 miles) off the coast of Taiwan. Iriomote Island lies at the end of the Ryukyu chain of islands, which run in a southwesterly direction from the southern end of Japan. The Ryukyu chain of islands is known as the "Galapagos of the Orient" because a long period of isolation from the mainland has caused many of the species found there to evolve distinctive characteristics. Most, like the wild boar and flying fox, are considered to be subspecies of mainland relatives but a few, like the Iriomote cat, have been assigned to their own species. Some experts believe that the Iriomote cat is so different that it should even be given its own genus, but most argue that it is merely a leopard cat that has been isolated for a long time. The debate should soon be resolved by scientists currently using DNA analysis and molecular genetics to sort out felid relationships.

The majority of Iriomote Island is covered with evergreen broadleaf forest, and dense mangrove swamps grow in the river estuaries. Some 1,500 people farm sugar cane, rice and pineapples on the island's flat coastal plain. Despite the fact that it is found nowhere else in the world, the Iriomote cat does not seem to be very specialized in terms of habitat requirements — it lives all over the island, in both mountains and mangroves, and avoids only heavily populated areas.

Slightly larger and heavier than a domestic cat, the average male Iriomote cat weighs about 4 kilograms (9 pounds) and its head and body measures 51 to 56 centimeters (20 to 22 inches) in length with a tail about 30 centimeters (12 inches) long. Both males and females look alike but the females are slightly smaller, weighing about 3.25 kilograms (7 pounds). The Iriomote cat has a dark brown coat that is slightly grayer on the sides and legs. The entire coat is patterned with small black or dark brown spots. There are distinct white markings below each eye and on the inside of the eye next to the nose. The rounded ears have a white spot on the back.

Like most felids, the Iriomote cat is a loner, and feeding experiments have shown that each individual uses an area of 2 to 3 square kilometers (0.8 to 1.2 square miles), each of which overlaps the ranges of several other cats. After spending most of the daylight hours resting in a rock crevice or tree cavity, the Iriomote cat begins to hunt at dusk and is active for most of the night. The cat is an agile climber and almost certainly spends some of its time hunting in trees. It can also swim well (a captive animal was observed playing in water), and wild Iriomote cats have been seen swimming across rivers. These cats take a wide variety of prey and are capable of hunting on land, in trees, and in water. Rats, flying foxes, birds, skinks, and insects form the major part of their diet. The behavior of some of these prey species suggests that the Iriomote cat is also active during at least part of the daytime. Skinks spend the night hiding in crevices and are out and moving around only during the daytime, and flying foxes are only vulnerable to predation when they are at their daytime roosts.

A one-year study of an adult male Iriomote cat in the Okinawa Kodomonokuni Zoo showed that the animal was most active at dawn and dusk, and that it became more nocturnal during the summer and more diurnal during the winter. During the winter the captive Iriomote cat lost weight and spent more time urine marking. In the wild, Iriomote cats are believed to mate during the winter, and the cats can be heard vocalizing and fighting. The cats are also seen in pairs more frequently at this time of the year.

The female selects a secluded place such as a rock crevice or hollow tree for the natal den and may give birth to as many as four young. The kittens are born at the end of April or May, and seem to mature more rapidly than the kittens of domestic cats. Young Iriomote cats have been seen on their own when they are only three months old.

There are believed to be between 50 and 100 Iriomote cats on the 289 square kilometer (112 square mile) island, and the species has been declared a national treasure by the government of Japan. Japan has designated a third of the island as a national reserve, and the law now prohibits anyone from trapping the cat for any reason. Unfortunately, despite these measures, Iriomote cat numbers continue to decline. Each year some cats are killed in snares set to catch wild boar, and others fall victim to development and habitat loss.

In 1984, Shigeki Yasuma and the scientific committee of World Wildlife Fund Japan developed a recovery plan for the Iriomote cat. The plan pinpointed several major problem areas, including the government's supplemental feeding program, the presence of a debilitating eye disease, serious competition from feral domestic cats, and continued habitat destruction. Some progress has been made. The feeding program has been discontinued, and the eye disease has been found to be less serious than was previously thought. However, development pressure has intensified, and plans for roads, dams, and airports continue to threaten the existence of this rare felid.

▶ Only a single population of between 50 and 100 Iriomote cats (*Felis iriomotensis*) exists on the small, mountainous Japanese island of Iriomote, near Taiwan. This cat became known to scientists 25 years ago, but the island's people knew the cat and considered its meat a delicacy.

Tadaaki Imaizumi/Nature Production

▲ An enormous stone lion's head graces Nemrut Dag, a mountain in Turkey. This first century BC sculpture tops the cone-shaped tumulus covering the tomb of Antiochos 1 of Commagene. The lion symbolizes the ruler's kingship and his divine ancestry.

CATS AND

HUMANS

DOMESTIC CATS

Although the early history of the domestic cat (*Felis silvestris catus*) has been obscured by time, little doubt remains concerning its ancestry. Studies of mummified cat remains, excavated from the sacred sites of Ancient Egypt, have revealed only two types of animal. A very small proportion of the largest specimens probably belonged to the species *Felis chaus*, the jungle cat. But the vast majority are virtually indistinguishable from the North African race or subspecies of the wild cat, *F. silvestris libyca*. On the basis of present evidence, it is likely that all modern breeds of cats are descended from this subspecies.

DOMESTICATION

It is popularly believed that the cat was first domesticated in Egypt between four and five thousand years ago, but no authenticated artistic representations of cats apparently existed in Egypt before about 2000 BC. This suggests that either the Egyptians were unfamiliar with cats until this time, or, and perhaps more likely, that the artistic conventions of earlier periods did not include representations of cats. A recent discovery on the Mediterranean island of Cyprus, however, provides evidence of a much older association between cats and people. Archeologists excavating one of the earliest human settlements on Cyprus

(approximately 6000 BC) have unearthed the unmistakable remains of a cat's jawbone. Since wild cats did not occur naturally on the island, this animal almost certainly arrived there by sea with the first human colonists. In other words, it appears that Mediterranean peoples may have been in the habit of capturing and taming wild cats long before the species was properly domesticated.

Some authorities have argued that wild cats originally domesticated themselves by invading and colonizing human settlements in search of small prey such as rats and mice. Since these rodents were probably regarded as vermin, people might have tolerated and encouraged cats around their homes and granaries and, in the process, established a semidomestic population of urban cats which depended increasingly on humans for food and shelter. Conflicting with this idea, is the fact that all modern wild cats, at least as adults, are notoriously timid and intractable, and go out of their way to avoid human contact. The Cyprus discovery, on the other hand, implies that people may have taken a more active role in cat domestication by capturing these animals, probably as kittens, taming them, and keeping them as pets. The practise of keeping tamed wild animals as pets is extremely widespread among tribal peoples throughout the world, and it has been claimed that this peculiarly human habit could have formed the basis upon which many species were first domesticated.

CHANGING FORTUNES

Whatever the process of domestication, it is clear that by 1500 BC the cat was a common household animal in Egypt. Frescoes from the tombs of Theban nobles depicted cats engaged in a variety of activities, such as catching mice, eating fish, or sitting under their owner's chairs. Another common artistic theme illustrated cats hunting alongside their owners among the papyrus swamps of the Nile Delta. Some experts have taken this as documentary evidence that the Egyptians actually used cats for hunting and retrieving game, but anyone who has ever attempted to train a cat

▲▼ First domesticated in ancient Egypt, cats were venerated as sacred animals. Many were mummified (above) upon their natural or sacrificial deaths. Cats figured prominently in Egyptian art, as in this mosaic (below) from a Theban tomb.

Ronald Sheridan/Ancient Art & Architecture Collection

C.M. Dixon

The Granger Collection, New York

would be likely to treat this idea with considerable scepticism. More likely, the image of the hunting cat had a symbolic meaning for the artists of the day, and should not be taken too literally. At about this time, cats also began to play an increasingly prominent role in Egyptian religion.

In the early, predynastic period, local communities worshipped gods mainly in the form of animals. As time progressed, some of these local gods and goddesses acquired widespread popularity, and a few achieved national importance. Within this complex religious structure, cats occupied two important roles. The male cat was sacred to the sun god, Ra, and it was

believed that the sun god adopted the form of a tomcat during his daily battles with the serpent of darkness, Apep. It seems likely that the Egyptians were familiar with the sight of cats attacking and killing snakes, and therefore assumed that Ra would adopt this guise in order to perform the same task. Female cats were regarded as the representatives of the mother goddess, Bastet, whose main cult center was the northern Egyptian town of Bubastis. Later, they also became associated with several other female deities, including Hathor, Mut, and Sekhmet. As the icon of Bastet, the cat symbolized feminine virtues such as beauty, grace, fertility, and motherhood. Cats

► About 30 distinct breeds of domestic cat exist today. The Siamese cat is an ancient breed with origins in Asia, but most modern breeds were developed in the last century by European, largely British, cat fanciers.

Jean-Paul Ferrero/AUSCAPE International

► A short-haired tabby domestic cat with the stocky body shape characteristic of "British" or cold-climate breeds. Fanciers classify breeds as "British" or "foreign." Foreign, or hot-climate, breeds, such as the Siamese, have a slimmer shape and shorter coat than British breeds.

Angelo Gandolfi

► Long-haired cats appeared in Europe after 1500, when Persian longhairs appeared. Descended from long-haired Angora cats from Turkey, Persian longhairs were jealously maintained by fanciers in Italy but eventually reached France and England. Today's diverse colors of Persian longhairs are recent products of selective breeding.

Hans Reinhard/Bruce Coleman Ltd

were also associated with the moon — one of the sources of the earth's fertility — and with the 28-day lunar and menstrual cycle. Despite her regional origins, Bastet eventually became one of the most important goddesses of Egypt around 950 BC, and her cult was still flourishing at the time of the Roman conquest. According to the Greek writer Herodotus, who visited Egypt around 450 BC, the temple at Bubastis was a magnificent building and the focus of an annual festival that attracted hundreds of thousands of ardent worshippers. The temple also contained an immense statue of the goddess, and hundreds of live cats that were cared for by the priesthood.

The status of cats in Egypt at this time seems to have been roughly equivalent to that of cows in present-day India. Anyone causing the death of a cat, even by accident, was liable to be lynched by

angry mobs, and when a cat died of natural causes its owners would shave their eyebrows as a sign of mourning. Dead cats were also mummified and buried, presumably at their owner's expense, in vast underground repositories. One of these sacred burial grounds was unearthed in 1888 and was estimated to have contained the remains of 80,000 cats. Recent research, however, suggests that not all of these animals died a natural death. It appears that during the declining centuries of Egyptian influence, cats were deliberately killed or sacrificed for the purposes of mummification. The Egyptians also banned the export of cats to other countries, and occasionally dispatched special agents to buy and repatriate cats that had been smuggled abroad illegally. As a result, domestic cats were slow to reach other parts of the world, and even by Roman times they were still regarded, outside Egypt, as quite unusual animals.

The rise of Christianity in Europe heralded a fundamental shift in attitudes to cats. During the Middle Ages, the cat's links with the ancient, pagan cult of the mother goddess inspired a wave of persecution that lasted several hundred years. Branded as agents of the Devil, and the chosen companions of witches and necromancers, cats, especially black ones, were enthusiastically tortured and executed during Christian festivals all over Europe. It was also believed that witches disguised themselves as cats as a means of traveling around incognito, so anyone encountering a stray cat at night felt obliged to try and kill or maim the animal. By teaching people to associate cats with the Devil and bad luck, it appears that the Church provided the underprivileged and superstitious masses with a sort of universal scapegoat, something to blame for all of the many hardships and misfortunes of life. Fortunately for cats, such attitudes began to disappear gradually during the seventeenth and eighteenth centuries with the dawn of the so-called Age of Enlightenment. However, not until the middle of the nineteenth century did cats eventually begin to regain the popularity they once enjoyed in Ancient Egypt.

CATS TODAY

About 30 distinct breeds of cats are now recognized, although most can be subdivided into a range of different-colored varieties. All of these breeds fall into two broad categories: the British (European or American, depending on the country of origin) and the foreign. In general, the British type is stockier, with a relatively heavy coat, while the foreign breeds are characterized by the more svelte appearance typical of such breeds as the Siamese and Burmese. Cat breeds are also classified as either long-haired (Persians, Angoras) or short-haired, according to the length of the fur. Despite frequently exotic-sounding names, most modern breeds were created by Western cat "fanciers" and breeders during the last 120 years.

Jane Burton & Kim Taylor/Bruce Coleman Ltd.

Exceptions include the Siamese, Burmese, Birman and Korat (which appear to have originated in Southeast Asia), and the Persian, Angora and Lake Van cats that came originally from parts of the Middle East and southern Soviet Union.

For most of their history, cats have been subjected to far less human control than the majority of domestic animals and, as a result, have been allowed to breed more or less at random. Nevertheless, long before people began to take an active interest in selective breeding, a number of factors combined to introduce substantial variability in body shape and color into domestic cat populations. For example, when cats were first exported from Egypt to other parts of the globe, small founding colonies became geographically and genetically isolated from the ancestral stock. It is well known from studies of other animal populations that this kind of isolation tends to promote rapid genetic divergence. In addition, each isolated regional population was subjected to different local conditions, such as climate, in which natural selection will have favored those individuals best adapted to cope with the new conditions. Local selection pressures of this kind may account for the stocky, thick-coated northern (or British) breeds, and the slim, thin-coated foreign cats of Southeast Asia. Perhaps the most important determinant of variability, though, has been the almost universal (and largely unconscious) human tendency to favor abnormal or unusual-looking animals — animals bearing particular combinations of genes or gene mutations that altered their physical appearance. In cats, this process of selection for novelty has affected mainly the color and quality of the fur.

▲ Even with domestication, cats have lost none of their predatory instincts. Feral cats, which can reach densities of up to 2,000 individuals per square kilometer, may exert significant effects on populations of their rodent and lagomorph prey. Cats have also devastated populations of island birds.

CATS AND HUMAN MIGRATION

Mary Evans Picture Library

Over the last 2,000 years cats have accompanied people to virtually every corner of the globe. According to population geneticists, the descendants of some of these original feline colonists still bear traces of their historical and geographic origins on their genes.

Since the 1940s, over 300 separate studies have investigated the distribution of gene frequencies in domestic cat populations throughout the world. Some of these studies have revealed unexpected differences between neighboring populations of cats in the frequency of the various mutant alleles, or genes, affecting such physical attributes as coat coloration and quality, and the presence of extra toes on the feet (a condition known as polydactyly). For example, detailed examination of local populations of cats in the New England area of the United States revealed that most of them displayed rather similar genetic profiles, and that geographic changes in gene frequencies tended to be gradual rather than sudden. The cats of New York City, however, proved to be exceptional. In particular, New York City contained unusually low frequencies of ginger, tortoiseshell (or calico), and long-haired mutants compared with surrounding populations in New England, and unusually high frequencies of piebald animals. The city was also devoid of polydactylous (extra-toed) cats, although they are relatively common elsewhere in New England.

The geneticist Andrew Lloyd believes that these differences between the cats of New York and New England reflect the fact that these populations originated from different sources. New England, as its name suggests, was originally settled by English colonists who presumably brought their own varieties of English cats with them. Indeed, comparisons between modern

▲ The genetic origin of cats in different geographical regions often mirrors that of humans. Scientists believe that study of domestic cat genetics may help us to understand the movements of people through history.

populations of English and New England cats reveal some striking genetic similarities. New York (formerly known as New Holland) was founded by the Dutch in 1626 and remained an exclusively Dutch colony until it was taken over by the British later that century. As it turns out, the city's cats are genetically closer to the cats of Amsterdam in Holland than they are to all but four of the 24 different New England cat populations that have been examined.

Several other regional cat populations show similar traces of human involvement. For example, most of the cats found on the Portuguese islands of the Azores, Madeira, and Cape Verde in the Atlantic exhibit mutant allele frequencies similar to those of mainland Portugal. The only exception is Mindelo in the Cape Verde Islands, a town which developed into one of the world's largest coaling stations during the middle of the nineteenth century. The coal available at Mindelo was mined and shipped from Wales, and it appears that British cats accompanied the shipments and were occasionally left behind. Mindelo's cats display an unusually high frequency of blotched tabby coloration, the result of a genetic mutation that is thought to have originated in the British Isles.

The feline gene frequencies of New York or Mindelo are the result of relatively recent colonial exploits, but Lloyd suggests that it may one day be possible to retrace far more ancient and less well-known human migration routes by comparing the genetic profiles of cat populations.

James Serpell

▲ Examples of some common cat coat colors, and the main genes/gene combinations involved. Top row, left to right: Striped or mackerel tabby (wild-type *TT*); Burmese (c^bc^b); tortoiseshell and white female (*Oo* and *S-*); dominant white (*W-*; note odd-colored eyes). Bottom row, left to right: Ginger or sex-linked orange female (*OO*); gray (or blue) dilution (*dd*); blotched tabby and white (t^bt^b and *S-*); non-agouti black (*aa*).

MAIN ALLELES AFFECTING COAT COLOR IN CATS

Alleles	Name	Main effects on coloration
aa	non-agouti	Converts wild-type banded or agouti hairs to solid color, such as black, chocolate, gray, cream.
bb	chocolate	Converts black pigment to brown/chocolate.
c^sc^s or c^bc^b	Siamese or Burmese	Produces a condition known as Himalayan albinism in which extremities are more densely colored than the body. Effect is less pronounced in Burmese.
dd	dilution	Dilutes dense colors such as black or chocolate to produce, for example, grays, blues and creams.
I-	silver	Removes yellow or fawn pigment from wild-type agouti hairs to produce a silvery effect.
O-	sex-linked orange	Replaces black pigment with orange. Produces different effects according to sex: males are always orange (ginger), females may be ginger or tortoiseshell.
S-	piebald spotting	Produces variable amounts of white piebald spotting.
t^bt^b	blotched tabby	Converts wild-type "mackerel" tabby stripes to blotches.
W-	dominant white	Produces an all white cat with blue, yellow or odd-colored eyes (sometimes linked with deafness).

During the course of this century, numerous experiments by cat breeders and geneticists have revealed a great deal about the genetic inheritance of coat color and quality in domestic cats. For example, the ancestral or wild-type coloration of the cat is the striped or mackerel tabby pattern typical of *Felis silvestris*. This color pattern is controlled by the tabby gene, symbolized by the capital letter *T*. This gene is also known to occur in an alternative mutant form, t^b, which is recessive (in other words, its effect is suppressed) whenever it is paired with the dominant gene, *T*. Since every cat carries a pair of these tabby genes (or alleles), its appearance will depend on the particular combination it inherits from its parents. Cats with the combination *TT* or *Tt^b* will be mackerel tabbies (in the second case, the dominant *T* will mask the expression of its recessive partner). The combination t^bt^b will produce a so-called blotched tabby in which the tabby stripes broaden and

merge into broad black bands and blotches. Just to complicate matters all of these effects can be masked by the "agouti" gene, *A*, which controls the background coloration against which the tabby stripes are normally seen. Agouti coloration (named after the South American rodent of that name) is the typical "ticked" brown fur color found in many mammals in which only the tips of the hairs are pigmented black. The recessive mutation *a* (or non-agouti), causes the entire hair to be pigmented black, with the result that a tabby cat bearing the gene combination *aa* is entirely black in color because its black tabby stripes or blotches are no longer visible. It is now known that all of the variations in the coat colors of modern cats are controlled by about nine pairs of alleles, although other less well-understood genetic factors may occasionally modify the way in which these different genes are expressed in the physical appearance of the animal.

CATS AND CULTURE

SUSAN LUMPKIN

▲ Throughout human history, representations of cats have appeared in every medium and adorned objects of virtually every conceivable purpose. This lion-headed scent bottle was made in Corinth about 1640 BC.

No group of animals exerts a more powerful influence or compels more intense fascination from people than do cats. Our relationship with cats, whether predatory tigers or purring house cats, is ancient and universal. Indeed, it is impossible to imagine human culture without cats, so greatly have they influenced our art and literature, our myths and legends, our symbols and psyches, and our history.

LIONS

According to Greek legend, the sun god Apollo created the lion; and his twin sister, Diana, who was identified with the moon, created a miniature copy of it — the cat — to ridicule him. This legend shows that people have long recognized the similarity of lion and cat, despite their enormous size disparity, and it suggests that part of the appeal of house cats is that they symbolize mastering the awesome big cats. The legend also encapsulates cats as symbols of sun and moon, good and evil, life-giver and life-taker.

Lions were already in possession of the African plains when our ancestors first emerged from the forest to embark on a new way of life. To these poorly armed and virtually defenseless proto-humans, lions must have loomed large — as predators, as competitors, and even as teachers in the ways of hunting. And throughout human evolution people have encountered lions, which were once distributed throughout Africa, Europe, the Middle East and north Asia to Siberia, south Asia as far as India and Sri Lanka and, until about 10,000 years ago, in North America and into northern South America. Perhaps this is why lions — and by extension all cats — have, as Evelyn Ames observed, "impressed themselves so deeply on the human mind, if not its blood, it is as though the psyche were emblazoned with their crest."

Lions occupy a dominant role paralleled only by the domestic cat in the myths, symbols, legends, literature, and art of peoples throughout the world. Portraits of lions appear in Europe's Paleolithic cave paintings and engravings. The earliest portrait, dated 3000 BC, of the Egyptian goddess Bastet shows her as lion-headed, although later she was more often revealed as a cat. Since then lions have been depicted in every media and appear on objects from ancient coins and jewelry to modern cars and baseball caps.

Wherever they are used, lions symbolize strength and power. They are often associated with the sun. Bastet as a lion-headed goddess was described as the "flaming eye of the sun," but was considered more benign than her fierce lion-headed twin, Sekhmet, who was associated with war as well as the sun. In Mesopotamia, the lion was the symbol of Ishtar, the goddess of love and war. Much later, in medieval Europe, the lion appeared as a symbol of Christ. Coins from the

Mogul empire in India depict lions and the rising sun together.

In Africa, a staff carved with a lion figure often signified a chief's power, and the belief that eating lion meat and especially a lion's heart imbued people with great courage was widespread. Also widespread in Africa were beliefs about chiefs being reincarnated as lions and the souls of dead chiefs entering the bodies of lions. Similarly, the ability to kill lions was a testament to a hunter's prowess, with Heracles, Samson, and kings throughout history earning powerful reputations through hunting lions; interestingly, the hunting of these big cats was often forbidden to anyone but rulers. Many individuals — from Europe's Richard the Lionhearted to Ethiopia's Haile Selassie, dubbed "Lion of Judea" — have adopted the lion as a symbol of power. Lions also emblazon

▼ *A Lion Hunt* by Peter Paul Rubens (1577–1640). Rubens captures the tumult of a lion hunt in a painting full of intense writhing activity. The realism of the lions is typical of the period, when European artists were familiar with and fascinated by such exotic beasts.

European flags and coats of arms, and in the Netherlands, the lion is the national symbol. Today, lions continue to represent power — as mascots for football or other sporting teams, as corporate logos, and in advertising. (In a modern version of the Apollo and Diana legend, the purring cat logo of Mary Tyler Moore's MTM television production company pokes fun at the famous roaring lion logo that represents Hollywood's powerful MGM movie company.)

Lions are sacred to Buddhists as defenders of the law and as protectors of sacred buildings. In the latter capacity countless stone lions guard castles, churches, bridges, and public buildings throughout the world. Perhaps an extension of the notion of lions as defenders of the law is the theme of lions being magnanimous. This theme recurs throughout literature, from the famous story of Androcles and the Lion to the modern children's story, *The Lion, the Witch, and the Wardrobe*.

TIGERS

Tigers play a powerful symbolic role in Asia similar to that of lions in Africa and western Europe. Koreans dub the tiger "King of Beasts," and throughout Asia, tiger motifs connote the power of kings. In China, the markings on a tiger's forehead are interpreted as the Chinese character for "king"; tigers and dragons together symbolize the two great forces of nature *yin*, or evil, and *yang*, good. As with lions, the hunting of tigers in Asia was a sport reserved for potentates. Tigers were often kept in oriental courts and used as executioners, as lions were in Rome. Chinese emperors employed tigers in boar and deer hunts.

▲ The Egyptian cat-goddess Bastet in bronze, about 751– 656 BC. She is seen here holding her three emblems: a sistrum in her right hand symbolizing the worship of Isis, to whom cats were considered sacred; an aegis or shield to demonstrate her fierceness; and a rush basket to carry her kittens.

▶ In symbolic, metaphoric, and actual forms, cats figure prominently in world literature, as in the story of Prince Assad from the Arabian Nights. This illustration by E. J. Detmold of "whilst they were yet devouring the meat, she hastily filled his flagon" appeared in a 1924 edition of this classic tale.

▶ This poster advertising a French circus about 1887 uses the powerful image, universally recognized in Western culture, of Christians being fed to lions in the Roman Colosseum to entice people to attend. Part of the popular appeal of circuses is the drama inherent in people confronting big cats.

▶ (Far top right) *Tiger* by Katsushika Hokusai (1760 –1849). A print artist with a great love of nature, Hokusai belonged to Japan's Ukiyo-e school of artists. Ukiyo-e means "pictures of the fleeting world," which perfectly captures this image of a tiger.

▶ (Far right) Molded and glazed brick panel of a lion from sixth century Babylon, where lions were depicted as symbols of royal power. This lion's well-developed mane was characteristic of the now-extinct subspecies of lion in North Africa and perhaps the Middle East.

Perno/Explorer

Jenny Mills

▲ In Taoism, the forces controlling the universe are represented by the tiger and the dragon. *Yin*, or evil, is controlled by the tiger, while *yang*, or good, is controlled by the dragon. The role of the tiger is reversed in Buddhist thought, in which the tiger represents *yang*.

▶ Typical of Mogul art, this painting illustrating *Akbar-Nama* (c. 1580) portrays the Mogul Emperor Akbar the Great hunting tigers. Hunting tigers was a sport reserved for royalty, serving to enhance the ruler's powerful image by showing his mastery over even so fierce and strong an adversary as a tiger.

▶ (Far right) *Rêve causé par le vol d'une abeille autour d'une pomme-grenade une seconde avant l'éveil* by Salvador Dali, (1944). Concrete imagery in bizarre juxtaposition — an accurately depicted tiger leaping from the mouth of an equally realistic fish, for example — is typical of Dali's surrealism with its focus on dreams and the unconscious.

Victoria and Albert Museum, London/The Bridgeman Art Library, London

Tigers play a role in the religious beliefs of Asia. In Hinduism, Shiva is both destroyer and reproducer; as destroyer he is pictured wearing a tiger skin and riding a tiger. His consort is Parvati the Beautiful who, in her dark side, appears as Durga the Terrible riding a tiger. A disciple of Buddha also rides a tiger to demonstrate his supernatural powers and ability to overcome evil. In Java, the tiger symbolizes mercurial, violent power.

Asians are profoundly influenced by the tiger and its danger to people, and their belief systems reflect this. Those who live in the tiger's domain, view tigers with great respect as well as fear. Many forest tribes in India deified tigers and erected temples and other shrines for tiger worship. In Thailand and Malaysia, forest-living aborigines believe tigers to be the avengers of their Supreme Being; tigers will kill only those who violate tribal law. In Sumatra, where Islam was introduced 500 years ago, the tiger is believed to punish sinners on behalf of Allah. Throughout the villages of Southeast Asia, shamans (priests) and magicians adopt the guise of tigers to promote a powerful, fearsome image.

Like lions in Africa, tigers in Asia are commonly associated with soul transfer and reincarnation, and legends of were-tigers (people who turn themselves into tigers at will) are widespread. In some Asian cultures, groups of were-tigers are believed to live, in their human form, in complex village societies.

In modern Asia, tigers figure prominently in advertising (as they do in North America and Europe), and tiger brands of products from soap to matches and beer abound.

Being an Asian animal, tigers appeared later in European culture than lions. But once they became known, through travelers' tales and later through animals brought to Europe, the tiger's sinuous beauty and awesome power quickly fired the imaginations of writers and artists. Shakespeare often used tiger images, for example when Romeo expresses his desire for Juliet:

> The time and my intents are savage-wild,
> More fierce and more inexorable far
> Than empty tigers or the roaring sea.

and when Henry V exhorts his men to courage at the battle of Agincourt:

> But when the blast of war blows in our ears,
> Then imitate the action of the tiger;
> Stiffen the sinews, summon up the blood,
> Disguise fair nature with hard-favor'd rage;
> Then lend the eye a terrible aspect.

In 1936, Winston Churchill drew on the Chinese proverb, "He who rides a tiger is afraid to dismount" to warn of the impending dangers in Europe: "Dictators ride to and fro upon tigers which they dare not dismount. And the tigers are getting hungry."

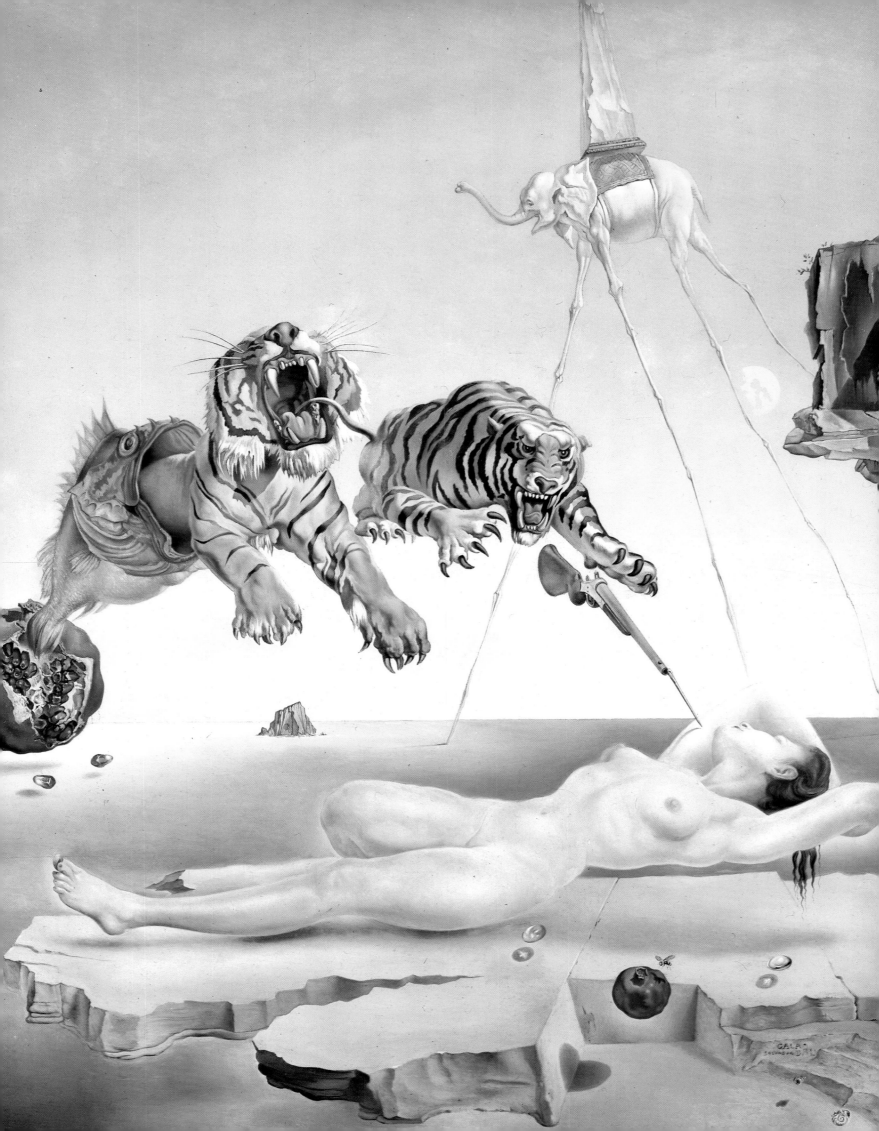

JAGUARS AND PUMAS

In the cultures of the Americas, jaguars and pumas occupy symbolic roles similar to those of lions and tigers in other parts of the world.

From Mexico to the Andes, art, religion, and culture were dominated by jaguar images.

▶ Jade figurines of jaguar spirit (800 – 400 BC), made by the Olmecs, who created the earliest known civilization in Mexico. The jaguar totem was the central theme of Olmec culture, as it would be for later Latin American civilizations like the Maya and Aztecs.

Werner Forman Archive/Dallas Museum of Fine Art

▶ A throne in the shape of a jaguar in the Temple of the Jaguar, part of the massive Maya sacred site of Chitchen Itza in Mexico's Yucatan Peninsula. Jaguars represented the Maya underworld, and evil gods, such as Jaguar God of the Night, take their form.

D. Donne Bryant Stock

Throughout Maya history, the jaguar symbolized the night sun of the underworld, which personified fear, night terrors, and death; jaguar motifs thus figure prominently on Maya funerary vessels. The Tucano Indians of the Amazon believed the sun created the jaguar as his earthly representative. The Olmecs of Mexico and many other peoples deified jaguars and built massive monuments devoted to their worship.

Everywhere, jaguars were associated with power and religion. Rulers in ancient Guatemala were given the title "Jaguar." Shamans were believed by some Indians to turn into jaguars after their death, and it was widely believed in Mexico, in an echo of the were-tiger legends of Asia, that some people could take on the shape of jaguars. The Arawak Indians in northeast South America today still perform man–jaguar transformation rituals to give a shaman the power to bring good or evil as the situation demands.

In the South American Andes and in North America, pumas rather than jaguars feature as feared and respected deities as well as cultural symbols. The ancient Peruvian city of Cuzco was laid out in the shape of a puma. Just as the jaguar represented the Maya underworld, so a widespread North American Indian legend has the puma in the form of an underwater panther ruling the watery underworld and controlling storms. The Cochiti Indians of present-day New Mexico carved a pair of life-sized pumas into the bedrock atop a mesa, in a puma shrine that a few Indians still visit today.

For European Americans, jaguars and pumas, as the largest cats in the Americas, took on the mystique of lions and tigers. American big-game hunters, for instance, looked to jaguars and pumas for the ultimate trophy. Jaguars and pumas have also come to represent fast cars and football teams.

OTHER WILD CATS

Everywhere that cats are found, people seem to have incorporated them symbolically into their culture. Leopards are common totemic animals in Africa, and were-leopard legends are known from Africa and India. In the Neolithic town of Catalhüyük, in present-day Turkey, evidence exists of leopard worship, and leopards are associated here and at other sites with fertility goddesses. Leopards are common elements in European heraldry and some experts believe that the lions that symbolize England were originally leopards.

In Norse mythology, Freyja, the goddess of love and beauty, is associated with the lynx and is often depicted riding one. The golden cat is sacred to some central African tribes and the clouded leopard to some Southeast Asians. In various societies, cheetahs and caracals were trained to stalk and capture prey. In parts of Europe and the Middle East, cheetahs once rivaled dogs as the favorite hunting companions of the rich.

CONCLUSION

Cats everywhere, especially big cats, evoke powerful emotions in humans — fear, awe, and longing. The image of beautiful, majestic big cats living as mighty predators is absolutely compelling, representing all that is powerful, wild, and free; so compelling, in fact, that big cats continue to live in the imagination of some: the extinct Bali tiger, for example, still exists in the minds of many Balinese; and, on a lighter note, erroneous reports of loose tigers or leopards regularly electrify rural communities in the United States. Sadly, without human action to conserve great cats, the awe these magnificent beasts inspire, and have inspired throughout history, will exist only in our collective memories.

◄ The belief in were-jaguars dates at least to the Olmecs in Latin America. Were-jaguars may have been the forerunners of Aztec and Maya rain gods. Today, vestiges of such beliefs remain, as in this Pre-Columbian festival for rain in which men dress as jaguars.

Nick Saunders/Barbara Heller

◄ Nearly life-sized ivory leopards, made from five elephant tusks, with copper discs forming the spots and eyes made of pieces of mirror, from nineteenth century Benin, Africa. The oba, or king, of Benin treated the leopard, with its courage and cunning, as the primary symbol of chieftainship.

The Granger Collection, New York

GREAT CATS IN WESTERN ART

LISA FLORMAN WEINBERG

▼ (Top) The tiger in this illumination from a twelfth century English Latin bestiary is typical of medieval symbolic representations of animals. (Bottom) *Hercules fighting with the Nemean lion* by Francisco de Zurbaran (1598 –1664) portrays the first of the mythical Greek hero's Labors.

The Granger Collection, New York

Prado, Madrid/The Bridgeman Art Library, London

On one side of a sculpted sarcophagus in the Istanbul Museum, a horseman wearing a distinctive lion-faced helmet charges into battle, spearing a hapless Persian who has recognized too late the wisdom of retreat. Not simply the expression of an artist's whim, the detail of the lion-skin helmet is in fact highly significant, for it serves to identify the rider as none other than Alexander the Great. At the same time the headgear represents a clever solution to the problem that confronted all early portraitists of that amazing man: how to convey to posterity both Alexander's handsome features *and* those other, less visible qualities that earned him his epithet.

Crowning Alexander with the features of a lion was a solution borrowed from earlier Greek images of Heracles, which customarily showed the mythical hero draped in the skin of the Nemean lion that he had slain as the first of his 12 great Labors. Even those images were artistic conceits, sanctioned by the belief that with animals in general, and perhaps large cats in particular, inward nature and outward appearance are more perfectly matched than they are with human beings. In either instance, Heracles in his lion skin or Alexander in Heracles' lion skin, leonine features were grafted onto the man to signal that he also possessed the *character* of a lion — its courage, its intelligence, its lethal potential.

The fact that large cats have continued to serve as symbols throughout much of the subsequent history of Western art is no doubt due to the invariably powerful visual impression the animals make. The ideas they have symbolized, however, have changed markedly over time, as have notions about which particular aspects of the cats' appearance and behavior are most symbolic. In the medieval world, for example, lions abounded with meaning, and not merely within the realm of art. God's own creations were seen as full of significance, each species embodying a moral or biblical lesson, there to be read by the pious and astute. Alongside their continuing associations with courage and strength, medieval lions also symbolized — in art as in the wild — Christ's resurrection, because of the common (mis)conception that the newborn lion lay dead for three days, until its father literally blew life into it.

During the Renaissance, people generally stopped hunting for such complex allegories within nature and turned instead to its empirical study. As one aspect of this awakened interest in the natural world, lions and other fabulous creatures were brought to Europe, to be marveled at and examined. Artists readily incorporated the knowledge gained from direct observation into their images of, for example, Daniel or Saint Jerome, both of whom were said to have tamed lions by the sheer strength of their piety and faith. In contrast to the schematic style of medieval art, the descriptive realism of Renaissance and Baroque works served to persuade those who saw them of the fundamental truth of the images; in that sense, they were much like the illustrations and photographs throughout this very book. But the need to be convincing was in some ways even more acute with a painting or sculpture of Daniel or Jerome, since the behavior of the docile lions that accompanied them threatened to make the entire image appear utterly unbelievable.

Through the incongruity of their actions, these Renaissance and Baroque lions reinforced the value their societies placed on restraint and pious humility. The lions of nineteenth century art, however, were altogether different beasts. The artists who created them admired large cats precisely for their lack of restraint, their wildness. Eugène Delacroix's painting *Horse Attacked by a Tiger,* was but one variation on a common theme, in which a cat, epitomizing instinct and raw emotion, devours a more "civilized" or domesticated animal. "The tigers of wrath are wiser than the horses of instruction," William Blake had written. Delacroix not only gave visible form to this opposition, he also rendered the speed and savagery of the tiger in the flashing bravura of his brushwork.

The lions and tigers in the paintings of the French "primitive" artist Henri Rousseau are the twentieth century heirs of Delacroix's cats. A similar Romantic celebration of life untouched by the stifling refinements of human society is manifest both in Rousseau's feline-filled jungles and in the cultivated "uncultivation" of his style. Despite his ambition to break with the traditions of Western art, Rousseau responded to the commanding physical presence of lions and tigers as so many artists had responded before him — with a desire to harness the cats' visual power to his own art.

Jean-Louis Charmet/Explorer

▲ *St. Blandine,* an anonymous watercolor for a catechism of the early twentieth century. The huge but docile lions serve to emphasize the saint's piety and faith, which proved strong enough to tame and even inspire the protection of ferocious lions in the Roman circus.

▼ *Horse Attacked by a Tiger* by Eugene Delacroix. Artists of the nineteenth century used big cats to represent instinct and raw emotion, admiring them for their wildness and savagery. The theme of this painting, in which a wild tiger is killing a domestic, or "civilized," horse, was a common one in this period of Western art.

The Louvre, Paris/Reunion Museé Nationaux

Eug Delacroix.

► *Tropical Story with a Tiger* by Henri Rousseau, 1891. Lions and tigers figure prominently in the "primitive" paintings of Rousseau. His fanciful jungles filled with big cats and other beasts were a celebration of life outside of the constraints of civilization.

The Granger Collection, New York

TIGERS AND LIONS IN ASIAN ART

JAN STUART

Cats are ubiquitous in world art, but they have been represented in some startlingly different styles. Indeed, art is rarely objective; rather, it reflects the culture of its origin. Thus the depictions of the big cats in Asian art reveal not only the artistic heritage of a people, but also attitudes and myths about the great felines.

Because of the cultural diversity of Asia, it is necessary to restrict the scope of discussion. And, as China exerted some influence on its eastern neighbors — Korea and Japan — as well as assimilating selected elements from the west — Central Asia and India — it provides a convenient example for inquiry into cats in Asian art. The two most common felines in Chinese art are the tiger and the lion; they embellish all popular art media including ceramics, embroidery, jade carving, painting, and stone sculpture. A study of these two cats in Chinese art reveals the complex relationship between real animals and cultural stereotypes. The image of an animal is often determined by the role it plays, such as, serving as a totem in man's search for a protective spirit, or symbolizing human qualities, such as dignity and valor. The nature of the real animal is almost divorced from its appearance in art, which may partially explain why a civilization like the Chinese would create admiring images of the great tiger, while simultaneously hunting it to virtual extinction in their own country.

TIGERS

The first feline depicted in Chinese art was the tiger, whose range once included all of China. Since antiquity, the tiger was cast in the role of King of the Beasts, which led to the fanciful convention of depicting the stripes on a tiger's head like the Chinese character for "king." Folk artists were especially fond of this convention.

During the Shang dynasty (1700–1050 BC) tigers enjoyed the rather dubious honor of serving as the "chief prey" in royal sporting hunts. In later times, the convention of placing a tiger pelt on the seat of an emperor or an exalted scholar continued the association between tigers and noble bearing.

Close examination of Shang culture reveals that the tiger was considered to be not only regal, but also beneficent. Shang art, especially ritual bronze vessels, repeatedly used faces and other bodily parts of tigers, birds, cattle, and dragons in its designs. When, occasionally, a human figure was included, a tiger was always present. One example is the wine vessel (*you*) now in the Musée Cernuschi, Paris, that depicts a small man hugging a tiger-like beast and placing his head in the cat's open jaws (below left). As the Shang people believed that ancestor spirits controlled their destinies and that tigers were potent messengers between the human and spirit worlds, this vessel probably represents a king or his appointed shaman (priest) using a tiger as a medium to communicate with the ancestors. By dressing in animal skins and using this kind of vessel in a ritual ceremony, the king could express his spiritual union with the unseen powers of the universe.

In the succeeding Zhou (Chou) dynasty (1050–221 BC), the bronzes became more sculptural and conveyed awe for the tiger's lethal power. A pair of tiger-shaped structural supports (below right) from the ninth century BC, now in the Freer Gallery of Art, Washington, D. C., illustrate this. They seem ready to rip open prey with their deadly fangs and talon-like claws. The convincing swell of the tiger's muscular shoulders and haunches and elegant dip at the center of the back make it obvious that the artisan knew his subject first-hand. During the latter part of the Zhou dynasty in the Warring States period (480–221 BC) artisans often depicted man and tiger in combat.

During the Han dynasty (206 BC–AD 220), images of powerful tigers persisted, but there was renewed emphasis on their beneficial powers. In the elaborate tombs of the period,

▼ Bronze wine vessel, Shang Dynasty (1700–1050 BC). A king or priest uses a tiger as messenger to communicate with ancestors in the spirit world.

▼ One of a pair of bronze tiger-shaped structural supports, ninth century, Zhou Dynasty (1050–221 BC), accurately rendering the tiger's lethal power.

Museé Cernuschi/Ville de Paris

Freer Art Gallery

images of tigers were used to deter evil spirits from disturbing the grave and the soul of the deceased.

After the Han dynasty, the tiger was most often portrayed as a protective guardian, and the mighty animals were also occasionally used for propaganda. Sometimes paintings of fighting tigers were commissioned by emperors, to show the imperial might and valor of the ruler.

Some twentieth-century artists have used the tiger as a national symbol. When China was threatened by Japanese domination, a painting of a roaring tiger symbolized China's fury and fighting spirit against the oppressor.

Another traditional guise of the tiger is as friend of Buddhist monks. Scenes of tigers either sleeping next to or subserviently sitting at a monk's feet demonstrated Buddhism's power to harmonize and tame nature's forces. In this role, the majestic and fierce tiger often took on the persona of a pussycat — soft, plump, and round.

LIONS

The lion, not native to China, first appeared in Chinese art during the first century AD, when Buddhism was introduced from India. Perhaps because of their rarity, lions became a great source of fascination, which led to their rise as one of the most enduringly popular art motifs. Two distinct styles for portraying lions evolved: one style realistically celebrated the cat's imposing strength, while the other approach was fantastical and, in the Han and Six dynasties (265–589 AD), included winged lions, called chimera.

Some of the exaggeration in the depiction of lions stems from the animals' scarcity in China. Real lions were known only as tribute brought by foreigners to the imperial court. The first record of an actual lion in China is dated 87 AD, when a Central Asian prince offered one in exchange for a Chinese princess, whom he wanted to marry. The Romans sent lions to China to trade for silk, but few artisans saw the real animals, and after the tenth century, when trade with the West declined, there were few, if any, live models.

Lions were most commonly depicted in Buddhist art. Continuing a tradition from India, Chinese artists usually portrayed the Buddha seated on a throne supported by a pair of lions, which were an emblem of the Sakya clan to which the historical Buddha belonged. Chinese temples were conventionally flanked by lion sculptures, a custom which in addition to Buddhist reference may also reflect Chinese knowledge in the ancient Near East and Mesopotamia. There, lions were symbols of power and authority and the guardians of sacred buildings. Gradually sculpted lions were also used to ennoble and protect the entrances to secular buildings, such as palaces, government offices or even private gardens. These lions were sometimes so exaggerated that Westerners thought they represented Pekingese pugs, which is the origin of the term "Fo Dog" (literally, "Buddhist Dog") and applies to the large lions by doors as well as portable images that were used on domestic Buddhist altars.

Palace architects, especially in the last two dynasties, the Ming (1368–1644) and the Qing (1644–1911) made great use of lions as protective spirits: stone and gilt bronze lions stood sentinel to palace courtyards and although these beasts did not have the wings of their earlier cousins, they were often as unrealistic. Typically a male and female lion were paired together, and both were given full manes. The male (below left) could be identified because he usually played with a brocaded ball, whereas the female (below right) had a cub beneath her paw (it was rumored that lions nursed from their mother's paws).

The lion was easily transformed in Chinese imagination into a mythical beast. It was only during the Tang dynasty (618–907), when thriving trade and military expansion brought China into close contact with "lion country," that artists depicted fierce, realistic looking lions. They symbolized Tang valor. After the fall of the Tang dynasty, China turned inward and artists reverted to portraying whimsical lions. The great cats became docile creatures embellished with more of a froufrou of curls than with true manes. It is these fantastical lions that have dominated Chinese art, suggesting that people, if China can be considered representative, prefer an artist's view of nature, which encodes cultural nuances, to the majesty of a real lion.

▼ Gilded bronze lions protecting the Gate of Supreme Harmony, The Forbidden City, Beijing, Qing Dynasty (1644–1911). The unrealistically maned female (right) holds a cub beneath her paw while the male (left) plays with a brocaded ball.

Tony Adina/Explorer

Rosi Baumgartner/Explorer

MAN-EATERS

CHARLES McDOUGAL

C.M. Dixon

▲ A Bengal tiger mauls an officer of the British East India Company in this wooden figure created for Tipu Sultan, an 18th century Indian ruler. Known as the Tiger of Mysore, Tipu Sultan was obsessed with tigers, and he loathed the British. This life-size model includes a mechanism that simulates the groans of the man and the roars of the tiger.

► Man-eating tigers appear rarely but regularly throughout their Asian range. Hunger, infirmity, or old age may force a tiger to suppress its normal tendency to avoid people. For these cats, people are prey more easily captured than deer or other wild creatures.

► Hong Kong policemen display the body of a man-killing tiger, shot in 1915 after killing two policemen searching for it. Once numerous on the mainland near Hong Kong, tigers often swam to the tiny, densely populated island. The last Hong Kong tiger was shot in 1942.

Humans and large cats evolved side by side during the Pleistocene (2 million–10,000 years ago). By virtue of their greater intelligence and a technology that produced ever more efficient weapons, humans eventually emerged as the dominant predator. Despite their superior size, power, and agility, the big cats came to regard humans with respect if not fear. They learned that avoiding bipedal man was the best strategy for survival. Humans do not form part of the natural prey of these great predators.

A relevant observation was made by the American biologist George Schaller during his study of the behavior of lions in Tanzania's Serengeti National Park. On those occasions when encounters with humans led lions to attack them, they attacked man as though he were another predator and not an item of prey. During the attack, the lion did not assume an aggressive facial expression, but instead the bared tooth defensive one, demonstrating an element of fear.

Despite their usual avoidance of human beings and their general reluctance to attack them, some exceptional cats do kill and eat people. Moreover, they have done so throughout history under a variety of circumstances. Cases of man-eating by tigers have been recorded from almost all parts of the tiger's range in Asia. Cases of man-eating by lions have been reported from nearly every part of Africa where that species is found. The Asian lion, however, even when its range was much more widespread, rarely preyed on people. Leopards have attacked and eaten humans in both Asia and Africa, although much less commonly than either tigers or lions. Even more rarely have the American jaguars killed people to obtain food. The shy and elusive snow leopard, the remaining *Panthera* species, has never been known to prey on man. The same is true of the cheetah, and for the other non-*Panthera* big cat, the puma, man-killing is very rare.

Exceptional cases apart, such as the Champawat Tigress and the Tsavo lions (see below), man-eating cats only supplement their normal diet with human prey and are not completely dependent on it.

TIGERS

Among the large cats, tigers have earned the greatest notoriety for preying on humans. A few individuals have claimed almost incredible numbers of victims — 436 in the case of the Champawat Tigress. The fierce beauty, combined with the solitary and secretive nature of the man-eating tiger, have enhanced its mystique. Adapted to a habitat characterized by thick cover, this cat is a cautious killer, seldom attacking unless everything is in its favor. Unlike the leopard, and,

to a lesser extent the lion, the man-eating tiger seldom penetrates human settlements in search of victims. Rather, humans are attacked on the tiger's own ground, and almost always during daylight. The person is rushed from behind at close quarters following a careful stalk, or they are ambushed at a place of the tiger's own choosing. Occasionally a person squatting or crouching in dense vegetation is killed when mistaken for another animal, and may be eaten.

Tigers have been responsible for the death of more humans than any other big cat. Prior to World War II the toll in British India alone, excluding the numerous Princely States, sometimes exceeded 1,500 deaths a year. This figure included all people killed during encounters with tigers, not only the victims of man-eaters. Perhaps the figures were occasionally inflated by conveniently blaming a murder on a tiger but, on the other side of the coin, many genuine cases were never reported.

Man-eating has always occurred under circumstances in which humans and tigers have come into conflict because of the disruption of the balance between tigers and their natural prey population. Man-eating is the ultimate expression of such conflict.

It is almost always the humans who have created the problem, directly or indirectly. Man-eating tigers are not a problem where suitable habitat is extensive, where sufficient natural prey is available, where the surrounding human population density is moderate, and where colonization or modification of the tiger's habitat is minimal, or even gradual. Such conditions existed over much of the Indian subcontinent before World War II; they still exist in some parts of Asia. The low incidence of man-eating was not due to lack of opportunity. For example, during the last century tigers were especially numerous in Burma's Tenasserim region. Nevertheless, according to contemporary reports, local people had no qualms about wandering in the heart of tiger country, even when alone. Attacks were almost unknown. During a year in which 800 people were killed by tigers in British India, only 16 were killed by these cats in the whole of Burma.

What then causes a tiger to become a man-eater? Not all man-eaters are old or infirm tigers too handicapped to capture natural prey. Many are in prime condition. Any factor that causes a tiger to subordinate its normal inclination to avoid humans, and its reluctance to attack them, can lead to man-eating. In the overwhelming majority of cases that factor is hunger.

The usual scenario is that the prospective man-eater is forced to survive in a marginal habitat where natural prey is scarce. This situation may result if a good habitat is degraded and the natural prey population decimated by people. It may also happen when weaker tigers — the young, the old, and the infirm — are pushed out to the periphery by more vigorous ones during competition for limited space in diminished prime habitat areas. In either case the tiger finds it difficult to secure sufficient natural food. Should the cat be old or disabled, or a female tiger with growing cubs to feed, the likelihood of it becoming a man-eater is increased. Most man-eaters begin by preying on village livestock. The first human victim is often a herdsman protecting his charges.

Today "problem tigers" are becoming a dilemma for conservationists, especially in the Indian subcontinent, but increasingly so in other regions as well. Tigers are flourishing in the special reserves which have been set aside to protect them and the ecosystems of which they are part. Reproduction is high and in some cases tiger populations are at saturation level. Often, however, tiger habitats adjacent to the reserves have been destroyed or degraded by the increasing demands of the surrounding human settlements. Tigers that gravitate to the periphery run out of habitat and into problems. "Problem tigers" give the species bad press and undermine local support for conservation, allowing politicians to ask, "Which are more important, tigers or people?"

A good example is Dudwa National Park in the Kheri district of India's Uttar Pradesh state, where tiger conservation has been very successful. Unfortunately, much of the area adjacent to Dudwa has been deforested for the cultivation of sugar cane. To a tiger, sugar cane looks like the tall grasses found in its natural habitat, so cats dispersing to the edge of the park often seek cover in the plantations. It is only a question of time before they encounter people at close quarters. In the decade from 1978 to 1987, 170 people were killed by tigers in the Kheri district.

A major trouble spot in the Indian subcontinent is the Sundarbans delta of the Ganges and Brahmaputra Rivers, which is nearly 10,000 square kilometers (3,860 square miles) of tidal mangrove forest that covers a multitude of islands formed by the many channels emptying into the Bay of Bengal. Sixty percent of the Sundarbans is in Bangladesh and 40 percent in India. It supports 500 to 600 tigers, the largest single population in

Raghu Rai/Magnum

Peter Jackson

Peter Jackson

▲ Nepalese villagers mourn the death of a schoolteacher, killed by a tiger at the edge of the Royal Chitwan National Park. As tiger populations in protected areas have grown, some tigers have been forced to the edges of reserves, and into inevitable encounters with the growing human population.

man-eating tiger. During a shorter career it kills fewer people than the tiger; nevertheless, a single lion killed 84 people in Ankole, Uganda, in the 1920s. Man-eating persists to the present day. Recently lions crossing from Mozambique into Tanzania's Tundara district killed 30 people in just one year.

Man-eating lions are often disabled or old, with worn-down or broken canine teeth and blunted claws. Such a cat begins to opt for easy prey in the form of domestic livestock. Sooner or later it finds itself face to face with a herdsman. Nevertheless, as is true of tigers, many man-eating lions suffer no disabilities — the Tsavo lions were in their prime. The area around Tsavo had been notorious for man-eaters long before the advent of the railroad. Man-eaters often appear in localities where game has been reduced by overhunting, or where natural prey is rendered temporarily difficult to hunt due to ecological or other factors. In Tanzania it was observed that more people were killed by lions during the rainy season, possibly because tall grass reduced the animals' normal hunting efficiency at this time. As is true of tigers, man-eaters are often females with a litter of growing cubs to feed.

It is debatable whether the cubs of a man-eater necessarily become man-eaters themselves once they are independent. If the scarcity of natural prey were a factor influencing the mother to prey on humans, the same circumstances would apply to the young, provided they remained in a similar marginal habitat. A commonly held belief is that once a big cat acquires the taste of human flesh it becomes an addiction, but there is probably nothing to this. There are documented cases of man-eaters that selected human prey when game was scarce, but reverted to natural prey once the ecological balance was restored.

Historically, only a few cases of man-eating can be attributed to the Asian subspecies of the lion, and these occurred in what was once Persia. Today a remnant population of Asian lions still occupies the Gir Forest of Gujarat in western India. For a long period, during which half of their prey consisted of domestic livestock, the Gir lions did not make the transition to man-eating. However, in 1988, following the removal of cattle from the area, the lions began to attack people. Within two years at least 15 people were killed and in some cases also eaten.

existence. The Sundarbans (meaning "beautiful forest") has long been notorious for its man-eaters. Writing in 1670, the French traveler François Bernier described how tigers climbed aboard boats in search of victims. Both India and Bangladesh have set aside special tiger reserves in the Sundarbans, and in these areas there are no permanent settlements. Nevertheless, every year thousands of local people are permitted to penetrate the mangroves to fish, gather honey, cut palm leaves, and collect wood. During the period 1975–85, 425 people were killed by tigers in the Indian Sundarbans and another 187 on the Bangladesh side. Here hunger does not appear to be the explanation, for natural prey is plentiful; man-eating is chiefly opportunistic. These man-eaters — a small proportion of the total population — are described as especially "ferocious" tigers. Generally they do not go out of their way to hunt for people, but should they encounter a human, they will kill and devour him.

LIONS
In the course of constructing the railroad across Kenya in 1898, a bridge had to be built across the Tsavo River. A pair of male lions killed and ate so many laborers during a period of nine months that work had to be halted for three weeks until the marauders were shot by Colonel J.H. Patterson. The lions had killed 28 Indians, "dozens of natives," and also wounded a European.

Generally speaking, the man-eating lion is a bolder animal than its tiger counterpart. It frequently operates at night, in contrast to the tiger, and sometimes even enters villages in search of victims. This very boldness makes the man-eating lion an easier animal to eliminate than the

LEOPARDS
"If the leopard were as big as the lion it would be ten times more dangerous." Such was the opinion of John Taylor, a hunter in Africa for 25 years, with a wealth of experience concerning man-eating lions and leopards. Neither in Asia nor in Africa do leopards commonly prey on people. But once it becomes a man-eater, the leopard exhibits an almost diabolical cunning.

Peter Beard/VISIONS

Perhaps the most notorious wild animal that ever lived was the man-eating leopard of Rudyaprayag. Between 1918 and 1926 it terrorized the route along which thousands of pilgrims annually ascended through the Garhwal Hills on their way to the Hindu shrines in the Himalayas, claiming 125 lives. This cat had the proverbial nine lives. Because its exploits were closely followed by the press, and questions even asked about it in the British House of Commons, no effort was spared to terminate its career, and a sizeable reward was placed on its head. Once it escaped when caught in a box trap, and again when sealed up in a cave — the entrance was opened by an incredulous local dignitary whereupon the leopard burst through

the crowd of 500 people that had gathered outside. It survived various types of poison, trip-guns set over kills, and a fusillade of bullets fired by two British officers who ambushed it crossing a suspension bridge. Once the jaws of a powerful spring trap snapped shut on the leopard's foreleg but caught it at the very point where one of the trap's metal teeth had accidentally been broken off on the trip up; the cat was able to extricate itself before the hunters arrived. "The best hated and most feared animal in all India," the large, old male was finally shot by Jim Corbett after a hunt that lasted months. Sixteen years earlier Corbett had killed the Panar man-eater, a leopard that claimed 400 victims but received far less publicity.

▲ Man-eating lions tend to be more aggressive in their pursuit of human victims than are tigers, but they become man-eaters for much the same reasons: hunger, age, and disability. There are exceptions, however. The infamous man-eaters of Tsavo, for example, who terrorized laborers building a bridge across Kenya's Tsavo River in the late 1800s, were male lions in their prime.

LEOPARDS AND HUMAN EVOLUTION

JOHN A. CAVALLO

Many theories of human evolution rest on whether or not our earliest human ancestors obtained animal flesh by hunting or by scavenging. A substantial number of researchers now agree that many of the remains, of wildebeest-sized and larger animals, at the earliest archeological sites, such as Olduvai Gorge in Tanzania, may have been scavenged by our early human ancestors from kills made, eaten, and abandoned by large predators such as lions, hyenas, and sabertooth cats. The remains of smaller Thomson's gazelle and impala-sized animals at this and other early sites are attributed to hunting by early hominids. The hunting argument is based on the fact that, with small prey, modern lions and hyenas usually leave little or nothing in the way of food remains for potential scavengers. Some paleoanthropologists have argued that scavenging by early hominids was an unproductive means of acquiring food because predators such as lions require expansive home ranges, and kills made by them are rare in any one particular area.

However, using information on leopard behavior and fossil evidence from a number of early hominid sites in Africa, I reasoned that scavenging from tree-stored leopard kills could have provided early hominids, especially our direct human ancestor, *Homo habilis*, with similar yields of animal flesh and marrow bones as could be obtained by hunting, but at lower risk from predation. I based this hypothesis on a combination of unique behaviors exhibited by modern leopards which are assumed to be ancient characteristics of these carnivores.

1. Due to competition from lions and hyenas, the solitary leopard stores one or more kills in trees and abandons them between feeds for varying periods of time during the day — the time when early hominids would have been foraging for food.

2. Leopards prey on animals similar in size to those remains attributed to hunting at the earliest archeological sites, and occasionally they kill larger species.

3. Leopard consumption of its prey is prolonged, and the theft of their tree-stored kills by other predators and vultures is infrequent compared to kills made on the ground by lions and hyenas. As a result, a kill can remain in a tree for some days.

4. Leopard kills may be easier to locate than those of other large carnivores because leopards maintain small ranges in riverine habitats that are generally of linear configuration. These factors would increase the likelihood of early hominids encountering tree-stored kills whilst foraging.

Since 1987 I have been testing this hypothesis in Tanzania's Serengeti National Park, by observing leopard behavior and collecting and analyzing the bones of their prey. My research has shown that tree-stored leopard kills could, indeed, have provided our early ancestors with a regular source of scavengeable animal carcasses from areas well within their daily foraging ranges. For example, during a two-month period in the dry season of 1988, 16 kills of small- to medium-sized antelope, made by two adult leopards (a male and female) with independent but overlapping home ranges, were recorded in one river valley, approximately 13 by 6.5 kilometers (8 by 4 miles). During the short rains of 1989, 14 tree-stored leopard kills of small and medium-sized antelope were found in a

10-kilometer stretch of river in 22 days of observations. Many of these carcasses, still retaining abundant flesh and marrow, were temporarily abandoned by the leopards for between 3 and 8.5 hours during a single day.

Although fossil evidence from South Africa documents leopard predation of both early hominids and baboons between 1 and 2 million years ago, the unique day–night shift in species dominance between leopards and baboons observed in Africa today suggests a similar division in behavior may have existed between leopards and early hominids. During the day, baboons readily drive off leopards and, on one occasion, were reported to have scavenged a tree-stored kill. At night, however, leopards frequently prey on baboons sleeping in trees. These data, in conjunction with anatomical evidence for the tree-climbing abilities of early hominids, suggest that while leopards were indeed predators of our early human ancestors, their kills may have provided hominids with a predictable source of animal flesh and marrow. In conjunction with plant foods, these rich sources of protein, obtained by scavenging rather than hunting, may have been the major influence on human evolution.

▼ Excavations of a cave complex from the Pleistocene of South Africa unearthed the fossil skull of a juvenile *Australopithecus*. Two small holes in the skull matched the lower canines of a leopard skull found in the same site. This suggests that leopards preyed on these early hominids, storing the carcasses in trees at the cave's mouth.

Corbett did not think that leopards became man-eaters for the same reasons as tigers. He cited two cases in which leopards began to prey on people in the wake of major epidemics; he believed they acquired the taste for human flesh by scavenging on corpses thrown into the jungle.

But the question is not so much why leopards become man-eaters. Rather, it is why do they not prey on human beings more often? A highly adaptable animal that has learned to live in proximity to people, the leopard often supplements its diet with village goats and dogs, attacking them with an audacity that is sometimes incredible. This is the big cat with the greatest familiarity with the human species — all the more reason to wonder why people are not attacked more often. The explanation may lie in the leopard's predatory adaptation itself. Although it preys on some of the larger mammals, such as deer, antelope, and wild pig, it is not completely dependent on them and can subsist quite well on small prey. The situation is different for the tiger and lion: they are dependent on large prey to survive. Although they are opportunistic predators that take small animals when possible, they cannot kill them in sufficient numbers to make up for a lack of large prey; leopards can and do, so hunger is less liable to be a factor subordinating leopards' natural reluctance to attack humans.

In India, man-eating leopards almost invariably operate at night, some even forcing entry into dwellings to kill; in Africa, they also hunt by day. It is at night, though, that they are most in their element, and when they are bolder than lions. "Human settlements hold no terrors for them," remarked Taylor.

JAGUARS

Although they are larger than leopards, jaguars are less prone to prey on humans. There are numerous authentic reports of jaguars killing people, but almost always under circumstances when they felt threatened or cornered, or occasionally when a human was mistaken for another animal.

A jaguar that deliberately hunts down and kills people for food is a rarity indeed. Some cases were reported during the last century and the early part of the present one. In parts of the Peruvian jungle, marauding jaguars were said to have become so numerous that the Indians had to move their settlements, one of which was abandoned for 100 years due to the depredations of man-eaters. Much of this information comes from travelers' tales based on local hearsay. Nevertheless, reliable reporters such as Charles Darwin wrote that many woodcutters along the Parana River were killed by these cats which occasionally even boarded boats at night. Alfred Wallace, the British naturalist and explorer, reported that a jaguar entered a house and attacked an Indian in his hammock.

There is little recent evidence of man-eating and what exists is from questionable sources. Leopold found no confirmed cases in Mexico. Beebe, who traveled widely in jaguar habitats in several Central and South American countries in the early 1900s, reported that he had never known a jaguar to attack a man.

In all parts of their range, jaguars prey on domestic livestock. They take many cattle on the treeless plains of Venezuela, which brings them into closer contact with people. Armed and mounted South American *vaqueros* are, however, a different proposition to the herdsmen that tigers encounter in India. Many jaguars are shot, and cattle-killers are promptly dealt with.

Attacks on cattle may be largely opportunistic and do not necessarily reflect a shortage of natural prey. Like the leopard, the jaguar can survive even when large prey are unavailable. In addition to larger mammals such as peccaries, deer, capybaras, and occasionally tapir, their diet includes anteaters, opossums, coatis, skunks, kinkajous, armadillos, agoutis, monkeys, caimans, crocodiles, iguanas, anacondas, boas, turtles, fish, and a variety of birds. Alan Rabinowitz, who studied jaguars in the Cockscomb Basin in Belize, found that over 50 percent of their diet was armadillos.

Their particular predatory adaptation apart, there is also the jaguar's separate evolution in the western hemisphere. Of the four big cats discussed, the jaguar displays the greatest antipathy towards preying on human beings.

SUMMARY

A big cat may turn man-eater whenever its normal reluctance to attack people is subordinated by some overriding factor. Aside from exceptional situations, such as the excessive aggression in Sundarbans tigers, that factor is almost always hunger. The perfect candidate to become a man-eater is a disabled cat living in a peripheral habitat where natural prey is scarce, especially if it is a female with dependent young. When prey is unavailable, tigers and lions are more likely to become man-eaters than leopards or jaguars because of their dependence on large prey.

Peter Beard/END OF THE GAME © 1988 Chronicle Books

▲ Famous African big game hunter Carl Akeley near the carcass of a man-eating leopard. Like the other big cats, leopards only rarely become man-eaters, but hunters' lore says that once a leopard turns to man-eating, it becomes more dangerous than the larger cats.

Raghu Rai/Magnum

◄ With the success of cat conservation programs, the numbers of tigers and other big cats in reserves have increased. To sustain this progress, mechanisms must be developed to protect people from predation. Too often, the only solution has been barriers and bullets.

FAMOUS HUNTERS OF MAN-EATERS

Peter Beard/VISIONS

Peter Beard/VISIONS

The British Library, London

▲ (Above) Colonel J.H. Patterson with the first of the two notorious man-eating lions of Tsavo he dispatched in 1898. (Above center) The second Tsavo man-eater, which Patterson killed 18 days later. Chief engineer for construction of a bridge over the Tsavo River, Patterson had to eliminate this terrifying pair of lions, who killed so many workers that work on the bridge temporarily stopped.

▶ Also a railroad engineer, Jim Corbett was a world-famous hunter of man-eating tigers in northern India. His numerous accounts of hunting man-eaters always revealed his enormous respect for the tiger. India's Corbett National Park is named in his memory.

JIM CORBETT AND THE MAN-EATERS OF KUMAON

Born in 1875 at Naini Tal in India, Jim Corbett spent his childhood and early youth in the forests of the Himalayan foothills, developing the unique jungle skills that enabled him to successfully hunt man-eaters alone and on foot. At the age of 32, he shot his first man-eater, the Champawat Tigress, which, having claimed 436 human lives, had taken more humans than any other man-eater in history. Three years later he killed the Panar Leopard, which had claimed 400 victims, a record for

man-eaters of that species. At the age of 63, on what he had solemnly promised would be his last day of man-eater hunting, he shot the Thak Tigress. Imitating the call of a male, Corbett lured the tigress to him, killing her at point-blank range just as darkness fell. The man-eating tigers and leopards he shot had collectively killed more than 1,300 humans.

As much a naturalist and lover of wildlife as a hunter, Corbett had a huge respect for the tiger, which he described as a "big hearted gentleman." Corbett was one of the first people in

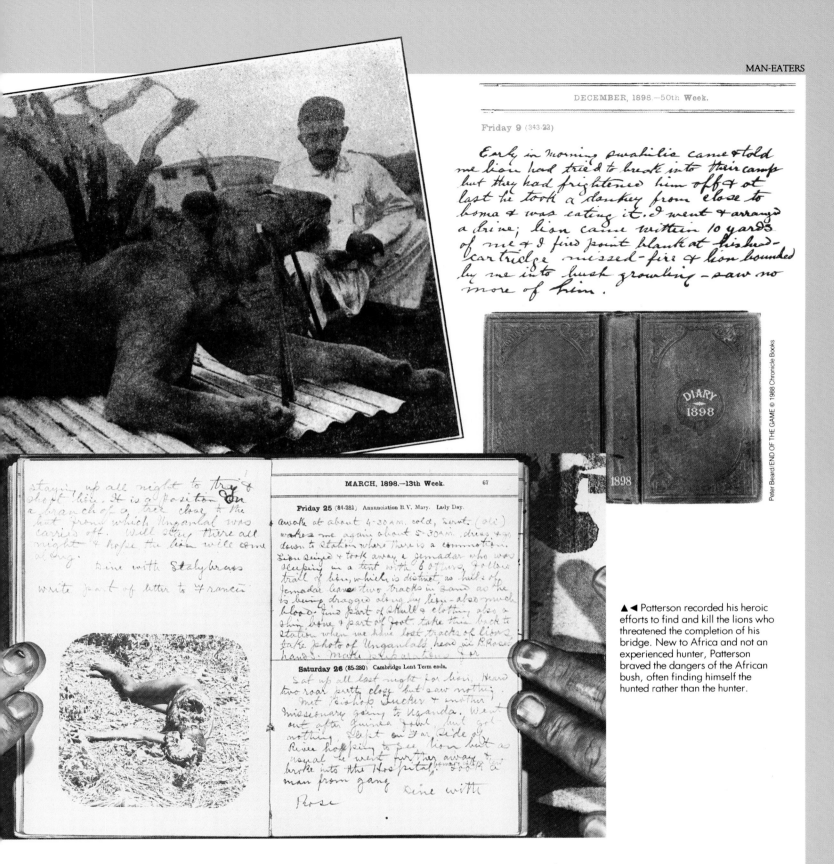

Peter Beard/END OF THE GAME © 1988 Chronicle Books

DECEMBER, 1898.—50th Week.

Friday 9 (343-22)

Early in morning swahilis came & told me lion had tried to break into their camp but they had frightened him off & at last he took a donkey from close to boma & was eating it. I went & arranged a drive; lion came within 10 yards of me & I fired point blank at his head - cartridge missed-fire & lion bounded by me into bush growling - saw no more of him.

▲ ◄ Patterson recorded his heroic efforts to find and kill the lions who threatened the completion of his bridge. New to Africa and not an experienced hunter, Patterson braved the dangers of the African bush, often finding himself the hunted rather than the hunter.

India to call attention to the need for conserving wildlife in general and the tiger in particular.

J.H. PATTERSON AND THE MAN-EATERS OF TSAVO

In contrast to Corbett, who was suited by background, temperament, and inclination to hunt man-eaters, Colonel Patterson, an engineer in charge of building a bridge over the Tsavo River in Kenya, just happened to be the man on the spot when two male lions began to prey on his laborers. Lacking experience, he took risks that Corbett would have avoided. He and the lions both had their share of narrow escapes. One of the lions miraculously escaped after being captured in a fall-door trap constructed of heavy metal. A stray bullet, which was meant for the lion, hit and severed a wire which secured the door, thus allowing the lion to squeeze through and escape. Later Patterson, perched on a flimsy platform, shot one of the man-eaters as it stalked him from below. The other he encountered on foot. Wounded, it charged and treed him, but he eventually killed it with his ninth bullet.

MAN VERSUS MAN-EATERS

PETER JACKSON

Raghu Rai/Magnum

Peter Jackson

▲ (Top) In India's Sundarbans forest at the mouth of the Ganges River, people are tackling the problem of man-eating tigers in innovative ways. Draped with human clothing, these life-sized mannequins are left in the tiger's forest habitat. The mannequins are wired to a car battery so that if a tiger attacks it receives a nasty shock. This may teach the tiger to avoid people in the future.

▲ A scroll depicting man-eating tigers in the Sundarbans. Long notorious for man-eating tigers, the immense mangrove forests of the Sundarbans are also one of the world's most important reserves for tigers. No permanent human dwellings exist in the Sundarbans' 10,000 square kilometers (3,900 square miles), but thousands of people enter the forest to collect honey, catch fish, and harvest timber.

▶ Another innovative defense against man-eating tigers used in the Sundarbans is wearing a face mask on the back of the head. Tigers usually approach their prey from behind; the mask essentially eliminates the behind of the person wearing it. The Indian government provides masks to forest users, who report that the masks are extraordinarily effective.

Being two-faced may be the best way to combat man-eating tigers in the mangrove forests of the Sundarbans, in the Indian subcontinent. Tigers have been notorious killers for hundreds of years in this vast delta region where the Ganges and Brahmaputra Rivers flow into the Bay of Bengal. But, since 1987, the Indian authorities have provided plastic face masks for forest workers to wear on the back of the head. As tigers normally stalk and attack their prey from behind, the face masks fool them into thinking they are observed. None of the several thousand men using the masks has been attacked, although tigers have been seen following them. The method imitates the way that some vulnerable species, including various butterflies and caterpillars, have evolved large eye-like spots that deter predatory birds.

Face masks may be the most effective defense so far against man-eaters, but the authorities have also tried shock therapy. Dummy figures, disguised as fishermen, honey collectors, and woodsmen, are dressed in clothes impregnated with human smell and wrapped with electrified wires. Any tiger that attacks them gets a sharp nonlethal shock. When placed at strategic points where individual tigers are behaving in a threatening manner, the dummies can teach them that human scent can lead to a painful experience.

Pigs are released as food for tigers that frequent areas close to villages, to prevent them attacking livestock or people. In addition, the authorities have banned collection of the fronds of the phoenix palm for thatching houses, in order to avoid confrontation with the tigers, which like to lie up in the dense vegetation and to give birth to their cubs there.

A German wildlife biologist, sent by the World Wide Fund for Nature (WWF) to investigate the man-eating problem in the Sundarbans, theorized that having to drink saline water might cause the unusual aggressiveness of these tigers. Although the theory has not been proven, ponds have been dug to collect fresh rainwater. The ponds are used by tigers and other wild animals, but they continue also to drink the saline waters in the creeks and rivers.

These new measures have reinforced the traditional use of fireworks to scare away any lurking tigers. But many of the fishermen, woodsmen, and honey collectors entering the Sundarbans still pray for protection at little shrines to jungle deities which are revered by both Hindus and Muslims. They may also be accompanied by shamans or priests who recite mantras to deter man-eaters.

The Sundarbans man-eaters are a unique phenomenon. In most cases human deaths result from accidental confrontations between tigers and people. A surprised animal attacks to defend itself and can cause fatal injuries. Such situations are well understood by conservation authorities in India and Nepal, who examine the circumstances of all attacks. If the attack was "accidental," then the tiger may be given the benefit of the doubt, but its movements are monitored thereafter. Live baits may be used to draw a tiger away from a potential area of conflict with people, or to reduce the danger from a female tiger when she is trying to feed small cubs where prey is scarce.

Raghu Rai/Magnum

CATS IN ZOOS

RONALD L. TILSON

In the past, large and small cats were nearly always kept in scandalous conditions in zoos, often locked alone in concrete and steel cages. It was little different from being in jail. Row upon row of cat cages still remain at many zoos, a distasteful reminder of an era when animals were collected and displayed as living trophies to be gawked at by a seemingly uncaring public. The food fed to the animals was atrocious as well, and because it lacked essential minerals, vitamins, and amino acids, there was little chance, if any, of successful reproduction. Social or psychological requirements of the species were not integrated with a knowledge of endocrine or hormonal function, thus further threatening reproduction. But during those times it was thought to be unimportant because replacement animals could readily be collected from the wild, and animal dealers were doing brisk business.

► This menagerie of big cats in small cages typifies the zoos of the nineteenth century. Poorly fed, lacking veterinary care, and living under unsanitary conditions, the cats rarely survived long and seldom reproduced. Still, they were popular with the public.

▼ At the turn of the century, some zoos, such as Regent's Park, London, were set in beautifully landscaped parks, but the animals lived in relative squalor. People commonly saw magnificent animals, like this cat, in iron-barred concrete cages.

Mary Evans Picture Library

PANTHER   FOX   TIGER   CIVET CAT   LION, LIONESS & CUBS   ICHNEUMON

Hulton-Deutsch

Times have changed. Most modern zoos are now designed with a concern for the welfare of the animals. Many zoos attempt to simulate the species' natural habitat, not so much for the animal's sake in every case, but because showing animals in natural social groups living in seemingly natural habitats enables zoos to contribute to the animal's conservation by increasing public awareness of and sympathy for vanishing species and their threatened habitats. Diets have improved immensely, and management practises have been fine-tuned to match each species' peculiarities. A telling statistic is that over 90 percent of all birds and mammals currently held in North American zoos are born in captivity, a tribute to the profession and a testimonial to what the modern zoo is all about.

Zoos have much to contribute, and as they grow beyond their current role as educational and recreational centers, they will become the primary link between people living in cities and towns, and earth's biological diversity. Zoos already exist in nearly every major city, many in developing nations where the majority of endangered species live. They are thus uniquely positioned to play a vital role in habitat preservation and species conservation.

COOPERATIVE ZOO-BREEDING PROGRAMS

North American zoos are a five-billion-dollar-a-year industry with more than 100 million visitors annually. Zoos and aquariums, which now collectively exhibit more than half a million animals, are now becoming a kind of biological (rather than biblical) Noah's Ark. Just over 10 years ago, the American Association of Zoological Parks and Aquariums (AAZPA), an organization that includes almost all North American zoos and similar institutions as members, established the Species Survival Plan (SSP) — specialized programs that try to maximize genetic diversity in small populations — for rare and endangered species represented in their collections. Already, SSPs are in place for 55 species, including some of the most endangered of the larger members of the cat family — Siberian and Sumatran tigers, snow leopards, clouded leopards, cheetahs, and Asian lions (paradoxically, all captive Asian lions in North America were discovered to be hybrids between Asian and African forms and thus are not currently being bred). More SSP species are being added as existing programs get under way. By the end of this century there should be at least 200 SSP programs in place; and by the middle of the next century it is hoped there may be another 1,000 programs established.

The birth of an SSP depends on the convergence of two significant issues: the survival needs of a species, and the degree of genetic diversity that can be maintained for the captive population of that species. The first issue involves the recognition that a particular species is in desperate need of protection beyond the traditional process of maintaining it in its natural environment. Important factors include how threatened a species is, the likelihood of its survival in captivity, and the probability of putting enough individuals together to have an effective breeding program. Input from the International Union for the Conservation of Nature and Natural Resources' (IUCN) various specialist groups (for cats it is called the Cat Specialist Group) is integrated with other relevant information to make these decisions. Once the AAZPA has approved the species for inclusion in an SSP, member zoos already possessing individuals of the species are asked to participate in the program, and a propagation committee is set up to devise the master plan, and to appoint a coordinator and studbook keeper who are to be responsible for implementing the program.

The master plan is the core of the SSP. It provides institution-by-institution and animal-by-animal recommendations on mate selection, animal relocations (from zoo to zoo, to produce better breeding combinations), breeding and surplusing (or non-breeding) schedules and, finally, technical and financial support for programs that advance the conservation of the species in its natural range.

The strength of any SSP master plan depends absolutely on accurate genetic, demographic, and biological information about every animal within the program. Three sources are available for compiling and cross-checking this information. The largest and most comprehensive is the International Species Information System (ISIS), a computerized inventory of records from 353 zoos, which is gradually incorporating more and more zoos from around the world into its network. ISIS now maintains a database on the sex, parentage, place of birth, and selected physiological norms for 49,000 mammals, 47,000 birds, 13,000 reptiles, 4,500 amphibians, 159,000 fish, and tens of

thousands of invertebrates. Information from this database is then checked against regional or international studbooks and, in a final confirmation of its accuracy, each participating institution verifies the facts. Once verification is accomplished, the propagation group can then begin serious planning for their particular species.

A series of complicated analyses needs to be performed before the propagation group can start making rational recommendations. These analyses include calculating the inbreeding coefficient — the proportion that one individual is related to another — for each individual in the population, as well as equalizing founder representation. The founders of a zoo population are the original wild-caught animals from whom the current population

▼ Pumas (*Felis concolor*) mating in a zoo exhibit. With urbanization and the disappearance of wildlife and wild lands, zoos are increasingly important as places for people to learn to appreciate the natural world. Zoos help preserve rare and endangered cats.

Robbi Newman/The Image Bank

▲ Naturalistic enclosures like the one occupied by these ocelots (*Felis pardalis*) permit the animals to behave as much like they do in the wild as possible. Preserving the natural behavior patterns of wild animals in zoos is as important as preserving their genetic diversity.

To ensure that the population's genetic variability is maximized, the propagation group must decide which animals are descended from the underrepresented founders and ensure that they have as many offspring produced as the overrepresented founders. While it is necessary to limit the number of descendants from the latter, the propagation group must also be careful not to lose any particular family line by not continuing to breed the more commonly represented founders in successive generations.

The second major issue that must be considered in managing the captive population is influenced by the captive carrying capacity — that is, the total amount of spaces available in all of the participating zoos for that particular species. In general, the SSP tries to maintain as much genetic diversity as possible, but because of space limitation has settled for maintaining 90 percent of that variability for 200 years as a reasonable goal. The more animals that are in the captive population, the more likely this goal can be achieved. But the "Zoo Ark" has limited spaces and there are just too many passengers that need to be brought aboard. For that reason there is often a compromise between what can be accomplished, given the available spaces, and what is optimal, given the genetic and demographic variables of the species under consideration.

Once the above information is available, the propagation group must identify which animals are to breed, when their breeding is to be scheduled, and at what facility. These institution-by-institution recommendations are then approved and the process begins. Cooperation among the various zoos involved is critically important if the program is to succeed. Construction of new exhibits, incompatibility of selected mates, unanticipated medical problems, and other unplanned-for contingencies are the rule rather than the exception, but through patience, compromise, and creative rescheduling none of these problems is insurmountable. The SSP remains a viable alternative to extinction.

Zoos in many regions of the world are organizing similar, well-planned, and tightly coordinated schemes for captive propagation. Programs like the North American SSPs are operating in Europe, Australia, and Japan; and more are being developed throughout the rest of the world. The next challenge is to integrate all of these programs into comprehensive global master plans for each endangered species.

LONG-TERM POPULATION MANAGEMENT

Collectively, zoos can hold only small populations, and the genetic and demographic goals of the most ambitious programs to date have a life span of about 200 years. Thus, if zoos managed only bird and mammal species that have SSPs, only some 300 species — or 20 percent of the vertebrate species in

is descended. It is presumed the founders are unrelated to each other and represent a reasonably well-distributed genetic sample of the species in the wild. If all existing zoo animals of the species are founders — that is, all born in the wild — then founder representation is already equal. This is seldom the case, as most animals in zoos are captive-born descendants of founders. Typically, a large proportion of zoo animals are descended from a few prolific founders who have many more living descendants than others and are thus more fully represented in the population's gene pool.

Miriam Austerman/Animals Animals

need of such programs — can be accommodated in North America's 100 "Zoo Arks." Expansion of the programs to include all of the space available in the world's fleet of 500 "Zoo Arks" (North America, Europe, Australia, and Asia) might increase the number to 900 species. Even with such an effort, however, there are already more threatened species than zoos can manage.

The size of this dilemma increases with time. If zoos aimed to add 10 new programs each year, about 150 programs would be created by the year 2000. This is not enough. By that time an estimated 1,500 species of birds and mammals (and another 500 reptiles) will need captive breeding programs to escape extinction.

It must be emphasized that the purpose of captive propagation is to reinforce, rather than replace, wild populations. All too often the general public expects individuals of endangered species at their local zoo to be released back into the wild. This is not the case. Instead, the captive population needs to be perceived as a reservoir of genetic material representing the species, not just individuals, that can periodically be used to reestablish populations that have been lost or to revitalize wild populations that have become depressed by genetic and demographic problems.

Taronga Zoo, Sydney

▲ A pair of jaguarundis (*Felis yagouaroundi*), one in gray color phase, and the other in red color phase. Thanks to years of research, many cats in zoos live longer, healthier lives than do their cousins in the wild. Zoo cats live alone, or in pairs, or in prides, depending on the nature of their natural social structure.

◄ No longer confined to barred cages, cats like these jaguars (*Panthera onca*) at Taronga Park, Sydney, are separated from zoo visitors by invisible or discreet barriers. This reduces the psychological distance between the cats and the people, and brings people into the cat's world rather than the reverse.

217

SIBERIAN TIGER SSP

The SSP for tigers is a good example of how North American zoos are working together to protect an endangered species. Small pockets of tigers remain in forest patches from India across China to the Soviet Union's eastern republics and south to Indonesia. Three of the recognized eight subspecies are now extinct; two others—the Siberian or Amur Tiger and the South China Tiger—are near extinction.

The free-ranging Siberian tiger population is divided into several small subpopulations, together numbering 193 studbook-registered Siberian tigers residing in North American zoos. The Tiger SSP manages 103 of these tigers in its breeding program, distributed among 48 participating institutions. This entire captive population is descended from 34 founders, eight of which are distinctly overrepresented in the genealogy of the present population. Another five founders are soon to be added: four wild-caught animals from the Moscow Zoo and a first-generation descendant of wild-caught parents from Tierpark Berlin Zoo.

The surplus, or non-breeding, Siberian tiger population in the Tiger SSP numbers 90 animals held at 40 different zoos. The success of the tiger master plan (designed to manage not only the Siberian subspecies of tiger, but also the Sumatran, Bengal and Indochinese subspecies) is contingent on surplus animals being removed to make room for new founder stock and animals resulting from recommended breedings. Ideally, these animals would be lost through attrition by natural causes, such as old age, but improvements in health care and management have greatly lengthened the average tiger's life span. The most recent demographic analysis shows a substantial number of surplus geriatric animals currently occupying space in North American zoos; nevertheless the breeding population remains relatively healthy.

Population analyses for Siberian tigers indicate that they have a generation time of seven years (the number of years from birth to the time that the first cub is born), sex ratios at birth are equal, and the litter size averages 2.5 cubs. An average neonatal mortality of 50 percent has not changed over the past 20 years. The total number of founders represented is 34; another 10 to 12 unrelated founders are needed, which would permit a captive population of 175 tigers to retain 90 percent of their genetic diversity for 200 years. By contrast, a population of 95 tigers would retain only 85 percent for 200 years, a level considered too low to be practical.

Given the current life-history characteristics of Siberian tigers, 10 animals must be added to the population each year to maintain the SSP population. Mortality prior to reproductive age (zero to four years) is 50 percent, so 20 offspring, or six to eight litters, must be produced per year (based on 2.5 offspring per litter). Since only about 75 percent of attempted pairings succeed, this means eight to ten pairings per year need to be scheduled by the Tiger SSP. This number serves as a guide upon which breeding recommendations will be made in the institution-by-institution analyses. Finally, the ultimate number of offspring to be produced by any individual tiger will depend upon a balance between the degree of founder representation of the animals and its family size. The Tiger master plan suggests the following:
- if the individual is underrepresented, then *five* surviving offspring should be produced;
- if average, then *three* surviving offspring should be produced;
- if the individual is overrepresented, then *one* surviving offspring should be produced.

For a subspecies like the Siberian tiger, a minimal population size of several thousand free-ranging animals is believed necessary for its long-term survival. This implies that if management units of tigers are to center around the five

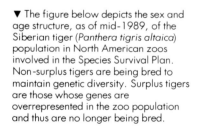

▼ The figure below depicts the sex and age structure, as of mid-1989, of the Siberian tiger (*Panthera tigris altaica*) population in North American zoos involved in the Species Survival Plan. Non-surplus tigers are being bred to maintain genetic diversity. Surplus tigers are those whose genes are overrepresented in the zoo population and thus are no longer being bred.

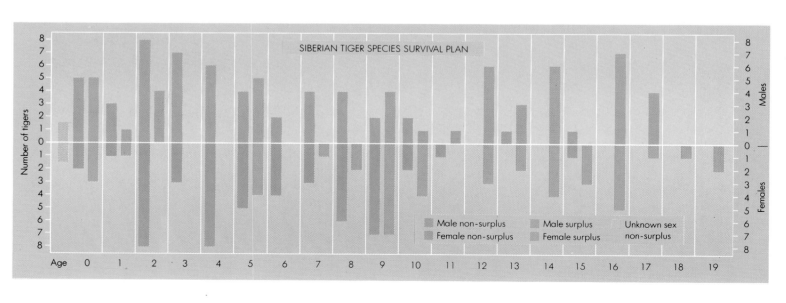

surviving subspecies, then a world population of 10,000 tigers is needed. These numbers are obtained from the emerging discipline of conservation biology, which ranks the relative importance of factors — the overall age of the population, their genetic diversity, and environmental distribution factors — that drive small populations to extinction. For a growing number of species, like tigers, we can estimate the survival probabilities of various population sizes. In all probability, all the free-ranging tiger populations throughout Asia (except possibly one population occupying the Sundarbans flood plain of India and Bangladesh) are too small and fragmented to ensure their survival in the future. What we are left with is the expectation that tigers will become extinct.

LINKS WITH THE WILD

Beyond the concerns for the captive population, the status of the wild Siberian tiger subpopulations needs to be recorded, as do the effects of current removal rates from the wild populations, and the contribution these tigers can make to captive populations. All animal populations, however large or small, are at some risk of extinction. The smaller the population, the greater the risk. To counter the trend toward smaller populations of wild tigers conservationists must come up with interactive strategies for managing fragmented wild populations and for using captive populations for backup and support. If captive breeding is used to help preserve a particular animal population, researchers need to develop a methodology for transferring genetic material between animals living in different areas.

Zoos are responding to such challenges in several ways; by growing larger, by building new facilities, by developing off-site breeding centers for endangered species, and by organizing cooperative programs with private facilities, such as exotic-animal ranches, that have more space and other resources not avail- . These actions increase the ov capacity, thus providi

Also, zoos are wo their captive carrying c reproductive technology embryo transfer, artific gamete freezing. If the moderately successfi effective size of a po living animals to thou maintaining them in li None of these technolog viewed as means of halting the extinction process, but as additional alternatives for conserving species.

In the future, wildlife reserves will become megazoos, governed by the same principles of conservation biology that increasingly govern today's zoo populations. It is not too futuristic to

ns of free- injectable enealogy and tion can be grated with l variables in a se. Information al wildlife biologists, directors, zoo directors, al executives, to politicians and nservation leaders, so that decisions onomic growth of the country could with due consideration of their impact upon animal conservation. Because so many endangered species are found in developing nations, there needs to be a massive transfer of technology and economic resources to help combat environmental deterioration and extinction.

▲ Nearly a decade old, the Siberian tiger Species Survival Plan has been a zoo success and a model for others. Species Survival Plans are now in place for Sumatran tigers as well as other big cats including Asian lions, cheetahs, snow leopards, and clouded leopards.

ADVANCES IN ARTIFICIAL REPRODUCTION

DAVID E. WILDT

Artificial insemination (AI) has been used for decades to more efficiently disperse the sperm of valuable farm livestock. Embryo transfer (ET) — the transfer of embryos from a genetically superior female to a more "common" surrogate mother — has also become routine, especially in cattle where a female normally produces only one calf each year. With ET, outstanding females can be treated with hormones to release many eggs. These multiple embryos can be flushed from the uterus and transferred into surrogate mothers which complete the pregnancy and nurse these genetically unrelated young, thus producing many more offspring than normal. In vitro fertilization (IVF), commonly referred to as "test-tube" fertilization, is another revolutionary technique which has been used to combat human infertility, allowing thousands of previously infertile couples to produce healthy babies. IVF involves the laboratory culture of sperm and eggs in a Petri dish under special environmental conditions.

These successes naturally have generated the question of whether reproductive "biotechnology" can be useful for conserving wildlife species including the great cats. The answer is an unequivocal "yes." Management of endangered species has become a sophisticated science. Animal pairings are now dictated by "genes," and most North American zoo breeding programs are regulated by Species Survival Plans (computerized, master guidelines) which ensure that genetic diversity is maximized. There is a need to rapidly disperse the genetic make-up of animals that are "underrepresented" in the population. The shipment or long-term frozen storage and use of sperm, eggs, and embryos would efficiently expand the gene pool, and artificial breeding would resolve the problem of pairing animals housed in different zoos that are separated by long distances. Shipping germ plasm would also reduce the many risks associated with transporting dangerous and often stress-susceptible species. A male and female designated for breeding may be behaviorally incompatible or may have some psychological or physical abnormalities that prevent mating. Artificial breeding can assist these animals.

At present, reproductive biotechnology is not being used for routinely managing the great cats. However, there is exciting progress and indications that some techniques will be available soon. Scientists are focusing on three strategies.

ARTIFICIAL INSEMINATION

There have been only a few successes using the conventional AI approach in which sperm are placed in the female's vagina. In the tiger, vaginally deposited sperm are not transported through the reproductive tract to the site of fertilization (oviduct). This appears to be due to the need for anesthesia which abnormally quietens the uterus and reduces contractions that normally assist in sperm transport. One alternative being tested at the National Zoo in Washington D. C. is the placement of sperm nearer to the site of fertilization using the technique of laparoscopy. A laparoscope is a fiber-optic telescope which is inserted through a small incision in the abdominal wall and used to view the reproductive organs. Laparoscopy can also be used to direct a needle through the abdominal wall and into the uterine horns. Tubing containing sperm can be threaded through the needle and into the uterus where the sperm are injected adjacent to the oviduct. This technique has been so successful in domestic cats (pregnancy rates are five times greater than using vaginal AI) that it soon will be tested in the great cats.

IN VITRO FERTILIZATION AND EMBRYO TRANSFER

IVF, one of the most powerful tools available to conservation biologists, eliminates concerns about behavioral incompatibility, and, unlike AI, does not require identifying the time of sexual activity (estrus) or ovulation. Like AI, IVF could be used to infuse new genes into genetically stagnant felid populations; sperm from free-living males could be used to inseminate eggs from zoo females. In 1988, the National Zoo achieved a milestone by producing the first-ever carnivore offspring (domestic cat kittens) by IVF and ET. Females were injected with a hormone to synchronize and stimulate ovarian activity. Using a laparoscope, eggs from ovarian follicles were aspirated through the abdominal wall. Collected sperm were washed and cultured with the eggs in a laboratory incubator. Thirty hours later, the eggs were examined for embryo formation and transferred to surrogate females. Five of six cats became pregnant. The Cincinnati Zoo reported the birth of an Asian wild cat kitten by similar procedures in 1989 while National Zoo scientists also produced leopard cat and puma (including the rare Florida panther) embryos by IVF. The most consistent success has been with the tiger. The National Zoo, in Washington D.C., in collaboration with the Henry Doorly Zoo in Omaha and the Minnesota Zoological Gardens in Apple Valley, has generated tiger embryos and the first-ever tiger offspring by in vitro fertilization.

IVF is also an important tool for testing male fertility. The sperm of different cat species are capable of binding and even penetrating the eggs of each other. Scientists at the National Zoo have taken advantage of this quirk in nature and are using domestic cat eggs and IVF to test the fertility status of the great cats. Males producing less robust and more abnormal sperm are less likely to attach to domestic cat eggs. Thus, this test provides a new method for choosing animals which are more likely to contribute to zoo breeding programs.

EGG RESCUE

To ensure that all genetically valuable animals contribute to the breeding population, every avenue must be explored. One frustration is the loss of genetic potential due to age, terminal illness, or unexpected death. Until recently, there were no methods for salvaging the genetic material of such animals. Recently, however, immature ovarian eggs have been "rescued" from animals which die unexpectedly. These eggs can be cultured or "matured" in the laboratory, subjected to IVF, and the embryos transferred to surrogate mothers. Generating life from recent death has resulted in live births in several livestock and laboratory animal species. National Zoo scientists have begun salvaging eggs from cat species. In the domestic cat, about half the ovarian eggs can be rescued and about a third of these form embryos after IVF. Pilot studies have begun with other

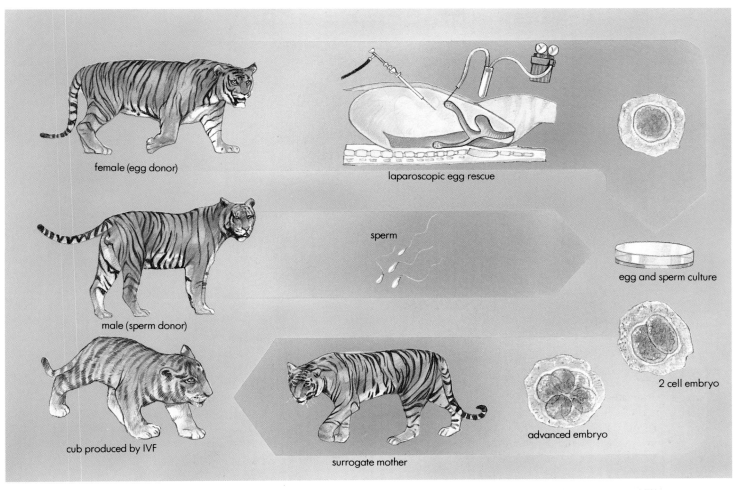

female (egg donor)

laparoscopic egg rescue

male (sperm donor)

sperm

egg and sperm culture

cub produced by IVF

surrogate mother

advanced embryo

2 cell embryo

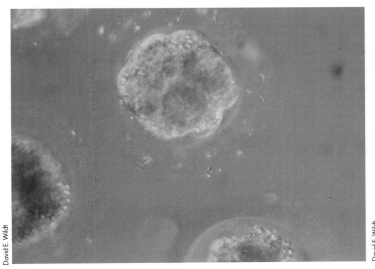

David E. Wildt

David E. Wildt

species, and a North American network is in place involving the cooperation of more than 30 zoos. Ovaries from animals which die unexpectedly are shipped to the National Zoo where the eggs are harvested, studied, and used to produce embryos.

Biotechnology is on the edge of assisting in the breeding and conservation of rare cat species. The extent of progress will depend largely on more funding for this innovative field of science. The real challenge will be to apply existing technology as soon as possible before more genetic diversity is lost.

▲ (Top) Artificial reproduction may help to increase the numbers of endangered cats. One new technique involves in vitro fertilization (IVF) and embryo transfer (ET): eggs are collected by laparoscopic surgery (after hormonal injections have induced ovulation in the female), placed in a special medium with sperm collected from a male, and incubated until embryos begin to grow. The embryos are inserted into another female tiger, the surrogate mother. (Above left) Tiger embryos produced by IVF before their transfer from the Petri dish to the surrogate mother. (Above right) One of the first three tiger cubs born following IVF and ET. This milestone came after years of effort by scientists at the National Zoo, Washington D. C., working in collaboration with the Minnesota Zoological Gardens, and the Henry Doorly Zoo in Omaha, Nebraska.

DO WILD CATS HAVE A FUTURE?

JEFFREY A. McNEELY

Cats have coexisted with people for a long time. Judging from the behavior of contemporary hunter–gatherer societies, it is quite likely that the earliest human hunters may have earned much of their meat from chasing lions off their kills, or robbing the tree-larders of leopards. Later on, the great cats became symbols of chief and king, venerated and even worshipped by the common people, and made the object of great royal hunts.

▼ Artist Salvador Dali with his pet ocelot (*Felis pardalis*) Baby in 1969. No one knows precisely how many nondomestic pet cats people keep worldwide but at least 3,000 big cats are kept as pets in Italy alone. The pet trade contributed significantly to the decline of cats in the wild until the mid-1970s, when most nations became parties to the Convention on International Trade in Endangered Species of Wild Fauna and Flora (CITES).

Wild cats are also very much a part of our present culture. As symbols of power, grace, and cunning, the great cats are so important that countries as culturally different as the United Kingdom, India, and Singapore use them as national symbols. Some of the most powerful international businesses find the big cats helpful in marketing: for Exxon, the petroleum giant, the tiger communicates the power of its products; the jaguar, cougar, and lynx have all been appropriated to help sell automobiles; and cinema-goers have been greeted by MGM's roaring lion for over 50 years.

Real wild cats also fascinate people. The main attraction for most tourists who visit Africa's national parks are the lions; one study found that visitors to Kenya's Amboseli National Park spent some 30 percent of their wildlife-viewing time watching them. Many of the estimated 500 million annual visitors to zoos throughout the world head first for the big cats, and circus acts with lions, tigers, and leopards still bring gasps of awe from the crowds. Some people like to have cats around them. Reportedly, at least 3,000 lions, tigers, and leopards are kept as pets in Italy. Domestic cats worldwide may number more than 100 million, and in the United States the bill for cat food amounts to US$1.5 billion per year; a further $200 million a year is spent on cat-box fillers.

But do wild cats have a future in our increasingly crowded and complex modern society? What are the factors that are threatening the survival of this great family of hunters?

THE SURVIVAL OF WILD CATS: PROBLEMS AND PROMISE

Judging from the impressions of teeth in hominid fossils, big cats were important predators of early humans, and even today are sometimes significant predators of people. More generally, wild cats today are seen as our competitors, preying on chickens, goats, and cattle. It is perhaps understandable that many rural communities would be happy to see them exterminated, and modern technology gives them the means to do so. Using guns, poison, snares, traps, hunting dogs, and a wide range of other technology, shepherds, ranchers, and farmers, from Tibet to Bolivia, are removing the competition. They are also expanding their flocks into more remote areas, and replacing the wild prey of cats with domestic animals, thereby making conflicts inevitable. Rural people are often able to enlist support from governments in their efforts to protect their livestock. In 1988, for example, some 200 pumas were legally shot under a controversial government predator control program run by the United States Department of Agriculture.

With farmers already killing cats to protect their livestock, the fur trade can be the factor that seriously threatens a once-secure population of cats. In the early 1970s, the United States alone imported 25,000 large-cat skins and 130,000 ocelot skins per year, supplementing the domestic North American annual harvest of over 83,000 bobcats and 25,000 lynxes. In 1980, Europe imported nearly half a million skins of medium and small cats; and from Bolivia alone almost 100,000 cat skins were legally exported during 1984 and 1985. Though exports of at least some species are now prohibited in many countries under the Convention on International Trade in Endangered Species (CITES), the trade in cat skins is still thriving — China's 1988 export quota for leopard cat skins, for example, was 150,000.

As a result of widespread persecution by humans, cats have become one of the most threatened major groups of land animals. The *Red List of Threatened Animals* produced by the International Union for Conservation of Nature and Natural Resources (IUCN) — the international authority on the status of threatened species — lists three species and eight subspecies as "endangered," the highest category of threat, and another ten as "vulnerable" or "rare." Already in this century, a number of subspecies and local populations have disappeared, including the Indian cheetah; the Bali, Javan, and Caspian tigers; the Taiwanese clouded leopard; and the alpine lynx. Against this onslaught, what hope is there for the survival of wild cats? In fact, quite a lot.

First of all, despite the many disturbing trends, some cats are doing quite well. Population estimates of the widespread smaller cats are hard to come by, but judging from the tens of thousands of skins which enter the fur trade annually, some of them might number in the millions. Even some of the big cats are relatively common, such as the African lion which numbers perhaps 200,000 individuals, and the African leopard, which one optimistic computer model suggests may have a population as high as 700,000.

▼ Lion cubs (*Panthera leo*) in Kenya's Kora Game Reserve. Favorites among tourists visiting game reserves and national parks, lions have real economic value. Estimates suggest that each adult male lion in Amboseli National Park earns for Kenya about US$515,000 in foreign exchange each year — giving Kenya a real incentive to protect its wildlife and wildlands.

Betty Press/Animals Animals

Popperfoto

Hulton-Deutsch

▲ Queen Elizabeth and Prince Philip on one of Nepal's last great tiger hunts in 1961. Today, tiger hunting is banned and many former tiger hunters like Prince Philip have led the way in efforts to save the tiger and other endangered wildlife. Throughout the world, stalking wild animals with cameras and camcorders is replacing stalking them with firearms.

Some species thrive in a very wide range of habitats: the puma once ranged throughout North and South America wherever sufficient food could be found, with different forms ranging in size from 30 kilograms (66 pounds) up to nearly 100 kilograms (220 pounds). The leopard is found from Africa to Java and Siberia, inhabiting arid deserts, torrid tropical rainforests, and frigid subarctic forests. European wild cats range from northern Scotland through Europe and the Middle East into South Africa, and east as far as parts of India and China.

Many cats are able to survive and even prosper in close proximity to people. In 1988, four leopards were caught in a single night in Nairobi

during an attempt to trap an escaped leopard, which itself was not found. In 1989, a lynx entered the city of Leningrad, causing an uproar among local people. After searching for three days, police located the lynx in a park. Some people wanted it shot — an all-too-common response of urban dwellers exposed to wild predators — but conservationists vigorously defended it. While the argument raged, the lynx sneaked back into the nearby forest. A Siberian tiger which recently strolled into central Vladivostok, the biggest city in the eastern Soviet Union, was not so lucky — he was chased by a helicopter until he was cornered and shot.

Some cats may even benefit from human activities. When the Plant Protection Department of Israel's Ministry of Agriculture organized a large-scale poisoning campaign against jackals, the numbers of hares and partridges increased, leading to a significant increase in the population of caracals, their main predators.

Once human hunting pressure has been removed, cats can make quite impressive comebacks. The remarkable return of the Bengal tiger in India as a result of Project Tiger is perhaps the best known, but several other examples are noteworthy. The lynx became extinct in the Alps early in this century, but was reintroduced in Switzerland in the early 1970s and has now reoccupied about two-thirds of the Swiss Alps; the current population is estimated at about 100, and is causing new conflicts with sheep farmers. Even so, lynxes are also being reintroduced in the Vosges mountains of France, and similar programs are being considered in Austria, Germany, and Italy.

AN INTERNATIONAL PROGRAM TO CONSERVE THE CATS

Cats are well equipped to survive, and even prosper, if humans allow them to do so. Five major actions are required:
BUILD STRONGER PUBLIC SUPPORT
Support is required from two quite different publics: the urban-dwelling public whose knowledge of wild cats is based primarily on books, films, zoo visits, and other media; and the rural people who actually live among the cats. They require quite different approaches. The politically and economically influential sectors of society, who enjoy wild cats vicariously, generally support conservation efforts (though their attitude would surely be somewhat different if wild cats were preying on their pet dogs). Their support needs to be further strengthened through more public information which will help maintain support for wild cats.

The rural people pose a far more challenging problem — their actions can bring life or death to the wild cats. Those who advocate conservation of cats need to recognize the conflicts that are inevitable when predators live among rural people whose livelihood depends on maintaining livestock. Of course, cats have long been competitors with humans, but the people who have a history of living among the great cats have found means of accommodation. The Minangkabau of Sumatra, for example, give high status to "tiger magicians" who are responsible for maintaining the balance between village welfare and the tigers that roam the nearby forest; they have found that tigers help keep down the population of crop-raiding pigs and monkeys, and can serve a number of cultural roles as well. Other rural people have learned how to manage their livestock in ways that can reduce predation from cats, such as keeping the animals in barns or corrals at night, controlling where livestock drop their calves, or allowing cats to consume completely the animal they have killed (so they do not need to kill another one to fill their bellies).

But as the human population increases and more people move into the wilderness strongholds of the big cats, more conflicts are inevitable. These conflicts can be reduced only by ensuring that rural people have an interest in conserving cats, by designing economic incentives which bring benefits to the rural people.

One controversial approach is safari hunting of those big cats that have been proven to be significant predators on livestock. In Mongolia, safari hunting of snow leopards is part of the management strategy for these cats. An annual quota of just five animals, all of which must be established livestock predators, has been set, and the proceeds are channeled to livestock owners. In Belize, jaguar hunting is being discussed as a solution to the problem of jaguars that take livestock. In Zimbabwe, safari hunters are being used to remove problem leopards, with the profits from the hunt going to the local people. While many will not see this as an ideal solution, the alternative — which is often the case today — is that herdsmen take the law into their own hands and end up killing far more snow leopards, jaguars, or leopards than would ever be killed in a formal hunting program. The problem is accurately identifying the cats to be hunted. Also, even with legal hunting, some parts of the urban public have difficulty in understanding that hunting can be part of conservation.

In some cases, existing government programs such as management of public lands can be linked to conservation of cats. For example, in the United States, public rangeland is leased for just over $20 per year per head of cattle, a subsidized price that is granted in return for sharing the range with wildlife. Part of the lease agreement should be an acceptance on the part of the rancher that he will absorb reasonable losses of livestock to predators in return for the subsidy. In other cases, payment of compensation for livestock losses should be considered.

Tom Nebbia

D. Donne Bryant Stock

▲ ◄ Western consumers' demand for goods made of cat skins — from a decorative mounted lion, on sale in a Botswana bazaar, to ocelot pelts for women's coats, displayed in a market in Ecuador — continues to drain many wild populations of cats. Spotted cats such as ocelots and snow leopards are particularly hard hit.

Rural people also need to be able to benefit from the interest urban people have in conserving the wild cats. One important means is through tourism to national parks. Each of the adult male lions in Kenya's Amboseli National Park has been shown to bring in approximately US$515,000 in foreign exchange annually; the present value to the national economy of each male lion is equivalent to a herd of 30,000 zebu cattle. The challenge is to ensure that local people earn some of these benefits. Conflict between cats and humans cannot be completely eliminated, but it can be minimized by sound management of livestock, cats and other wildlife, and by ensuring that local people have an economic stake in conserving the cats.

OPERATION TIGER

PETER JACKSON

In 1969, this message shocked the General Assembly of the International Union for Conservation of Nature and Natural Resources (IUCN) in Delhi: "Only 2,500 tigers left in India, and numbers declining rapidly." Already seven subspecies of the tiger were regarded as endangered by the IUCN. Now the Indian (Bengal) tiger, which may have numbered 40,000 at the turn of the century, joined the list of species threatened with extinction. In response to the assembly's call for urgent conservation measures, the Indian government, headed by the then Prime Minister Indira Gandhi, banned tiger hunting and export of skins. But an all-India census, in 1972, indicated that the tiger population had dropped below even 2,000 animals. Guy Mountfort, a founder trustee of the World Wide Fund for Nature (WWF), appealed for US$1,000,000 to finance tiger conservation in Asia, under the banner of "Operation Tiger." He flew to Delhi to meet Mrs Gandhi, who set up a task force to prepare a detailed program.

On 1 April 1973, India's Project Tiger was launched at a ceremony in Corbett National Park. In charge was Kailash Sankhala, the Indian forester and tiger expert who had raised the alarm in 1969. Project Tiger adopted an ecological approach based on protection, not only of the tiger, but also of its prey animals and their habitat. Eight reserves were established initially, and this number was later increased to 18. Despite the sacrifice of valuable revenue, India's State governments were persuaded to stop logging forests in the reserves. Antipoaching squads were trained, and controls put on the destructive grazing of livestock. Villages were even moved out of some reserves, and dams were built to create reservoirs for wild animals. The Indian government put substantial funds into the project, while WWF's appeal provided hard currency for the purchase of Jeeps, radio networks to help combat poachers and forest fires, firearms, jet patrol boats for the Sundarbans reserve in the Ganges–Brahmaputra delta, camels for the Ranthambhore reserve on the edge of the Thar desert, night-viewing devices, cameras, and slide projectors for educational programs. By 1978, a census reported as many as 3,000 tigers in India, showing that the decline in numbers had been reversed. Five years later, the census estimated 4,000 tigers, and in 1989 a few hundred more.

Operation Tiger funds, which eventually exceeded US$1,800,000, also flowed to Bangladesh, Indonesia, Nepal, and Thailand to finance improved tiger protection and management. In Nepal, WWF funds supported an intensive long-term study of tiger behavior and ecology by a team of American and Nepalese scientists under the auspices of the Smithsonian Institution in Washington.

Meanwhile, despite all efforts, the Javan tiger became extinct in the early 1980s in the wake of its former neighbor, the Bali tiger, unseen since the 1940s. Iran, financing its own conservation efforts, was unable to find any evidence of the continued existence of the Caspian tiger, already reported to be extinct in the Soviet Union and Afghanistan. In China, tigers were still treated as pests and even as a source of bones for traditional medicine, despite last-ditch efforts to protect them.

But elsewhere, the great cat has been given a new lease of life. Degraded vegetation in protected forests has been rejuvenated, and deer, antelope, and other wild animals have increased in numbers. Furthermore, publicity about Project Tiger has strengthened the conservation movement as a whole in India and increased public awareness.

Much has been achieved, but the situation of the tiger and other wildlife must be reassessed in this last decade of the twentieth century. In India alone, the human population has increased by over 200 million since Project Tiger was launched. Impoverished local people have largely exhausted resources of timber, grazing, and forest products outside reserves. They look hungrily at the flourishing vegetation in the reserves. Their crops are raided by wild animals, and sometimes people are killed by tigers. Hostility to wildlife conservation has grown. Thus Project Tiger, one of the most successful of all species conservation programs, now faces a crisis. Unless the condition of people around the reserves is improved, and they can be taught to appreciate the importance and benefits of wildlife conservation, the tiger's decline to extinction may be resumed.

CONSERVE THE HABITATS OF WILD CATS
One of the best ways to minimize conflicts between humans and cats is to separate the two. Where cats have plentiful wild prey, they seldom bother with domestic stock. In Belize, for example, field studies have shown that cattle grazing outside the forest are usually safe from jaguars, but cattle which range freely in the forest often fall prey to the big cats. Therefore, if sufficiently large areas are conserved so that the jaguar does not have to leave the forest, conflicts with local people could be reduced.

The great majority of the world's 4,000 major protected areas contain at least some cats, and some contain as many as six or seven species. While few protected areas will be sufficiently large to hold the 500 to 1,000 individuals that may be required to maintain a viable population of a species, they do provide the most secure habitats for both cats and their wild prey. Therefore, protected areas must be considered of particular importance for the future of wild cats. Every protected area needs a management plan that states why the area has been established and how it is to be managed to attain its objectives. For protected areas containing important populations of cats, explicit measures are required for ensuring that the populations are well managed.

But protected areas are not enough. In India, for example, established wildlife reserves constitute only about 15 percent of potential tiger habitat, and more than half the total tiger

Fiona Sunquist

population lives outside these reserves. Further, since cat populations tend to grow quickly if they are protected, they will soon spill over into the surrounding countryside. Therefore, protected areas should be surrounded by other kinds of natural or seminatural habitats which can provide fodder, fuel, building materials, medicinal plants, water, and other products for local people.

MANAGE CAPTIVE POPULATIONS TO ENHANCE CONSERVATION

The zoos of the world have a vested interest in ensuring that cats survive; cats provide one of the main attractions for visitors. Zoos also serve as a refuge of last resort for some cats. For example, no more than about 20 to 30 Amur leopards remain in the wild in the Soviet Union and China, but 82 are held in captivity. Only about 50 South China tigers remain in the wild, but 52 are held in zoos. In order to ensure that these captive populations are well managed, zoos have established studbooks which register purebred specimens and encourage the exchange of breeding stock.

Zoos can contribute to conservation in several additional ways:
● maintain sufficient captive populations to ensure that only a minimum number of animals needs to be taken from the wild;
● breed endangered species with a view to returning them to the wild, should that extreme and difficult step ever become necessary;
● educate visitors about cats in the wild, thereby contributing to public support for conservation efforts;
● carry out research on cat biology — such as breeding biology (especially artificial insemination and embryo transfers), capture, and relocation techniques — which can improve the management of cats in the wild;
● hold training courses on cat management for those responsible for wildlife management;
● provide an alternative to killing problem animals — the Colombo Zoo in Sri Lanka, for example, has 43 leopards, some of which were taken from the wild as livestock raiders.

▲ Scientists studying tigers (*Panthera tigris*) in Nepal's Royal Chitwan National Park, site of a twenty-year investigation of tiger ecology and behavior, the longest such project for a big cat after lions. The knowledge gained has helped maintain Nepal's tigers and accommodate the needs of local people while preserving tigers and tiger habitat.

► Cheetahs in Kenya's Masai Mara Game Reserve, which is contiguous with Tanzania's enormous Serengeti National Park and one of the few areas where cheetahs enjoy large expanses of unfragmented habitat. Elsewhere in Africa and the Middle East, economic development has left small populations of cheetahs isolated on relatively small habitat islands. The smaller and more isolated the habitat island, the greater the risk that the cheetah will not survive there.

D. Parer & E. Parer-Cook/AUSCAPE International

THE REINTRODUCTION OF THE LYNX
IN SWITZERLAND

URS BREITENMOSER

▲ Twenty wild Eurasian lynx (*Lynx lynx*) from Czechoslovakia were released in Switzerland in the early 1970s. Today, about 100 lynx live there. These animals are closely monitored, through radiotelemetry (top) or video recordings of heat detectors (middle), to measure their success. The best indicator though, is effective reproduction in the wild. The female lynx pictured above with her cubs was part of the release program.

The Eurasian lynx *(Lynx lynx)* is a medium-sized, spotted cat, which inhabits the forests of the northern hemisphere. In western and central Europe, the lynx has become extinct in recent centuries, but since 1970 several attempts to reintroduce the lynx have been made. Reconstruction of the lynx population in Switzerland is one of the few cases of a successful reintroduction of a big predator.

In the last two centuries, many large game species — ungulates, or hooved mammals, as well as predators — became extinct in Switzerland. As a result of natural repopulation and releases during the past 80 years, ungulate populations have recovered, and today, ungulates are more abundant than ever.

Between 1971 and 1976, about 20 wild lynxes from Czechoslovakia were released in Switzerland, creating two small populations which grew and spread to a total area today of 10,000 square kilometers (4,000 square miles) in the Alps and 5,000 square kilometers (2,000 square miles) in the Jura Mountains. There are now about 100 individuals.

Reintroduction of lynxes was surrounded by controversy — hunters complained of lynx predation of roe deer and chamois, and farmers blamed the cat for killing too many sheep.

Lynx typically have large home ranges. In the established populations in the Jura Mountains and the Northern Alps, home ranges cover 100 to 150 square kilometers (38 to 58 square miles) for females, and 200 to 400 square kilometers (77 to 154 square miles) for males. The home ranges of a single male and a single female overlap almost completely, and within this area, no other adult lynx lives permanently.

The lynx is a perfect predator of smaller ungulates. In Switzerland, a lynx kills 50 to 60 roe deer or chamois per year. The lynx approaches its victim carefully to make a sneak attack. This hunting tactic may be the reason for the large home ranges. When the lynx stays for a few days in any region, the wariness of the ungulates increases and another attack by the lynx would be very difficult. Therefore, the lynx has to turn to a part of its home range where it has not hunted for a long time.

At the beginning of the recolonization, and still today along the periphery of the population, ranges were much smaller than the norm, and the lynx hunted over a very limited area. The ungulates had not yet readapted to the presence of a large predator and were easy to catch. Therefore, during the period of recolonization, the predator can have a considerable influence on prey abundance by dispersing and reducing the ungulate populations, but subsequently the lynx itself has to react to the readaptation of the prey animals, and so lynx home ranges increase. Once a lynx population is established, its density is very low. In Switzerland, numbers are not more than one individual per 100 square kilometers (2.5 per 100 square miles).

Experience with the reintroduction of the lynx in Switzerland shows the importance of predators for the regulation of some ungulate populations.

DEVELOP AND USE KNOWLEDGE ABOUT CATS IN THE WILD

Living with wild cats in an increasingly complex and overcrowded world will require that we know how cats live, how our activities are affecting them, and how they contribute to the functioning of the ecosystems of which they are part. Such information will provide the basis for public support, and contribute to the decisions that wildlife managers will need to take when they are faced with problems such as inbreeding in small populations, livestock raiding, critically low populations, and apparent imbalances between predator and prey.

Long-term research and monitoring programs therefore need to be established throughout the range of the cats, with a body of scientists to keep the programs active. Such a body has already been established. IUCN's Cat Specialist Group consists of some 112 of the world's leading experts on the cats; under the chairmanship of noted tiger expert Peter Jackson, the Cat Specialist Group produces a regular newsletter, prepares conservation action plans, and advises governments and organizations on important cat conservation questions.

CONTROL THE INTERNATIONAL TRADE IN CATS AND THEIR PRODUCTS

Once effective management programs for cats have been implemented, some international trade in cats and their products (especially skins) may be essential to build the necessary support among the rural people who are expected to participate in conservation programs. In North America, for example, the harvest of bobcat and lynx skins earns rural hunters some US$15 million per year. Some experts even feel that removing the commercial value from skins is the surest way to make cats disappear from those parts of their range where they are unprotected.

On the other hand, the trade in skins has often been abused and some cats have been reduced to such low levels that additional harvests could spell extinction. For snow leopards, tigers, and rare subspecies of leopards (such as the Amur leopard), noncommercial status is essential to survival. Most people now feel a certain revulsion toward wealthy people adorned in furs of the big cats, a change in fashion which came none too soon.

The seeming conflict between conservation and trade needs to be addressed through more effective monitoring of wild populations, credible and enforceable quotas on skins from species that can bear some trade, and sophisticated measures for enforcing the quotas that are established. This may require occasional demonstrations of resolve, such as the July 1988 burning in Brazil of thousands of confiscated animal skins, among them jaguar, puma, and ocelot.

CONCLUSION

It is hard to imagine a world without wild cats. Their combination of beauty, power, efficiency, and grace symbolizes wild nature for many, and our lives would be the poorer for their absence.

But there is no reason why we cannot continue to enjoy their presence. Conservation programs have shown that any wild cat can be conserved if people are willing to make the necessary effort. Under any credible scenario of the human future, sufficient wild spaces will exist to support adequate populations of the feline predators that help define healthy ecosystems. Ensuring that wild cats occupy these wild spaces is very much in our hands, and, indeed, sound resource management demands that cats be part of a comprehensive program to conserve biological diversity for the benefit of humanity, now and far into the future.

◄ A Eurasian lynx (*Lynx lynx*) in a Swiss cornfield. One problem with reintroducing cats is that most remaining areas of natural habitat lie in close proximity to agricultural land. Wary of wild predators that might kill livestock, farmers and ranchers often oppose reintroduction efforts.

Urs Breitenmoser

THE USES OF CATS IN NATIVE FOLK MEDICINE

In 1983, a Seminole Indian in Florida, USA, was tried and convicted of killing a Florida panther, an endangered subspecies. His unsuccessful defense? The panther, he argued, is a vital part of Seminole healing rituals. The big cat's tail, claws, and bits of hide were required to enhance the effectiveness of the tribe's medicine pouch (a deerskin sack which contains herbs, roots, and animal parts).

The big cats — tigers, lions, jaguars, and panthers — are considered by rural people to be brave, strong, and dangerous, three qualities that many people would like to share. Through sympathetic magic, many traditional healers seek to give their patients these qualities by preparing medicines based on the relevant parts of the big cats; the use of sexual parts to cure reproductive ailments is perhaps the most widespread example.

The big cats are also often thought to possess their own magic, which they can pass on to humans. Since rural folk often believe that many ills are produced by spirits, rituals to deal with the spirits often involve the cats — or parts of them — as major players. And to the extent that illnesses frequently have a psychological component, the patient may perceive a powerful force that a scientist seeking objective proof would have difficulty in documenting.

Perhaps the most developed feline pharmacopoeia is found in tropical Asia, where the tiger is the supreme symbol of power and cunning. Shamans, or medicine men, in traditional tribal societies and doctors in civilizations such as China and India use tigers for both prevention and cure. In China, tigers are painted on Buddhist temple walls to scare away malignant spirits, tiger scrolls are hung in houses to keep disease devils out, mothers paint tigers on their children's mumps-swollen cheeks, and the shoes of small children are embroidered with tiger heads to prevent fevers.

These symbolic representations are powerful and easy to use because they do not involve actually harvesting a tiger. The actual parts of the tiger, however, are thought to be even more effective. For example, the tail is ground and mixed with soap as an ointment for skin diseases, and sitting on a tiger skin rug cures fevers caused by ghosts. Tiger brain is mixed with oil and rubbed on the body to cure laziness and acne. Tiger gallstones are mixed with honey to cure abscesses, and when applied to the eyes will stop persistent watering. Eyeballs rolled into pills are a sure cure for convulsions, and eating the meat will make a

person immune to snakebite. When added to wine, tiger bones make a powerful Taiwanese tonic. Tiger penises are considered effective aphrodisiacs by aging Chinese gentlemen, and the demand for these is so strong in Asia that a thriving market in counterfeit tiger penises has sprung up. Made in Hong Kong from ox and deer tendons, they sell for about US$15 each.

Tiger parts are also worn to give hunters courage. Many a British hunter's trophy from his tiger kill mysteriously lost its whiskers and claws as the native bearers took the opportunity to collect protection against the time they would next be expected to drive the dangerous cats under the hunter's guns. The whiskers are used as a charm to give courage and immunize against bullets, while claws are carried in the pocket or worn as amulets for the same purpose. Tiger claws find a major market in the towns of Thailand, where youths seek every advantage to give them courage in a country where firearms are freely available. In the Central Highlands of Indochina, the small bones of the tiger's shoulder (the clavicles) prevent tiger attacks and give their owner physical superiority over his foes, while in China the tiger's floating ribs are carried as a good-luck talisman.

Given their great value in medicine, tigers are sometimes hunted specifically for the market, but the local people who live among tigers are seldom the hunters. The same qualities that give the great cats their power in folk medicine also protect them from the local people. "Live and let live" is their attitude, and the cats are often considered to harbor the spirits of deceased chiefs who watch over the village. Only if a tiger becomes a man-eater or takes too many local pigs, cattle, or goats will local people normally hunt them. A shaman who claims the ability to communicate with spirits through trances and can use this ability to cure spirit-caused diseases may need to kill a tiger on occasion, but this harvest would seldom endanger the species.

In many parts of Africa, lions are similarly protected. In Zambia's Luangwa Valley, for example, lions are seen metaphorically as chiefs, so any lion killed must be presented to the chief; any commoner who kills a lion has to go through an intricate purification process. Lion claws and teeth placed in a chief's grave ensure that the spirit of the chief will be reincarnated in a lion which will then protect the land and control the fertility of crops and animals. Such a lion is protected — or at least avoided — by normal villagers.

But the spread of agriculture and growing human populations bring more people into the areas which formerly supported the great cats and smaller populations of tribal peoples. The big cats are becoming so rare that they need to be protected by law, making them unavailable for legal use as medicine. This causes the kinds of conflicts faced today by the Seminoles in Florida. Arguing that they had long relied on panthers for ceremonial and medicinal purposes without endangering the species, Pete Osceola, a Seminole medicine man, summarized his tribe's position: "We did not make the panther endangered. We showed the beauty of the panther's skin to the white man and he found it pleasing. He started killing the panther for skin alone. The rest went to waste. In his greed for beauty, he has made it endangered."

British Library

► Capes and coats made of cat fur form the ceremonial apparel of many traditional people. As cats decline, such practices may have to be curtailed, and this part of people's heritage may subsequently be lost, further eroding cultural diversity.

Bill Leimbach/South American Pictures

▲▼ Once obtained only at great risk to the hunter, the body parts of tigers play a key role in traditional Asian medicine. Such use posed little threat to tiger populations until modern weapons enabled people to kill great numbers of tigers for the large profits to be made in many markets.

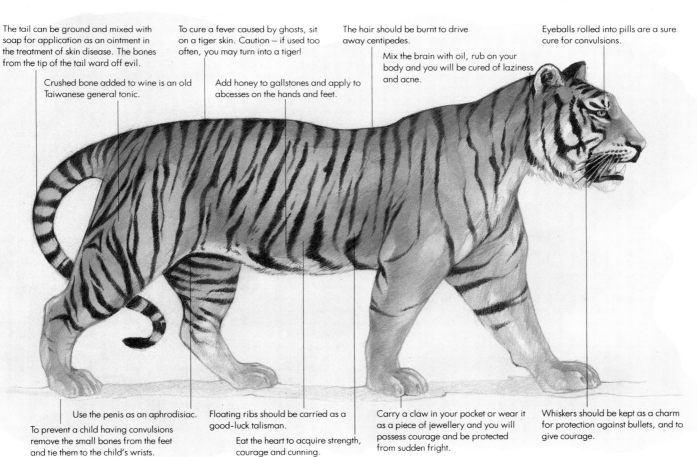

The tail can be ground and mixed with soap for application as an ointment in the treatment of skin disease. The bones from the tip of the tail ward off evil.

To cure a fever caused by ghosts, sit on a tiger skin. Caution — if used too often, you may turn into a tiger!

The hair should be burnt to drive away centipedes.

Eyeballs rolled into pills are a sure cure for convulsions.

Mix the brain with oil, rub on your body and you will be cured of laziness and acne.

Crushed bone added to wine is an old Taiwanese general tonic.

Add honey to gallstones and apply to abcesses on the hands and feet.

Use the penis as an aphrodisiac.

To prevent a child having convulsions remove the small bones from the feet and tie them to the child's wrists.

Floating ribs should be carried as a good-luck talisman.

Eat the heart to acquire strength, courage and cunning.

Carry a claw in your pocket or wear it as a piece of jewellery and you will possess courage and be protected from sudden fright.

Whiskers should be kept as a charm for protection against bullets, and to give courage.

ACKNOWLEDGMENTS

The Consulting Editors would like to thank Dr Roslyn Walker, Curator, National Museum of African Art, Smithsonian Institution; Dr Jan Stuart, Assistant Curator, Freer Gallery of Art and Arthur M. Sackler Gallery, Smithsonian Institution; and Dr. Colin Groves, Reader in Anthropology, Australian National University.

Every effort has been made to acknowledge copyright holders of all material published in this book, but in the event of an omission please contact Weldon Owen.

The photographers take full responsibility for identifying the species pictured on page 176, captioned as the Andean mountain cat (Felis jacobita) and the kodkod (Felis guigna).

THE CATS AND HOW THEY CAME TO BE
page 17, **The phylogeny of cats and cat-like carnivorans**
Table adapted from *The Big Cats, The Paintings of Guy Coheleach,*

Abradale Press/Harry N. Abrams, Inc., Publishers, New York, 1982, page 15.
page 27, **Smilodon attacking a young mammoth**
Illustration adapted from Mark Hallett's illustrations of *Smilodon* prey capture techniques in William A. Akersten's "Canine Function in Smilodon", *Contributions in Science,* No. 356, Natural History Museum of Los Angeles County, 1985, pages 13 and 18.

HOW CATS WORK
page 56, **A natural jackknife**
Illustration adapted from *The Big Cats, The Paintings of Guy Coheleach,* Abradale Press/Harry N. Abrams, Inc., Publishers, New York, 1982, page 19.

MAN-EATERS
page 208, **Leopards and human evolution**
Illustration adapted from "The Search for Our Ancestors", *National Geographic,* November 1985, Volume 168, Number 5, page 607.

NOTES ON CONTRIBUTORS

BRIAN BERTRAM
Dr. Brian Bertram spent four years at the Serengeti Research Institute, Tanzania, studying the ecology and social organization of lions and leopards. He worked at the Zoological Society of London as Curator of Mammals, and then of Invertebrates and of the Aquarium. Currently he is Director General of the Wildfowl and Wetlands Trust in the UK.

URS BREITENMOSER
Urs Breitenmoser completed his Diploma and Ph.D. thesis with the Lynx Project, through the University of Berne. Since 1986 he has worked as a research assistant with the Swiss Foundation for Scientific Research. He is a member of the International Union for Conservation of Nature and Natural Resources' (IUCN) Cat Specialist Group and Reintroduction Specialist Group.

JOHN DAVID BYGOTT
As a Staff Scientist at the Serengeti Research Institute, Dr. David Bygott conducted studies on the behavior and ecology of lions in Serengeti and Ngorongoro. He is now a partner in his own business, and publishes both scientific and popular articles. He is also a professional tour guide and lecturer, and has illustrated many books.

T. M. CARO
Dr. T. M. Caro has studied the development of play and teaching in domestic cats, and, more recently, has studied the behavior and ecology of free-living cheetahs in the Serengeti National Park. Currently he is preparing a monograph on cheetahs, and is an Assistant Professor at the University of California, teaching conservation biology.

JOHN CAVALLO
John Cavallo is a Ph.D. candidate in anthropology at Rutgers University, New Brunswick. He is a professional archeologist who uses animal behavior and ecology to address archeological problems. He is interested in applying behavioral and ecological data to wildlife management and conservation.

RAVI CHELLAM
Ravi Chellam has completed a Masters degree in wildlife biology and has done four years of field work for his Ph.D. in India's Gir Forest, studying predation ecology and ranging patterns of Asian lions.

LOUISE H. EMMONS
Dr. Louise Emmons has spent 20 years studying the ecology, behavior, and systematics of tropical rainforest mammals in Africa, Asia, and the Neotropics. She has conducted field studies of squirrels, porcupines, rodents, bats, cats, and tree shrews and is now a Research Associate at the Smithsonian Institution, Museum of Natural History in the Division of Mammals.

JEANNETTE PATRICIA HANBY
Dr. Jeannette Hanby completed her Masters degree and Ph.D. in Animal Behavior, and as a Staff Scientist at the Serengeti Research Institute, Tanzania, studied the ecology and behavior of lions in Serengeti and Ngorongoro. She is now a partner in a business that produces material for education and tourism. She is also a professional tour leader and lecturer and has written a number of scientific papers and books.

FRED P. HEALD
Dr. Heald practiced general surgery in rural California for 30 years. After retiring, he undertook voluntary laboratory work in vertebrate paleontology. Since 1980 he has been describing and studying pathologic bones of *Smilodon* and *Canis dirus* at the George C. Page Museum, California.

PETER JACKSON
Peter Jackson's interest in wildlife began as a hobby during 18 years as Chief Correspondent of Reuters in India. In 1970 he was appointed Director of Information of the World Wide Fund for Nature (WWF), and he also managed Operation Tiger when it was launched in 1972. He is Chairman of the Cat Specialist Group of the IUCN.

RODNEY JACKSON

Rodney Jackson is an associate scientist in wildlife ecology with the Woodlands Mountain Institute of West Virginia, and he works to preserve habitats surrounding Mt. Everest in Nepal and Tibet. He is on the Advisory Board of the International Snow Leopard Trust of Seattle, Washington, and he is a director of the California Institute of Environmental Studies.

A. J. T. JOHNSINGH

Dr. A. J. T. Johnsingh completed his Ph.D. on the ecology and behavior of dholes in Bandipur Tiger Reserve, Karnataka, India. He initiated the Elephant Project for the Bombay Natural History Society and since 1985 has been Associate Professor at the Wildlife Institute of India, Dehradun. He is a member of the IUCN's Cat, Canid and Asian Elephant Specialist Groups.

K. ULLAS KARANTH

K. Ullas Karanth currently works as a wildlife biologist at the Center for Wildlife Studies, Mysore, India, and is completing his Ph.D. at Bangalore University. He is a honorary wildlife warden, and has carried out research on tigers, leopards, and dholes in Nagarhole National Park, India.

GILLIAN KERBY

After completing a first degree in biology, Dr. Gillian Kerby completed her Ph.D. in the Animal Behavior Research Group, Department of Zoology, at the University of Oxford. The focus of her research was the social behavior of farm cats. Currently, Dr. Kerby works as an environmental consultant to the agricultural industry.

RICHARD A. KILTIE

Dr. Richard A. Kiltie is an Associate Professor in the Zoology Department at the University of Florida, USA. His research has primarily been with mammals and birds, and he has worked on aspects of functional morphology, community ecology, reproductive behavior, behavioral ecology and the evolution of coloration.

M. KAREN LAURENSON

After completing her degree in Veterinary Medicine, M. Karen Laurenson became involved in research on cheetahs and wild dogs in Serengeti National Park, Tanzania. She is now a Ph.D. student in zoology at Cambridge University, completing her thesis on cheetahs with a view to refining management procedures for their conservation.

SUSAN LUMPKIN

Dr. Susan Lumpkin received her Ph.D. in biological psychology, specializing in animal behavior, at Duke University. She was awarded a Smithsonian Institution Post-doctoral Fellowship for advanced study in mammalian behavior at the National Zoological Park, and has written on animal behavior and conservation. She is currently Director of Communications at Friends of the National Zoo, and is editor of its *ZooGoer* magazine.

DAVID W. MACDONALD

Dr. David Macdonald is the head of the Wildlife Conservation Research Unit at the University of Oxford. For the past three years he has studied the social behavior of farm cats, and his research has resulted in a 50 minute BBC documentary on the subject. He has studied many species of mammals, and has produced various books, including the *Encyclopedia of Mammals.*

CHARLES McDOUGAL

Dr. Charles McDougal gained a Ph.D. in anthropology but, in the last three decades, has concentrated his interest on natural history. He has had first-hand experience with tigers and leopards, first as a hunter and later to study them. He lived in the Royal Chitwan National Park in Nepal for 12 years, and, still based in Nepal, is now a Research Associate of the Smithsonian Institution.

JEFFREY A. McNEELY

Jeffrey A. McNeely is Chief Conservation Officer for IUCN. He spent three years running the WWF program in Indonesia, and since 1980, has been based at IUCN in Switzerland, where he has written and edited a dozen books on conservation issues. His major interest is in influencing government policies in favor of biological and cultural diversity.

ROBIN MEADOWS

Robin Meadows has a Masters degree in biology, and a Graduate Certificate in Science Communication. She works as a science writer, both freelance and for the University of California's Toxic Substances Program. She is also a contributing editor to Friends of the National Zoo's *ZooGoer* magazine.

JILL MELLEN

Dr. Jill Mellen teaches courses and workshops on the application of behavioral research to zoo animal management. She gained her Ph.D. at the University of California at Davis, and her dissertation examined factors influencing reproductive failure in small captive exotic felids. She is currently Conservation Research Coordinator at the Washington Park Zoo, Portland, USA, and she is a member of the IUCN Cat Specialist Group.

S. DOUGLAS MILLER

Dr. S. Douglas Miller is currently Regional Executive and Director of the National Wildlife Federations's Alaska Natural Resources Center in Anchorage. He has a Ph.D. in wildlife biology, and has lectured at North Carolina State University. He also worked at the US Fish and Wildlife Service as the Assistant Leader of the Massachusetts Cooperative Wildlife Research Unit.

SRIYANIE MIThTHAPALA

Sriyanie Miththapala received her B.Sc. from the University of Colombo, Sri Lanka, and is currently working on a Ph.D. in wildlife and range sciences at the University of Florida, Gainesville, in collaboration with the National Zoological Park, Smithsonian Institution. As the focus of her dissertation she examines genetic and morphological variation in leopards.

NANCY NEFF

Dr. Nancy Neff's primary research interests are in methods of evolutionary analysis, focusing, in particular, on the problems of felid and nimravid evolution. She has a Ph.D. in biology and spent six years as Assistant Professor of Biology at the University of Connecticut. She has written a number of books, journal articles, and book reviews, and is currently a software design engineer for an avionics engineering firm.

STEPHEN J. O'BRIEN

Dr. Stephen J. O'Brien heads the Laboratory of Viral Carcinogenesis at the National Cancer Institute in Maryland, USA. He also co-chairs the International Committee on Comparative Gene Mapping and is the editor of *Genetic Maps.* His studies in genetic analysis and molecular evolution have concentrated on the cat family, particularly the African cheetah, and pandas.

WARNER C. PASSANISI

Warner C. Passanisi is currently a Ph.D. student in the Department of Zoology at the University of Oxford, England. For the past three and a half years he has been studying the social organization and reproductive tactics of free-ranging domestic cats found on farms around Oxford.

GUSTAV PETERS

After studying zoology, genetics, and ethnology Dr. Gustav Peters received his Ph.D. in 1975. He worked as a research assistant on acoustic communication in the Felidae until 1980 and then took up his current position as Assistant Curator of Mammals at the Alexander

Koenig Institute and Zoological Museum in Bonn. He is a member of the IUCN Felid Specialist Group, and the Mustelid and Viverrid Specialist Groups.

JOHN SEIDENSTICKER
Dr. John Seidensticker was one of the pioneers of radiotelemetry use in the study of large, solitary-living cats. He was founding principal investigator of the Smithsonian–Nepal Tiger Ecology Project and an ecologist and park planner for the Indonesia–World Wildlife Program. As a wildlife ecologist and Curator of Mammals at the National Zoological Park, Smithsonian Institution, he studies the consequences of habitat insularization and change on populations of large and medium-sized mammals and their response to confined environments. He has been a member of the IUCN Cat Specialist Group since 1974.

JAMES A. SERPELL
Dr. James A. Serpell is author of numerous popular and scientific publications on companion animal behavior and human/animal relationships, including the book *In the Company of Animals*. He has completed a degree in zoology and a Ph.D. in animal behavior. Currently, he is Director of the Companion Animal Research Group at the Cambridge Veterinary School, England.

CHRISTOPHER A. SHAW
Christopher Shaw has been working in the field of Vertebrate Paleontology since 1967 and at Rancho La Brea since 1969. His research focuses on the sabertooth cat. He is now Collection Manager at George C. Page Museum, California, where he is responsible for the identification, cataloguing, and storage of all fossils and archival material.

JAN STUART
Dr Jan Stuart is Assistant Curator of Chinese Art at the Freer Gallery and the Arthur M. Sackler Gallery, Smithsonian Institution. She has led tours to China for the Smithsonian National Associates Program, taught for the Smithsonian Resident Associates Program, written for *ZooGoer* and *Asian Art,* and was a contributing author to *Images of the Mind.*

FIONA C. SUNQUIST
Fiona C. Sunquist is a wildlife writer and photographer, a Roving Editor for *International Wildlife Magazine,* and a consultant to the Special Publications Division of National Geographic Society. Her articles and photographs have been published in various international magazines,

and she was co-author of the book *Tiger Moon.* She and her husband, Mel, have studied carnivore biology on three continents.

MEL SUNQUIST
Dr. Mel Sunquist received a Ph.D. in wildlife ecology from the University of Minnesota in 1979. Since 1965 he has been engaged in research on mammalian ecology and behavior using radio-tracking techniques. He is a member of the IUCN Cat Specialist Group, Florida's Panther Technical Advisory Council, and is on the Research Advisory Board of the International Society for Endangered Cats.

RONALD L. TILSON
Dr. Ronald Tilson has a Ph.D. in ecology and has worked as a conservation biologist in Southeast Asia for more than 20 years. He is currently Director of Conservation at the Minnesota Zoo, and is on the graduate faculty group in the Department of Wildlife Conservaton at the University of Minnesota. He is a member of the IUCN Cat Specialist Group, and coordinator of the AAZPA's Siberian Tiger Species Survival Plan.

BLAIRE VAN VALKENBURGH
Dr. Blaire Van Valkenburgh received her Ph.D. from the Johns Hopkins University in 1984 and then worked as instructor of human anatomy and embryology at the Johns Hopkins School of Medicine. She is presently at the UCLA Department of Biology, and her research interests include morphology, ecology, and behavior of fossil and living carnivorous mammals.

LISA FLORMAN WEINBERG
Lisa Florman Weinberg is completing her Ph.D. in art history at Columbia University in New York City, where she specializes in the art of ancient Greece and modern European painting. Her interest in animals in art developed from her association with *ZooGoer* magazine, to which she has contributed several essays.

DAVID E. WILDT
Dr. David Wildt is Head of the Reproductive Physiology Program at the Smithsonian Institution's National Zoological Park. He studies a variety of animals, but his greatest interest is cats. He has published more than 100 papers and at present serves as reproductive research coordinator for species recovery programs for the cheetah, tiger, Florida panther, maned wolf and black-footed ferret.

INDEX

Illustrations are indicated in *italics*.